HARDPRESS.NET
HOME OF HARD-TO-FIND BOOKS

Service Book for Public Worship
by Harvard University. Chapel

Address:
HardPress
8345 NW 66TH ST #2561
MIAMI FL 33166-2626
USA
Email: info@hardpress.net

ngt

Service Book

A

SERVICE-BOOK

FOR

PUBLIC WORSHIP.

PREPARED ESPECIALLY FOR USE IN THE CHAPEL OF HARVARD
UNIVERSITY.

CAMBRIDGE:
JOHN BARTLETT.
1858.

CAMBRIDGE:
METCALF AND COMPANY, PRINTERS TO THE UNIVERSITY.

PREFACE.

THE object of this Service-Book is to make our public worship more interesting, more reverential, more various, more congregational, and more effectual in promoting the sacred purposes for which the worship is offered.

It is believed that the designed manner of using it will be understood, on a little attention to the contents, without explanation. Though the circumstances have required a considerable deviation from the "Book of Common Prayer," that is recognized as the most complete body of liturgical exercises in our language. No entire service, for a day or season of devotion, is found arranged in order. That arrangement is left to the liberty and choice of the minister or the congregation. By way of suggestion, an "Order" is given on the page next after the table of Contents.

The passages intended to be given as responses to the minister, by the congregation, or by the choir, or by both together, as may be found expedient in different cases, — including always the *Amen*, — are printed in italics.

In the lessons from the Holy Scriptures, the passages and sentences are not always presented entire, as they occur in the Bible. It has only been endeavored to offer services in Scriptural language, with no such alterations or omissions as would materially affect the original meaning.

For convenience, the term " Prophecies " is used in an extended but not unauthorized sense, and is applied to any parts of Scripture which convey " praise or religious instruction in an elevated form of expression."

CAMBRIDGE, October, 1858.

CONTENTS.

A REGULAR ORDER.

1. INTRODUCTORY SENTENCES.
   Congregation sit.

2. THE "EXHORTATION AND CONFESSION," OR THE "GENERAL CONFESSION."
   Congregation sit, bowing the head, or kneel.

3. THE LORD'S PRAYER.
   Congregation sit, bowing the head, or kneel.

4. A CHANT OR ANTHEM.
   Congregation stand.

5. THE BEATITUDES, OR COMMANDMENTS. (At discretion.)
   Congregation sit.

6. COLLECT AND PROPHECIES FOR THE DAY.
   Congregation sit.

7. HYMN.
   In singing, Congregation stand.

8. PRAYER, BY THE MINISTER, OR SELECTED.
   Congregation sit, bowing the head, or kneel.

9. READING FROM THE NEW TESTAMENT, OR FROM ONE OF THE HISTORICAL BOOKS OF THE OLD TESTAMENT.
   Congregation sit.

10. HYMN.

In singing, Congregation stand.

11. LITANY, OR SPECIAL PRAYERS, OR BOTH.

Congregation sit, bowing the head, or kneel.

12. PSALMS FOR THE DAY.

Congregation sit.

13. "TE DEUM," OR ANTHEM, OR CHANT.

Congregation stand.

14. BENEDICTION.

Congregation stand.

*** If a Sermon is included in this service, it may be inserted after 13, when 5, 9, and 10 should be omitted, and a Chant or Hymn be sung after the Sermon.

*** Services for Special Days and Ordinances may be substituted, or introduced, at discretion.

*** It is recommended that the hymns be sung by the Congregation. Also, that the minister generally name the Day, and the page where each part of the service occurs.

*** Could a general rule for postures be followed, a proper correspondence between the attitude and the act would seem to require the worshippers to *stand in praise or singing*, to *sit in instruction or reading*, and to *kneel or bow in confession and prayer*.

SENTENCES OF INTRODUCTION.

THE hour cometh, and now is, when the true worshippers shall worship the Father in spirit and in truth; for the Father seeketh such to worship him. God is a spirit, and they that worship him must worship him in spirit and in truth.

The Lord is in his holy temple: let all the earth keep silence before him.

When the wicked man turneth away from his wickedness that he hath committed, and doeth that which is lawful and right, he shall save his soul alive.

Come unto me, all ye that labor and are heavy laden, and I will give you rest. Take my yoke upon you, and learn of me, for I am meek and lowly of heart; and ye shall find rest unto your souls.

Again I say unto you, that if two of you shall agree on earth, as touching any thing that they shall ask, it shall be done for them of my Father which is in heaven.

For where two or three are gathered together in my name, there am I in the midst of them.

Seek ye the Lord while he may be found; call ye upon him while he is near.

Let the wicked forsake his way, and the unrighteous man his thoughts: and let him return unto the Lord, and he will have mercy upon him; and to our God, for he will abundantly pardon.

Not every one that saith unto me, Lord, Lord, shall enter into the kingdom of heaven, but he that doeth the will of my Father which is in heaven.

Blessed are they which do hunger and thirst after righteousness: for they shall be filled.

1

Blessed are the pure in heart: for they shall see God.

Likewise I say unto you, There is joy in the presence of the angels of God over one sinner that repenteth.

The Lord is good unto them that wait for him; to the soul that seeketh him.

It is good that a man should both hope and quietly wait for the salvation of the Lord.

This is life eternal, that they might know Thee the only true God, and Jesus Christ whom thou hast sent.

Jesus said, I am the bread of life: he that cometh to me shall never hunger; and he that believeth on me shall never thirst.

Labor not for the meat which perisheth, but for that meat which endureth unto everlasting life, which the Son of Man shall give unto you: for him hath God the Father sealed.

As the Father raiseth up the dead and quickeneth them, even so the Son quickeneth whom he will.

Hear what Christ the Lord said: He that heareth my word and believeth on Him that sent me hath everlasting life, and shall not come into condemnation; but is passed from death unto life.

My brethren, have not the faith of our Lord Jesus Christ, the Lord of glory, with respect of persons. For if there come unto your assembly a man with a gold ring, in goodly apparel; and there come in also a poor man in vile raiment; and ye have respect to him that weareth the gay clothing, and say unto him, Sit thou here in a good place; and say to the poor, Stand thou there, or sit here under my footstool: are ye not then partial in yourselves, and are become judges of evil thoughts?

The wind bloweth where it listeth, and thou hearest the sound thereof, but canst not tell whence it cometh or whither it goeth: so is every one which is born of the Spirit.

Thus saith the Lord, Behold, I stand at the door and knock: if any man hear my voice, and open the door, I will come to him.

If any of you lack wisdom, let him ask of God, that giveth to all men liberally, and upbraideth not, and it shall be given him. But let him ask in faith, nothing wavering. For he that wavereth is like a wave of the sea driven of the wind and tossed.

Verily I say unto you, that in this place is one greater than the temple. Know ye not that ye are the temple of God, and that the Spirit of God dwelleth in you?

Stand in the gate of the Lord's house, and proclaim there this word, and say, Hear ye the word of the Lord, all ye that enter in at these gates to worship the Lord. Thus saith the Lord of hosts, Amend your ways and your doings, and I will cause you to dwell in this place. Obey my voice, and I will be your God, and ye shall be my people.

The Lord reigneth; let the earth rejoice! Righteousness and judgment are the habitation of his throne. Enter into his gates with thanksgiving, and into his courts with praise. Be thankful unto him and bless his name.

For ye are not come unto the mount that might be touched, and that burned with fire, nor unto blackness, and darkness, and tempest, but ye are come unto Mount Sion, and unto the city of the living God, the heavenly Jerusalem, and to an innumerable company of angels, to the general assembly and church of the first-born, which are written in heaven, and to God the Judge of all, and to the spirits of just men made perfect, and to Jesus the mediator of the new covenant, and to the blood of sprinkling, that speaketh better things than that of Abel. See that ye refuse not him that speaketh.

The Lord is risen indeed. If ye then be risen with Christ, seek those things which are above, where Christ sitteth on the right hand of God.

Now is Christ risen from the dead, and become the first fruits of them that slept. For as in Adam all die, even so in Christ shall all be made alive. Thanks be to God, which giveth us the victory through our Lord Jesus Christ.

For we have not an high-priest which cannot be touched with the feeling of our infirmities : but was in all points tempted like as we are, yet without sin. Let us therefore come boldly unto the throne of grace, that we may obtain mercy, and find grace to help in time of need.

To the Lord our God belong mercies and forgivenesses, though we have rebelled against him ; neither have we obeyed the voice of the Lord our God, to walk in his laws which he set before us.

Repent ye, for the kingdom of heaven is at hand.

From the rising of the sun unto the going down of the same, the Lord's name is to be praised.

Let our prayers be set forth in his sight as incense; and the lifting up of our hands as an evening sacrifice.

Ask, and it shall be given you; seek, and ye shall find; knock, and it shall be opened unto you.

Even the youths shall faint and be weary, and the young men shall utterly fall; but they that wait on the Lord shall renew their strength, they shall mount up with wings as eagles, they shall run and not be weary, they shall walk and not faint.

Let us search and try our ways, and turn again to the Lord.

Rend your heart, and not your garments, and turn unto the Lord your God: for he is gracious and merciful, slow to anger, and of great kindness, and repenteth him of the evil.

Wherewith shall I come before the Lord, and bow myself before the High God? He hath showed thee, O man, what is good; and what doth the Lord require of thee but to do justly, and love mercy, and walk humbly with thy God?

If thou bring thy gift to the altar, and there remember that thy brother hath aught against thee, leave there thy gift upon the altar, and go thy way; first be reconciled to thy brother, and then come and offer thy gift.

The kingdom of God is not meat and drink, but righteousness, and peace, and joy in the Holy Ghost.

Take heed, brethren, lest there be in any of you an evil heart of unbelief in departing from the living God.

Wherefore lift up the hands which hang down, and the feeble knees; following peace with all men, and holiness, without which no man shall see the Lord.

And be ye doers of the word, and not hearers only deceiving your own selves.

O, come, let us worship and bow down, and kneel before the Lord our Maker. For he is our God, and we are the people of his pasture, and the sheep of his hand.

Min.   The Lord be with you!
Cong.   *And with thy spirit!*
Min.   Lift up your hearts.
Cong.   *We lift them up unto the Lord.*

EXHORTATION AND CONFESSION.*

DEARLY beloved brethren, the Scripture moveth us in sundry places to acknowledge and confess our manifold sins and wickedness, and that we should not dissemble nor cloak them before the face of Almighty God our Heavenly Father ; but confess them with an humble, lowly, penitent, and obedient heart; to the end that we may obtain forgiveness of the same, by his infinite goodness and mercy. And although we ought, at all times, humbly to acknowledge our sins before God ; yet ought we chiefly so to do, when we assemble and meet together to render thanks for the great benefits we have received at his hands, to set forth his most worthy praise, to hear his most holy word, and to ask those things which are requisite and necessary, as well for the body as the soul. Wherefore I pray and beseech you, as many as are here present, to accompany me, with a pure heart and humble voice, unto the throne of the heavenly grace, saying with me, —

ALMIGHTY and most merciful Father, We have erred and strayed from thy ways like lost sheep. We have followed too much the devices and desires of our own hearts. We have offended against thy holy laws. We have left undone those things which we ought to have done ; And we have done those things which we ought not to have done. But thou, O Lord, have mercy upon us miserable offenders. Spare thou those, O God, who confess their faults. Restore thou those who are penitent, according to thy promises declared unto mankind in Christ Jesus our Lord. And grant, O most merciful Father, that we may hereafter live a godly, righteous, and sober life; To the glory of thy holy name. *Amen.*

---

* The *Confession* to be said by the minister and congregation together.

GENERAL CONFESSION.

WITH a true heart and sincere repentance, let us make humble confession of our unworthiness: —

If we say we have no sin, we deceive ourselves and the truth is not in us ;

If we confess our sins, God is faithful and just to forgive us our sins, and to cleanse us from all unrighteousness.

I will arise and go to my Father, and say unto him, Father, I have sinned against Heaven, and in thy sight, and am no more worthy to be called thy son.

For the good that I would, I do not; but the evil which I would not, that I do.

God be merciful to me a sinner.

Create in me a clean heart, O God, and renew a right spirit within me.

Lord, if thou wilt, thou canst make me clean.

Speak the word only, and thy servant shall be healed.

Enter not into judgment with thy servant, O Lord!

For in thy sight shall no man living be justified.

Hide thy face from my sins! and blot out all mine iniquities! The sacrifices of God are a broken spirit.

A broken and a contrite spirit, O God, thou wilt not despise.

THE LORD'S PRAYER.

Our Father, who art in heaven, Hallowed be thy name. Thy kingdom come; Thy will be done on earth, as it is in heaven. Give us this day our daily bread. And forgive us our trespasses, As we forgive those who trespass against us. And lead us not into temptation, But deliver us from evil. For thine is the kingdom, and the power, and the glory, For ever and ever. *Amen.*

THE COMMANDMENTS.

Thou shalt have no other gods before me.

Thou shalt not make unto thee any graven image, or any likeness of anything that is in heaven above, or that is in the earth beneath, or that is in the water under the earth: thou shalt not bow down thyself to them, nor serve them : for I the Lord thy God am a jealous God, visiting the iniquity of the fathers upon the children, unto the third and fourth generation of them that hate me ; and showing mercy unto thousands of them that love me and keep my commandments.

Thou shalt not take the name of the Lord thy God in vain : for the Lord will not hold him guiltless that taketh his name in vain.

Remember the Sabbath day to keep it holy.   Six days shalt thou labor, and do all thy work ; but the seventh is the Sabbath of the Lord thy God : in it thou shalt not do any work, thou, nor thy son, nor thy daughter, thy man-servant, nor thy maid-servant, nor thy cattle, nor thy stranger that is within thy gates : for in six days the Lord made heaven and earth, the sea and all that in them is, and rested the seventh day : wherefore the Lord blessed the Sabbath day, and hallowed it.

Honor thy father and thy mother ; that thy days may be long upon the land which the Lord thy God giveth thee.

Thou shalt not kill.

Thou shalt not commit adultery.

Thou shalt not steal.

Thou shalt not bear false witness against thy neighbor.

Thou shalt not covet thy neighbor's house, thou shalt not covet thy neighbor's wife, nor his man-servant, nor his maid-servant, nor his ox, nor his ass, nor anything that is thy neighbor's.

HEAR also what our Saviour Christ saith : —

The first of all the commandments is, Hear, O Israel! The Lord our God is one Lord : and thou shalt love the Lord thy God with all thy heart, and with all thy soul, and with all thy mind, and with all thy strength.

This is the first commandment. And the second is like, namely, this :

Thou shalt love thy neighbor as thyself.

There is none other commandment greater than these.

O Lord, Open thou our eyes !

And we shall behold wondrous things out of thy law !

O Lord, have mercy upon us !

And write all these thy commandments, we beseech thee, in our hearts.

BEATITUDES.

Jesus opened his mouth and taught them, saying : —
Blessed are the poor in spirit ;
For theirs is the kingdom of Heaven.
Blessed are they that mourn ;
For they shall be comforted.
Blessed are the meek ;
For they shall inherit the earth.
Blessed are they which do hunger and thirst after righteousness ;
For they shall be filled.
Blessed are the merciful ;
For they shall obtain mercy.
Blessed are the pure in heart ;
For they shall see God.
Blessed are the peacemakers ;
For they shall be called the children of God.
Blessed are they which are persecuted for righteousness' sake ;
For theirs is the kingdom of Heaven.
Blessed are ye when men shall revile you, and persecute you, and
shall say all manner of evil against you falsely, for my sake ;
Rejoice, and be exceeding glad : for great is your reward in
Heaven : for so persecuted they the prophets which were before you.

O Lord, touch our hearts,
That we may know the mysteries of the kingdom of Heaven !

SERVICES FOR THE CHRISTIAN YEAR.

FIRST SUNDAY IN ADVENT.

COLLECT.

ALMIGHTY God, give us grace that we may cast away the works of darkness, and put upon us the armor of light, now in the time of this mortal life, in which thy Son, Jesus Christ, came to visit us in great humility; that in the last day, when he shall come again in his glorious majesty, to judge both the quick and the dead, we may rise to the life immortal, through him who liveth and reigneth with thee evermore. *Amen.*

PROPHECIES.

ISAIAH.

And it shall come to pass in the last days, that the mountain of the Lord's house shall be established in the top of the mountains, and shall be exalted above the hills; and all nations shall flow unto it.

And many people shall go and say, Come ye, and let us go up to the mountain of the Lord, to the house of God; and he will teach us of his ways, and we will walk in his paths: for out of Zion shall go forth the law, and the word of the Lord from Jerusalem.

And he shall judge among the nations, and shall rebuke many people, and they shall beat their swords into plough-shares, and their spears into pruning-hooks: nation shall not lift up sword against nation, neither shall they learn war any more.

Come ye, and let us walk in the light of the Lord.

The lofty looks of man shall be humbled, and the haughtiness of men shall be bowed down; and the Lord alone shall be exalted in that day.

For the day of the Lord of hosts shall be upon every one that is proud and lofty, and upon every one that is lifted up; and he shall be brought low;

And the loftiness of man shall be bowed down, and the haughtiness of men shall be made low: and the Lord alone shall be exalted in that day.

In that day a man shall cast his idols of silver, and his idols of gold, which they made each one for himself to worship, to the moles, and to the bats;

For fear of the Lord, and for the glory of his majesty, when he ariseth to shake terribly the earth.

Arise, shine; for thy light is come, and the glory of the Lord is risen upon thee.

For, behold, darkness shall cover the earth, and gross darkness the people: but the Lord shall arise upon thee, and his glory shall be seen upon thee.

And the Gentiles shall come to thy light, and kings to the brightness of thy rising.

Lift up thine eyes round about, and see: all they gather themselves together, they come to thee: thy sons shall come from far, and thy daughters shall be nursed at thy side.

Then thou shalt see, and flow together, and thine heart shall fear, and be enlarged; because the abundance of the sea shall be converted unto thee, the forces of the Gentiles shall come unto thee.

They shall bring gold and incense; and they shall show forth the praises of the Lord.

The flocks shall come up with acceptance on mine altar, and I will glorify the house of my glory.

Who are these that fly as a cloud, and as the doves to their windows?

Surely the isles shall wait for me, and the ships, to bring thy sons from far, their silver and their gold with them, unto the name of the Lord thy God, and to the Holy One of Israel, because he hath glorified thee.

And the sons of strangers shall build up thy walls, and their kings shall minister unto thee : for in my wrath I smote thee, but in my favor have I had mercy on thee.

Therefore thy gates shall be open continually: they shall not be shut day nor night.

The glory of Lebanon shall come unto thee, the fir-tree, the pine-tree, and the box together, to beautify the place of my sanctuary; and I will make the place of my feet glorious.

The sons also of them that afflicted thee shall come bending unto thee; and all they that despised thee shall bow themselves down at the soles of thy feet; and they shall call thee, The City of the Lord, The Zion of the Holy One of Israel.

Whereas thou hast been forsaken and hated, so that no man went through thee, I will make thee an eternal excellency, a joy of many generations.

Thou shalt also know that I the Lord am thy Saviour and thy Redeemer, the Mighty One of Jacob.

For brass I will bring gold, and for iron I will bring silver, and for wood brass, and for stones iron : I will also make thy officers peace, and thine exactors righteousness.

Violence shall no more be heard in thy land, wasting nor destruction within thy borders: but thou shalt call thy walls Salvation, and thy gates Praise.

The sun shall be no more thy light by day; neither for brightness shall the moon give light unto thee : but the Lord shall be unto thee an everlasting light, and thy God thy glory;

Thy sun shall no more go down; neither shall thy moon

2

withdraw itself: for the Lord shall be thine everlasting light, and the days of thy mourning shall be ended.

Thy people also shall be all righteous: they shall inherit the land for ever, the branch of my planting, the work of my hands, that I may be glorified.

A little one shall become a thousand, and a small one a strong nation: I the Lord will hasten it in his time.

O Lord, open thou our ears!

That we may hear meekly thy word, and receive it with pure affection.

PSALMS.

To the king, O God, give thy justice,
And to the son of a king thy righteousness!
Yea! and he shall judge thy people with equity,
And thine oppressed ones with justice.
For the mountains shall bring forth peace to the people,
And the hills, through righteousness.
He shall defend the oppressed of the people ;
He shall save the needy,
And break in pieces the oppressor.
They shall fear thee as long as the sun and moon shall endure,
From generation to generation.
He shall be like rain descending on the mown field ;
Like showers which water the earth.
In his days shall the righteous flourish,
And great shall be their prosperity, as long as the moon shall
    endure.
He shall have dominion from sea to sea,
And from the river to the ends of the earth.
They that dwell in the desert shall bow before him,
And his enemies shall lick the dust.
The kings of Tarshish and of the isles shall bring presents ;
The kings of Sheba and Seba shall offer gifts ;
Yea, all kings shall fall down before him ;
All nations shall serve him.

For he shall deliver the poor who crieth for aid,
And the oppressed who hath no helper.
He shall spare the weak and the needy,
And save the lives of the poor.
He shall redeem them from deceit and violence,
And their blood shall be precious in his sight.
He shall prosper, and to him shall be given of the gold of
    Sheba ;
Prayer also shall be made for him continually,
And daily shall he be praised.
There shall be an abundance of corn in the land ;
Even on the tops of the mountains its fruit shall shake like
    Lebanon,
And they of the cities shall flourish as the grass of the earth.
His name shall endure for ever ;
His name shall be continued as long as the sun.
By him shall men bless themselves ;
All nations shall call him blessed.
Blessed be God, Jehovah, the God of Israel,
Who alone doeth wonderful things !
Blessed be his glorious name for ever !
Let the whole earth be filled with his glory.   *Amen and Amen.*

JEHOVAH said to my lord,
" Sit thou at my right hand,
Until I make thy foes thy footstool."
Jehovah will extend the sceptre of thy power from Zion ;
Thou shalt rule in the midst of thine enemies !
Thy people shall be ready, when thou musterest thy forces,
    in holy splendor ;
Thy youth shall come forth like dew from the womb of the
    morning.
Jehovah hath sworn, and he will not repent :
" *Thou art a priest for ever,*
After the order of Melchisedeck ! "

The Lord is at thy right hand,
He shall crush kings in the day of his wrath.
He shall execute justice among the nations ;
He shall crush the heads of his enemies over many lands.
He shall drink of the brook in the way ;
Therefore shall he lift up his head.

BENEDICTION VII.

SECOND SUNDAY IN ADVENT.

COLLECT.

BLESSED Lord, who hast caused all holy scriptures to be written for our learning ; grant that we may in such wise hear them, read, mark, learn, and inwardly digest them, that, by patience and comfort of thy holy Word, we may embrace and ever hold fast the blessed hope of everlasting life, which thou hast given us in our Saviour Jesus Christ.   *Amen.*

PROPHECIES.

ISAIAH AND JEREMIAH.

Now will I sing to our well-beloved a song of my beloved touching his vineyard.   My well-beloved hath a vineyard in a very fruitful hill :
And he fenced it, and gathered out the stones thereof, and planted it with the choicest vine, and built a tower in the midst of it, and also made a wine-press therein : and he looked that it should bring forth grapes, and it brought forth wild grapes.
And now, judge, I pray you, betwixt me and my vineyard.
What could have been done more to my vineyard that I have

not done in it? wherefore, when I looked that it should bring forth grapes, brought it forth wild grapes?

And now, go to; I will tell you what I will do to my vineyard: I will take away the hedge‾ thereof, and it shall be eaten up: and break down the wall thereof, and it shall be trodden down.

And I will lay it waste: it shall not be pruned nor digged; but there shall come up briers and thorns: I will also command the clouds that they rain no rain upon it.

For the vineyard of the Lord of hosts is the house of Israel, and the men of Judah his pleasant plant: and he looked for judgment, but behold oppression; for righteousness, but behold a cry.

Woe unto them that join house to house, that lay field to field, till there be no place, that they may be placed alone in the midst of the earth!

In mine ears said the Lord of hosts, Of a truth, many houses shall be desolate, even great and fair, without inhabitants.

Woe unto them that shall rise up early in the morning, that they may follow strong drink; that continue until night, till wine inflame them!

And the harp and the viol, the tabret and pipe, and wine, are in their feasts: but they regard not the work of the Lord, neither consider the operation of his hands.

Therefore my people are gone into captivity, because they have no knowledge; and their honorable men are famished, and their multitude dried up with thirst.

Therefore hell hath enlarged herself, and opened her mouth without measure: and their glory, and their multitude, and their pomp, and he that rejoiceth, shall descend into it.

And the mean man shall be brought down, and the mighty man shall be humbled, and the eyes of the lofty shall be humbled:

2 *

But the Lord of hosts shall be exalted in judgment, and God, that is holy, shall be sanctified in righteousness.

Woe unto them that call evil good, and good evil; that put darkness for light, and light for darkness; that put bitter for sweet, and sweet for bitter!

Woe unto them that are wise in their own eyes, and prudent in their own sight!

Woe unto them that are mighty to drink wine, and men of strength to mingle strong drink:

Which justify the wicked for reward, and take away the righteousness of the righteous from him!

Therefore, as the fire devoureth the stubble, and the flame consumeth the chaff, so their root shall be as rottenness, and their blossom shall go up as dust. Because they have cast away the law of the Lord of hosts, and despised the word of the Holy One of Israel.

The people that walked in darkness have seen a great light: they that dwell in the land of the shadow of death, upon them hath the light shined.

For thou hast broken the yoke of his burden, and the staff of his shoulder, the rod of his oppressor.

For every battle of the warrior is with confused noise, and garments rolled in blood; but this shall be with burning and fuel of fire.

For unto us a child is born, unto us a son is given, and the government shall be upon his shoulder; and his name shall be called Wonderful, Counsellor, The mighty God, The everlasting Father, The Prince of Peace.

Of the increase of his government and peace there shall be no end, upon the throne of David, and upon his kingdom, to order it, and to establish it with judgment and with justice, from henceforth even for ever. The zeal of the Lord of hosts will perform this.

Behold, the days come, saith the Lord, that I will make a new covenant with the house of Israel, and with the house of Judah;

Not according to the covenant that I made with their fathers, in the day I took them by the hand, to bring them out of the land of Egypt ;

But this shall be the covenant that I will make with the house of Israel ; after those days, saith the Lord, I will put my law in their inward parts, and write it in their hearts ; and will be their God, and they shall be my people.

And they shall teach no more every man his neighbor, and every man his brother, saying, Know the Lord : for they shall all know me, from the least of them unto the greatest of them, saith the Lord : for I will forgive their iniquity, and I will remember their sin no more.

Thus saith the Lord, which giveth the sun for a light by day, and the ordinances of the moon and of the stars for a light by night, which divideth the sea when the waves thereof roar ; the Lord of hosts is his name.

O Lord, open thou our lips !
And our mouth shall show forth thy praise !

PSALMS.

OPEN to me the gates of righteousness : I will go unto them, and I will praise the Lord ;

This gate of the Lord, into which the righteous shall enter.

I will praise thee ; for thou hast heard me, and art become my salvation.

The stone which the builders refused is become the head stone of the corner.

This is the Lord's doing ; it is marvellous in our eyes.

This is the day which the Lord hath made ; we will rejoice and be glad in it.

Save now, I beseech thee, O Lord ! O Lord, I beseech thee, send now prosperity.

Blessed be he that cometh in the name of the Lord : we have blessed you out of the house of the Lord.

God is the Lord, which hath showed us light ;

Thou art my God, and I will praise thee : thou art my God, I will exalt thee.

O give thanks unto the Lord ; for he is good ; for his mercy endureth for ever.

Praise ye the Lord. Praise God in his sanctuary: praise him in the firmament of his power.

Praise him for his mighty acts : praise him according to his excellent greatness.

Praise him with the sound of the trumpet : praise him with the psaltery and harp.

Praise him with stringed instruments and organs.

Let everything that hath breath praise the Lord. Praise ye the Lord.

BENEDICTION II.

THIRD SUNDAY IN ADVENT.

COLLECT.

O GOD, the Father of Jesus Christ our Lord, who at his first coming didst send a messenger to prepare his way before him ; grant that the ministers of thy word may likewise so prepare and make ready his way, by turning the hearts of the disobedient to the wisdom of the just, that, at his second coming to judge the world, we may be found an acceptable people in thy sight. And this we beg in the name of Jesus Christ, through whom we ascribe unto thee all honor and glory, now and ever. *Amen.*

PROPHECIES.

ISAIAH AND JEREMIAH.

IN that day shall this song be sung in the land of Judah : We have a strong city ; salvation will God appoint for walls and bulwarks.

Open ye the gates, that the righteous nation which keepeth the truth may enter in.

Thou wilt keep him in perfect peace, whose mind is stayed on thee : because he trusteth in thee.

Trust ye in the Lord for ever: for in the Lord Jehovah is everlasting strength.

For he bringeth down them that dwell on high; the lofty city, he layeth it low; he layeth it low even to the ground; he bringeth it even to the dust. ·

The foot shall tread it down, even the feet of the poor, and the steps of the needy.

The way of the just is uprightness: thou, most upright, dost weigh the path of the just.

Yea, in the way of thy judgments, O Lord, have we waited for thee; the desire of our soul is to thy name, and to the remembrance of thee.

With my soul have I desired thee in the night; yea, with my spirit within me will I seek thee early: for when thy judgments are in the earth, the inhabitants of the world will learn righteousness.

Let favor be shown to the wicked, yet will he not learn righteousness: in the land of uprightness will he deal unjustly, and will not behold the majesty of the Lord.

Lord, when thy hand is lifted up, they will not see: but they shall see, and be ashamed for their envy at the people; yea, the fire of thine enemies shall devour them.

Lord, thou wilt ordain peace for us: for thou also hast wrought all our works in us.

For precept must be upon precept, line upon line, here a little, and there a little.

Wherefore hear the word of the Lord, ye scornful men,

Because ye have said, We have made a covenant with death, and with hell are we at agreement; when the overflowing scourge shall pass through, it shall not come unto us: for we have made lies our refuge, and under falsehood have we hid ourselves.

Therefore thus saith the Lord God, Behold, I lay in Zion for a foundation a stone, a tried stone, a precious corner-stone, a sure foundation.

Judgment also will I lay to the line, and righteousness to the plummet; and the hail shall sweep away the refuge of lies, and the waters shall overflow the hiding-place.

And your covenant with death shall be disannulled, and your agreement with hell shall not stand; when the overflowing scourge shall pass through, then ye shall be trodden down by it.

This also cometh forth from the Lord of hosts, which is wonderful in counsel, and excellent in working.

Woe be unto the pastors that destroy and scatter the sheep of my pasture! saith the Lord.

Therefore thus saith the Lord God of Israel against the pastors that feed my people, Ye have scattered my flock, and driven them away, and have not visited them: behold, I will visit upon you the evil of your doings, saith the Lord.

And I will gather the remnant of my flock out of all countries whither I have driven them, and will bring them again to their folds; and they shall be fruitful and increase.

And I will set up shepherds over them, which shall feed them; and they shall fear no more, nor be dismayed, neither shall they be lacking, saith the Lord.

Behold, the days come, saith the Lord, that I will raise unto David a righteous Branch, and a King shall reign and prosper, and shall execute judgment and justice in the earth.

In his days Judah shall be saved, and Israel shall dwell safely, and this is his name whereby he shall be called, The Lord our Righteousness.

Therefore, behold, the days come, saith the Lord, that they shall no more say, The Lord liveth, which brought up the children of Israel out of the land of Egypt;

But, The Lord liveth, which brought up, and which led, the seed of the house of Israel out of the north country, and from all countries whither I had driven them; and they shall dwell in their own land.

Now unto the King eternal, immortal, invisible, the only wise God ;

Be honor and glory through Jesus Christ, for ever and ever.

PSALMS.

PRESERVE me, O God : for in thee do I put my trust.

O my soul, thou hast said unto the Lord, Thou art my Lord : my goodness extendeth not to thee ;

But to the saints that are in the earth, and to the excellent, in whom is all my delight.

Their sorrows shall be multiplied that hasten after another god : their drink-offerings of blood will I not offer, nor take up their names into my lips.

The Lord is the portion of mine inheritance, and of my cup : thou maintainest my lot.

The lines are fallen unto me in pleasant places ; yea, I have a goodly heritage.

I will bless the Lord, who hath given me counsel; my reins also instruct me in the night seasons.

I have set the Lord always before me : because he is at my right hand, I shall not be moved.

Therefore my heart is glad, and my glory rejoiceth ; my flesh also shall rest in hope :

For thou wilt not leave my soul in hell ; neither wilt thou suffer thine Holy One to see corruption.

Thou wilt show me the path of life : in thy presence is fulness of joy ; at thy right hand there are pleasures for evermore.

I will declare thy name unto my brethren : in the midst of the congregation will I praise thee.

Ye that fear the Lord, praise him : all ye the seed of Jacob, glorify him ; and fear him, all ye the seed of Israel.

For he hath not despised nor abhorred the affliction of the afflicted, neither hath he hid his face from him ; but when he cried unto him, he heard.

My praise shall be of thee in the great congregation: I will pay my vows before them that fear him.

The meek shall eat and be satisfied; they shall praise the Lord that seek him: your heart shall live for ever.

All the ends of the world shall remember and turn unto the Lord; and all the kindreds of the nations shall worship before thee.

For the kingdom is the Lord's; and he is the governor among the nations.

All they that go down to the dust shall bow before him: and none can keep alive his own soul.

A seed shall serve him; it shall be accounted to the Lord for a generation.

They shall come, and shall declare his righteousness unto a people that shall be born, that he hath done this.

BENEDICTION XX.

FOURTH SUNDAY IN ADVENT.

COLLECT.

O LORD, raise up, we pray thee, thy power, and come among us, and with great might succor us; that whereas, through our sins and wickedness, we are hindered in running the race which is set before us, thy bountiful grace and mercy may speedily help and deliver us, through Jesus Christ our Lord. *Amen.*

PROPHECIES.

ISAIAH.

HEAR, ye that are far off, what I have done; and ye that are near, acknowledge my might.

The sinners are afraid ; fearfulness hath surprised the hypo-crites : who among us shall dwell with the devouring fire ? who among us shall dwell with everlasting burnings ?

He that walketh righteously, and speaketh uprightly ; he that despiseth the gain of oppressions, that shaketh his hands from holding bribes, that stoppeth his ears from hearing of blood, and shutteth his eyes from seeing evil ;

He shall dwell on high : his place of defence shall be the mu-nitions of rocks ; bread shall be given him, his waters shall be sure.

Thine eyes shall see the King in his beauty : they shall be-hold the land that is very far off.

Behold, a king shall reign in righteousness, and princes shall rule in judgment.

And a man shall be as an hiding-place from the wind, and a covert from the tempest ; as rivers of water in a dry place ; as the shadow of a great rock in a weary land.

And the eyes of them that see shall not be dim : and the ears of them that hear shall hearken.

The heart also of the rash shall understand knowledge, and the tongue of the stammerers shall be ready to speak plainly.

The vile person shall no more be called liberal, nor the churl said to be bountiful.

For the vile person will speak villany, and his heart will work iniquity, to practise hypocrisy, and to utter error against the Lord, to make empty the soul of the hungry ; and he will cause the drink of the thirsty to fail.

The instruments also of the churl are evil : he deviseth wicked devices to destroy the poor with lying words, even when the needy speaketh right.

But the liberal deviseth liberal things ; and by liberal things shall he stand.

Upon the land of my people shall come up thorns and briers, yea, upon all the houses of joy in the joyous city :

Until the spirit be poured upon us from on high, and the

3

wilderness be a fruitful field, and the fruitful field be counted for a forest.

Then judgment shall dwell in the wilderness, and righteousness remain in the fruitful field.

And the work of righteousness shall be peace; and the effect of righteousness, quietness and assurance for ever.

And my people shall dwell in a peaceable habitation, and in sure dwellings, and in quiet resting-places,

And there shall come forth a rod out of the stem of Jesse, and a Branch shall grow out of his roots:

And the spirit of the Lord shall rest upon him, the spirit of wisdom and understanding, the spirit of counsel and might, the spirit of knowledge, and of the fear of the Lord;

And shall make him of quick understanding in the fear of the Lord; and he shall not judge after the sight of his eyes, neither reprove after the hearing of his ears:

But with righteousness shall he judge the poor, and reprove with equity for the meek of the earth: and he shall smite the earth with the rod of his mouth, and with the breath of his lips shall he slay the wicked.

And righteousness shall be the girdle of his loins, and faithfulness the girdle of his reins.

The wolf also shall dwell with the lamb, and the leopard shall lie down with the kid; and the calf, and the young lion, and the fatling together; and a little child shall lead them.

They shall not hurt nor destroy in all my holy mountain; for the earth shall be full of the knowledge of the Lord, as the waters cover the sea.

Praise ye the Lord.

The Lord's name be praised.

PSALMS.

WHY do the heathen rage, and the people imagine a vain thing?

The kings of the earth set themselves, and the rulers take counsel together, against the Lord, and against his anointed, saying,

Let us break their bands asunder, and cast away their cords from us.

He that sitteth in the heavens shall laugh; the Lord shall have them in derision.

Then shall he speak unto them in his wrath, and vex them in his sore displeasure.

I will declare the decree: the Lord hath said unto me, Thou art my Son, this day have I begotten thee.

Ask of me, and I shall give thee the heathen for thine inheritance, and the uttermost parts of the earth for thy possession.

Thou shalt break them with a rod of iron; thou shalt dash them in pieces like a potter's vessel.

Be wise now, therefore, O ye kings; be instructed, ye judges of the earth.

Serve the Lord with fear, and rejoice with trembling.

Kiss the son, lest he be angry, and ye perish from the way, when his wrath is kindled but a little. Blessed are all they that put their trust in him.

Praise ye the Lord. I will praise him with my whole heart in the assembly of the upright, and in the congregation.

The works of the Lord are great, sought out of all them that have pleasure therein.

His work is honorable and glorious: and his righteousness endureth for ever.

He hath made his wonderful works to be remembered: the Lord is gracious, and full of compassion.

He hath given meat unto them that fear him: he will ever be mindful of his covenant.

He hath showed his people the power of his works, that he may give them the heritage of the heathen.

The works of his hands are verity and judgment: all his commandments are sure.

They stand fast for ever and ever, and are done in truth and uprightness.

He sent redemption unto his people : he hath commanded his covenant for ever ; holy and reverend is his name.

The fear of the Lord is the beginning of wisdom : a good understanding have all they that do his commandments : his praise endureth for ever.

BENEDICTION X.

SUNDAY ON OR NEXT AFTER CHRISTMAS.

COLLECT.

ALMIGHTY God, who hast given us thy only begotten Son to take our nature upon him, and as at this time to be born of a pure Virgin; grant that we, being regenerate and made thy children by adoption and grace, may daily be renewed by thy Holy Spirit, through the same our Lord Jesus Christ, that the light of his doctrine and life may shine into our hearts, and dispel our darkness, and direct our steps, and lead us at last to the unspeakable glories and felicities of thy heavenly kingdom ; which we beg in the name of our Saviour, ascribing to thee everlasting praises. *Amen.*

PROPHECIES.

ISAIAH.

THE wilderness, and the solitary place, shall be glad; and the desert shall rejoice, and blossom as the rose.

It shall blossom abundantly, and rejoice even with joy and singing ; they shall see the glory of the Lord, and the excellency of our God.

Strengthen ye the weak hands, and confirm the feeble knees.

Say to them that are of a fearful heart, Be strong, fear not; behold, your God will come with vengeance, even God with a recompense; he will come and save you.

Then the eyes of the blind shall be opened, and the ears of the deaf shall be unstopped :

Then shall the lame man leap as an hart, and the tongue of the dumb sing : for in the wilderness shall waters break out, and streams in the desert.

And the parched ground shall become a pool, and the thirsty land springs of water : in the habitations of dragons, where each lay, shall be grass, with reeds and rushes.

And an highway shall be there, and a way, and it shall be called, The way of holiness ; the unclean shall not pass over it ; but it shall be for those : the wayfaring men, though fools, shall not err therein.

No lion shall be there, nor any ravenous beast shall go up thereon ; it shall not be found there : but the redeemed shall walk there.

And the ransomed of the Lord shall return, and come to Zion with songs, and everlasting joy upon their heads : they shall obtain joy and gladness, and sorrow and sighing shall flee away.

Comfort ye, comfort ye, my people, saith your God.

Speak ye comfortably to Jerusalem, and cry unto her, that her warfare is accomplished, that her iniquity is pardoned : for she hath received of the Lord's hand double for all her sins.

The voice of him that crieth in the wilderness, Prepare ye the way of the Lord, make straight in the desert a highway for our God.

Every valley shall be exalted, and every mountain and hill shall be made low : and the crooked shall be made straight, and the rough places plain.

And the glory of the Lord shall be revealed, and all flesh

3 *

shall see it together: for the mouth of the Lord hath spoken it.

The voice said, Cry. And he said, What shall I cry? All flesh is grass, and all the goodliness thereof is as the flower of the field:

The grass withereth, the flower fadeth: because the spirit of the Lord bloweth upon it: surely the people is grass.

The grass withereth, the flower fadeth: but the word of our God shall stand for ever.

Behold, the Lord God will come with a strong hand, and his arms shall rule for him; behold, his reward is with him, and his work before him.

He shall feed his flock like a shepherd; he shall gather the lambs with his arm, and carry them in his bosom.

Who hath measured the waters in the hollow of his hand, and meted out heaven with the span, and comprehended the dust of the earth in a measure, and weighed the mountains in scales, and the hills in a balance?

Who hath directed the spirit of the Lord, or being his counsellor hath taught him?

With whom took he counsel, and who instructed him, and taught him in the path of judgment, and taught him knowledge, and showed to him the way of understanding?

Behold, the nations are as a drop of a bucket, and are counted as the small dust of the balance: behold, he taketh up the isles as a very little thing.

And Lebanon is not sufficient to burn, nor the beasts thereof sufficient for a burnt-offering.

All nations before him are as nothing; and they are counted to him less than nothing, and vanity.

To whom then will ye liken God? or what likeness will ye compare unto him?

The workman melteth a graven image, and the goldsmith spreadeth it over with gold, and casteth silver chains.

He that is so impoverished that he hath no oblation,

chooseth a tree that will not rot; he seeketh unto him a cunning workman to prepare a graven image, that shall not be moved.

Have ye not known? have ye not heard? hath it not been told you from the beginning? have ye not understood from the foundations of the earth?

It is he that sitteth upon the circle of the earth, and the inhabitants thereof are as grasshoppers; that stretcheth out the heavens as a curtain, and spreadeth them out as a tent to dwell in;

That bringeth the princes to nothing: he maketh the judges of the earth as vanity.

To whom then will ye liken me, or shall I be equal? saith the Holy One.

Lift up your eyes on high, and behold who hath created these things, that bringeth out their hosts by number: he calleth them all by names, by the greatness of his might, for that he is strong in power; not one faileth.

Why sayest thou, O Jacob, and speakest, O Israel, My way is hid from the Lord, and my judgment is passed over from my God?

Hast thou not known, hast thou not heard, that the everlasting God, the Lord, the Creator of the ends of the earth, fainteth not, neither is weary? there is no searching of his understanding.

He giveth power to the faint; and to them that have no might he increaseth strength.

Even the youths shall faint and be weary, and the young men shall utterly fall:

But they that wait upon the Lord shall renew their strength; they shall mount up with wings as eagles; they shall run and not be weary, and they shall walk and not faint.

O Lord, open thou our ears!

That we may hear meekly thy word, and receive it with pure affection.

PSALMS.

I said, I will take heed to my ways, that I sin not with my tongue : I will keep my mouth while the wicked is before me.

I was dumb with silence : I held my peace, even from good ; and my sorrow was stirred.

My heart was hot within me ; while I was musing, the fire burned : then spake I with my tongue.

Lord, make me to know mine end, and the measure of my days, what it is ; that I may know how frail I am.

Behold, thou hast made my days as an hand-breadth, and mine age is as nothing before thee : verily, every man at his best state is altogether vanity.

Surely every man walketh in a vain show ; surely they are disquieted in vain : he heapeth up riches, and knoweth not who shall gather them.

And now, Lord, what wait I for ? my hope is in thee.

Deliver me from all my transgressions ; make me not the reproach of the foolish.

I was dumb, I opened not my mouth ; because thou didst it.

Remove thy stroke away from me. I am consumed by the blow of thine hand.

When thou with rebukes dost correct man for iniquity, thou makest his beauty to consume away like a moth ; surely every man is vanity.

Hear my prayer, O Lord, and give ear unto my cry ; hold not thy peace at my tears : for I am a stranger with thee, and a sojourner, as all my fathers were.

O spare me, that I may recover strength, before I go hence, and be no more.

Lord, thou hast been our dwelling-place in all generations.

Before the mountains were brought forth, or ever thou hadst formed the earth and the world, even from everlasting to everlasting, thou art God.

Thou turnest man to destruction; and sayest, Return, ye children of men.

For a thousand years in my sight are but as yesterday when it is passed, and as a watch in the night.

Thou carriest them away as with a flood; they are as a sleep: in the morning they are like grass which groweth up.

In the morning it flourisheth, and groweth up; in the evening it is cut down, and withereth.

For we are consumed by thine anger, and by thy wrath are we troubled.

Thou hast set our iniquities before thee, our secret sins in the light of thy countenance.

For all our days are passed away in thy wrath; we spend our years as a tale that is told.

The days of our years are threescore years and ten; and if by reason of strength they be fourscore years, yet is their strength labor and sorrow: for it is soon cut off, and we fly away.

So teach us to number our days, that we may apply our hearts unto wisdom.

O satisfy us early with thy mercy; that we may rejoice and be glad all our days.

Make us glad according to the days wherein thou hast afflicted us, and the years wherein we have seen evil.

Let thy work appear unto thy servants, and thy glory unto their children.

And let the beauty of the Lord our God be upon us: and establish thou the work of our hands upon us; yea, the work of our hands establish thou it.

BENEDICTION VII.

FIRST SUNDAY IN THE YEAR.

COLLECT.

O GOD, the unfailing source of light and mercy, who hast brought us to the beginning of this year, and art sparing us to love thee, and to keep thy commandments ; give us, we beseech thee, a solemn sense of the importance of time, and of diligence in improving the talents thou hast placed in our hands ; and enable us so faithfully to discharge our duty in this life, that, when we shall appear before thee at thy great tribunal, we may be found worthy of that eternal kingdom which thou hast promised by Jesus Christ our Lord. *Amen.*

PROPHECIES.

HABAKKUK.

O JEHOVAH, I have heard thy words, and tremble. O Jehovah, revive thy work in the midst of the years, in the midst of the years make it known, in wrath remember mercy!

God cometh from Teman, and the Holy One from Mount Paran ; his glory covereth the heavens, and the earth is full of his praise.

His brightness is as the light ; rays stream forth from his hand, and there is the hiding-place of his power.

Before him goeth the pestilence, and the plague followeth his steps.

He standeth, and measureth the earth ; he beholdeth, and maketh the nations tremble ; the everlasting mountains are broken asunder ; the eternal hills sink down ; the eternal paths are trodden by him.

I see the tents of Cushan in affliction, and the canopies of the land of Midian tremble.

Is the anger of Jehovah kindled against the rivers, is thy wrath against the rivers, is thy indignation against the floods, that thou ridest on with thy horses, upon thy chariots of victory?

Thy bow is made bare; thine arrows are satiated; the song of victory is sung. Thou causest rivers to break forth from the earth.

The mountains see thee and tremble; the flood of waters overflows; the deep uttereth his voice, and lifteth up his hands on high.

The sun and the moon stand still in their habitation; like their light thine arrows fly; like their brightness the lightning of thy spear.

Thou marchest through the land in indignation; thou thrashest the nations in anger.

Thou goest forth for the deliverance of thy people; for the deliverance of thine anointed; thou smitest the head of the wicked; thou destroyest the foundation even to the neck.

Thou piercest with thine arrows the heads of their leaders, who rushed like a whirlwind to scatter us; who exulted, as if they should devour the distressed in a hiding-place.

Thou ridest through the sea with thy horses, through the raging of mighty waters.

I have heard, and my heart trembleth; my lips quiver at the voice; that I shall remain to the day of trouble, when the invader shall come up against my people!

Although the fig-tree shall not blossom, and there shall be no fruit in the vine, the labor of the olive shall fail, and the fields shall yield no meat. The flock shall be cut off from the fold, and there shall be no herd in the stalls.

Yet will I rejoice in the Lord, I will joy in the God of my salvation.

O Lord, open thou our lips!
And our mouth shall show forth thy praise.

PSALMS.

BLESS the Lord, O my soul; and all that is within me, bless his holy name.

Bless the Lord, O my soul, and forget not all his benefits;

Who forgiveth all thine iniquities; who healeth all thy diseases;

Who redeemeth thy life from destruction; who crowneth thee with loving kindness and tender mercies;

Who satisfieth thy mouth with good things; so that thy youth is renewed like the eagles.

The Lord executeth righteousness and judgment for all that are oppressed.

He made known his ways unto Moses, his acts unto the children of Israel.

The Lord is merciful and gracious, slow to anger, and plenteous in mercy.

He will not always chide; neither will he keep his anger for ever.

He hath not dealt with us after our sins, nor rewarded us according to our iniquities.

For as the heaven is high above the earth, so great is his mercy toward them that fear him.

As far as the east is from the west, so far hath he removed our transgressions from us.

Like as a father pitieth his children, so the Lord pitieth them that fear him.

For he knoweth our frame; he remembereth that we are dust.

As for man his days are as grass; as a flower of the field, so he flourisheth.

For the wind passeth over it, and it is gone; and the place thereof shall know it no more.

But the mercy of the Lord is from everlasting to everlasting upon them that fear him, and his righteousness unto children's children;

To such as keep his covenant, and to those that remember his commandments to do them.

The Lord hath prepared his throne in the heavens; and his kingdom ruleth over all.

Bless the Lord, ye his angels, that excel in strength, that do his commandments, hearkening unto the voice of his word.

Bless ye the Lord, all ye his hosts; ye ministers of his that do his pleasure.

Bless the Lord, all his works, in all places of his dominion: bless the Lord, O my soul.

BENEDICTION IV.

FIRST SUNDAY AFTER EPIPHANY.

COLLECT.

O LORD, we beseech thee mercifully to receive the prayers of thy people who call upon thee; and grant that they may both perceive and know what things they ought to do, and also may have grace and power faithfully to fulfil the same, through Jesus Christ our Lord. *Amen.*

PROPHECIES.

ISAIAH.

THUS saith the Lord to his anointed, whose right hand I have holden, to subdue nations before him; and I will loose the loins of kings, to open before him the two-leaved gates, and the gates shall not be shut:

I will go before thee, and make the crooked places straight: I will break in pieces the gates of brass, and cut in sunder the bars of iron:

4

And I will give thee the treasures of darkness, and hidden riches of secret places, that thou mayest know that I, the Lord, which call thee by thy name, am the God of Israel.

For Jacob my servant's sake, and Israel mine elect, I have even called thee by thy name: I have surnamed thee, though thou hast not known me.

I am the Lord, and there is none else, there is no God besides me: I girded thee, though thou hast not known me:

That they may know from the rising of the sun, and from the west, that there is none besides me. I am the Lord, and there is none else.

I form the light and create darkness: I make peace, and create evil: I the Lord do all these things.

Drop down, ye heavens, from above, and let the skies pour down righteousness; let the earth open, and let them bring forth salvation, and let righteousness spring up together. I the Lord have created it.

Woe unto him that striveth with his Maker! Shall the clay say to him that fashioneth it, What makest thou? or thy work, He hath no hands?

Thus saith the Lord, the Holy One of Israel, and his Maker, Ask me of things to come concerning my sons; and concerning the work of mine hands command ye me.

I have made the earth, and created man upon it: I, even my hands, have stretched out the heavens, and all their host have I commanded.

I have raised him up in righteousness, and I will direct all his ways: he shall build my city, and he shall let go my captives, not for price nor reward, saith the Lord of hosts.

Verily, thou art a God that hidest thyself, O God of Israel, the Saviour.

They shall be ashamed, and also confounded, all of them: they shall go to confusion together, that are makers of idols.

But Israel shall be saved in the Lord with an everlasting salvation: ye shall not be ashamed nor confounded, world without end.

For thus saith the Lord that created the heavens, God himself, that formed the earth and made it, he hath established it, he created it not in vain, he formed it to be inhabited; I am the Lord, and there is none else.

I have not spoken in secret, in a dark place of the earth: I said not, Seek ye me, in vain. I the Lord speak righteousness, I declare things that are right.

Assemble yourselves and come; draw near together, ye that are escaped of the nations: they have no knowledge that set up the wood of their graven image, and pray unto a god that cannot save.

Tell ye, and bring them near; yea, let them take counsel together: who hath declared this from ancient time? who hath told it from that time? have not I the Lord? and there is no God else besides me; a just God and a Saviour there is none beside me.

Look unto me, and be ye saved, all the ends of the earth; for I am God, and there is none else.

I have sworn by myself, the word is gone out of my mouth in righteousness, and shall not return, That unto me every knee shall bow, every tongue shall swear.

Surely, shall one say, In the Lord have I righteousness and strength: even to him shall men come; and all that are incensed against him shall be ashamed.

In the Lord shall all the seed of Israel be justified, and shall glory.

Now unto the King eternal, immortal, invisible, the only wise God;

Be honor and glory through Jesus Christ, for ever and ever.

PSALMS.

As for God, his way is perfect: the word of the Lord is tried; he is a buckler to all those that trust in him.

For who is God save the Lord? or who is a rock save our God?

The Lord liveth; and blessed be my Rock; and let the God of my salvation be exalted.

Therefore will I give thanks unto thee, O Lord, and sing praises unto thy name.

Unto thee will I cry, O Lord, my rock; be not silent to me: lest, if thou be silent to me, I become like them that go down into the pit.

Hear the voice of my supplications, when I cry unto thee, when I lift up my hands toward thy holy oracle.

Draw me not away with the wicked, and with the workers of iniquity; which speak peace to their neighbors, but mischief is in their hearts.

Because they regard not the works of the Lord, nor the operation of his hands, he shall destroy them, and not build them up.

Blessed be the Lord, because he hath heard the voice of my supplications.

The Lord is my strength and my shield: my heart trusted in him, and I am helped; therefore my heart greatly rejoiceth, and with my song will I praise him.

The Lord is the saving strength of his anointed.

Save thy people, and bless thine inheritance: feed them also, and lift them up for ever.

BENEDICTION III.

SECOND SUNDAY AFTER EPIPHANY.

COLLECT.

ALMIGHTY and most merciful God, we beseech thee to grant us thy grace, that in all the relations of life we may do justly, and love mercy, and walk humbly before thee; so that at last we may be received to the society of the just made perfect in thy heavenly kingdom, through Jesus Christ our Lord. *Amen.*

PROPHECIES.

ISAIAH.

HEARKEN to me, ye that follow after righteousness, ye that seek the Lord.

For the Lord shall comfort Zion: he will comfort all her waste places, and he will make her wilderness like Eden, and her desert like the garden of the Lord; joy and gladness shall be found therein, thanksgiving, and the voice of melody.

Hearken unto me, my people, and give ear unto me, O my nation: for a law shall proceed from me, and I will make my judgment to rest for a light of the people.

My righteousness is near; my salvation is gone forth and mine arms shall judge the people; the isles shall wait upon me, and on mine arm shall they trust.

Lift up your eyes to the heavens, and look upon the earth beneath; for the heavens shall vanish away like smoke, and the earth shall wax old like a garment, and they that dwell therein shall die in like manner: but my salvation shall be for ever, and my righteousness shall not be abolished.

Hearken unto me, ye that know righteousness, the people in whose heart is my law; fear ye not the reproach of men, neither be ye afraid of their revilings.

For the moth shall eat them up like a garment, and the worm shall eat them like wool; but my righteousness shall be for ever, and my salvation from generation to generation.

Awake, awake, put on strength, O arm of the Lord; awake, as in the ancient days, in the generations of old.

Art thou not it which hath dried the sea, the waters of the great deep; that hath made the depths of the sea a way for the ransomed to pass over?

Therefore the redeemed of the Lord shall return, and come

4 *

with singing; and everlasting joy shall be upon their head: they shall obtain gladness and joy; and sorrow and mourning shall flee away.

I, even I, am he that comforteth you: who art thou, that thou shouldest be afraid of a man that shall die, and of the son of man which shall be made as grass;

And forgettest the Lord thy Maker, that hath stretched forth the heavens, and laid the foundations of the earth; and hast feared continually every day, because of the fury of the oppressor, as if he were ready to destroy? and where is the fury of the oppressor?

The captive exile hasteneth that he may be loosed, and that he should not die in the pit, nor that his bread should fail.

But I am the Lord thy God, that divided the sea, whose waves roared: The Lord of hosts is his name.

And I have put my words in thy mouth, and have covered thee in the shadow of mine hand, that I may plant the heavens, and lay the foundations of the earth, and say, Thou art my people.

Awake, awake; put on thy strength, O Zion; put on thy beautiful garments, O Jerusalem, the holy city: for henceforth there shall no more come unto thee the unclean.

Shake thyself from the dust; arise, and sit down: loose thyself from the bands of thy neck.

For thus saith the Lord, Ye have sold yourselves for naught; and ye shall be redeemed without money.

For thus saith the Lord God, My people went down aforetime into Egypt to sojourn there; and the Assyrians oppressed them without cause.

Now, therefore, what have I here, saith the Lord, that my people is taken away for naught? they that rule over them make them to howl, saith the Lord; and my name continually every day is blasphemed.

Therefore my people shall know my name: therefore they shall know in that day that I am he that doth speak; behold, it is I.

How beautiful upon the mountains are the feet of him that bringeth good tidings, that publisheth peace ; that bringeth good tidings of good, that publisheth salvation ; that saith unto Zion, Thy God reigneth !

Thy watchmen shall lift up the voice ; with the voice together shall they sing ; for they shall see eye to eye, when the Lord shall bring again Zion.

Break forth into joy, sing together, ye waste places of Jerusalem : for the Lord hath comforted his people, he hath redeemed Jerusalem.

The Lord hath made bare his holy arm in the eyes of all the nations ; and all the ends of the earth shall see the salvation of our God.

Praise ye the Lord.
The Lord's name be praised.

PSALMS.

PRAISE ye the Lord.   Blessed is the man that feareth the Lord, that delighteth greatly in his commandments.

His seed shall be mighty upon earth : the generation of the upright shall be blessed.

Wealth and riches shall be in his house ; and his righteousness endureth for ever.

Unto the upright there ariseth light in the darkness : he is gracious, and full of compassion, and righteous.

A good man showeth favor, and lendeth ; he will guide his affairs with discretion.

Surely he shall not be moved for ever : the righteous shall be in everlasting remembrance.

He shall not be afraid of evil tidings : his heart is fixed, trusting in the Lord.

His heart is established, he shall not be afraid.

He hath dispersed : he hath given to the poor ; his righteousness endureth for ever :

The wicked shall see it, and be grieved; the desire of the wicked shall perish.

Praise ye the Lord. Praise, O ye servants of the Lord, praise the name of the Lord.

Blessed be the name of the Lord, from this time forth and for evermore.

From the rising of the sun, unto the going down of the same, the Lord's name is to be praised.

The Lord is high above all nations, and his glory above the heavens.

Who is like unto the Lord our God, who dwelleth on high;

Who humbleth himself to behold the things that are in heaven, and in the earth?

BENEDICTION VII.

THIRD SUNDAY AFTER EPIPHANY.

COLLECT.

O THOU most holy and perfect God, teach us to love one another with pure hearts fervently; to exercise forbearance and forgiveness toward our enemies; to recompense to no man evil for evil; and to be merciful, as thou, Father in heaven, art merciful. Grant this, we humbly beseech thee, in the name of Jesus Christ our Lord. *Amen.*

PROPHECIES.

PROVERBS.

A WISE man will hear, and will increase learning; and a man of understanding shall attain unto wise counsels;

The fear of the Lord is the beginning of knowledge: but fools despise wisdom and instruction.

My son, hear the instruction of thy father, and forsake not the law of thy mother:

For they shall be an ornament of grace unto thy head, and chains about thy neck.

My son, if sinners entice thee, consent thou not.

If they say, Come with us, let us lurk privily for the innocent without cause: we shall find all precious substance, we shall fill our houses with spoil: cast in thy lot among us; let us all have one purse, —

My son, walk not thou in the way with them; refrain thy foot from their path:

For their feet run to evil, and make haste to shed blood.

So are the ways of every one that is greedy of gain; which taketh away the life of the owners thereof.

Wisdom crieth without; she uttereth her voice in the streets;

She crieth in the chief place of concourse, in the openings of the gates: in the city she uttereth her words, saying,

How long, ye simple ones, will ye love simplicity, and the scorners delight in their scorning, and fools hate knowledge?

Turn you at my reproof; behold, I will pour out my spirit unto you, I will make known my words unto you.

Because I have called, and ye refused; I have stretched out my hand, and no man regarded;

But ye have set at naught all my counsel, and would none of my reproof;

I also will laugh at your calamity; I will mock when your fear cometh.

When your fear cometh as desolation, and your destruction cometh as a whirlwind; when distress and anguish cometh upon you;

Then shall they call upon me, but I will not answer; they shall seek me early, but they shall not find me:

For that they hated knowledge, and did not choose the fear of the Lord:

They would none of my counsel; they despised all my reproof:

Therefore shall they eat of the fruit of their own way, and be filled with their own devices.

For the turning away of the simple shall slay them, and the prosperity of fools shall destroy them.

But whoso hearkeneth unto me shall dwell safely, and shall be quiet from fear of evil.

O Lord, open thou our ears!

That we may hear meekly thy word, and receive it with pure affection.

PSALMS.

BLESSED is he that considereth the poor: the Lord will deliver him in time of trouble.

The Lord will preserve him, and keep him alive; and he shall be blessed upon the earth: and thou wilt not deliver him unto the will of his enemies.

The Lord will strengthen him upon the bed of languishing: thou wilt make all his bed in his sickness.

I said, O Lord, be merciful unto me; heal my soul; for I have sinned against thee.

Mine enemies speak evil of me, When shall he die, and his name perish?

And if he come to see me, he speaketh vanity: his heart gathereth iniquity to itself; when he goeth abroad, he telleth it.

All that hate me whisper together against me: against me do they devise my hurt.

Yea, mine own familiar friend, in whom I trusted, which did eat of my bread, hath lifted up his heel against me.

But thou, O Lord, be merciful unto me, and raise me up, that I may requite them.

By this I know that thou favorest me, because mine enemy doth not triumph over me.

And as for me, thou upholdest me, and settest me before thy face for ever.

Blessed be the Lord God of Israel from everlasting, and to everlasting. Amen, and Amen.

As the hart panteth after the water-brooks, so panteth my soul after thee, O God.

My soul thirsteth for God, for the living God: when shall I come and appear before God?

My tears have been my meat day and night, while they continually say unto me, Where is thy God?

When I remember these things, I pour out my soul in me: for I had gone with the multitude; I went with them to the house of God, with the voice of joy and praise, with a multitude that kept holy day.

Why art thou cast down, O my soul? and why art thou disquieted in me? Hope thou in God; for I shall yet praise him for the help of his countenance.

O my God, my soul is cast down within me: therefore will I remember thee.

Deep calleth unto deep at the noise of thy water-spouts: all thy waves and thy billows are gone over me.

Yet the Lord will command his loving-kindness in the daytime, and in the night his song shall be with me, and my prayer unto the God of my life.

I will say unto God my rock, Why hast thou forgotten me? why go I mourning because of the oppression of the enemy?

As with a sword in my bones, mine enemies reproach me; while they say daily unto me, Where is thy God?

Why art thou cast down, O my soul? and why art thou disquieted within me? Hope thou in God; for I shall yet praise him, who is the health of my countenance, and my God.

BENEDICTION II.

FOURTH SUNDAY AFTER EPIPHANY.

COLLECT.

O GOD, who knowest us to be set in the midst of so many and great dangers, that, by reason of the frailty of our nature, we cannot always stand upright; grant to us such strength and protection as may support us in all dangers, and carry us through all temptations, through Jesus Christ our Lord. *Amen.*

PROPHECIES.

ISAIAH.

BEHOLD, the Lord's hand is not shortened, that it cannot save; neither his ear heavy, that it cannot hear:

But your iniquities have separated between you and your God, and your sins have hid his face from you, that he will not hear.

For your hands are defiled with iniquity: your lips have spoken lies, your tongue hath muttered perverseness.

None calleth for justice, nor any pleadeth for truth: they trust in vanity, and speak lies: they conceive mischief, and bring forth iniquity.

Their feet run to evil: their thoughts are thoughts of iniquity; wasting and destruction are in their paths.

The way of peace they know not; and there is no judgment in their goings: they have made them crooked paths: whosoever goeth therein shall not know peace.

Therefore is judgment far from us, neither doth justice overtake us: we wait for light, but behold obscurity; for brightness, but we walk in darkness.

We grope for the wall like the blind, and we grope as if we had no eyes: we stumble at noonday as in the night; we are in desolate places as dead men.

We look for judgment, but there is none; for salvation, but it is far off from us.

For our transgressions are multiplied before thee, and our sins testify against us: for our transgressions are with us; and as for our iniquities, we know them:

In transgressing and lying against the Lord, and departing away from our God, speaking oppression and revolt, conceiving and uttering from the heart words of falsehood.

And judgment is turned away backward, and justice standeth afar off: for truth is fallen in the street, and equity cannot enter.

Yea, truth faileth; and he that departeth from evil maketh himself a prey: and the Lord saw it, and it displeased him that there was no judgment.

And he saw that there was no man, and wondered that there was no intercessor; therefore his arm brought salvation unto him; and his righteousness, it sustained him.

For he put on righteousness as a breastplate, and an helmet of salvation upon his head; and he put on the garments of vengeance for clothing, and was clad with zeal as a cloak.

According to their deeds, accordingly he will repay, fury to his adversaries, recompense to his enemies.

So shall they fear the name of the Lord from the west, and his glory from the rising of the sun. When the enemy shall come in like a flood, the Spirit of the Lord shall lift up a standard against him.

And the Redeemer shall come to Zion, and unto them that turn from transgression, saith the Lord.

As for me, this is my covenant with them, saith the Lord: My spirit that is upon thee, and my words which I have put in thy mouth, shall not depart out of thy mouth, nor out of the mouth of thy seed, nor out of the mouth of thy seed's seed, saith the Lord, from henceforth and for ever.

O Lord, open thou our lips!

And our mouth shall show forth thy praise.

PSALMS.

HEAR this, all ye people; give ear, all ye inhabitants of the world:

Both low and high, rich and poor, together.

My mouth shall speak of wisdom; and the meditation of my heart shall be of understanding.

I will incline mine ear to a parable; I will open my dark saying.

Wherefore should I fear in the days of evil, when the iniquity of my heels shall compass me about?

They that trust in their wealth, and boast themselves in the multitude of their riches;

None of them can by any means redeem his brother, nor give to God a ransom for him;

That he should still live for ever, and not see corruption.

For we see that wise men die, likewise the fool and the brutish person perish, and leave their wealth to others.

Their inward thought is, that their houses shall continue for ever, and their dwelling-places to all generations: they call their lands after their own names.

Nevertheless, man a being in honor abideth not: he is like the beasts that perish.

This their way is their folly: yet their posterity approve their sayings.

Like sheep they are laid in the grave; death shall feed on them; and the upright shall have dominion over them in the morning; and their beauty shall consume in the grave from their dwelling.

But God will redeem my soul from the power of the grave; for he shall receive me.

Be not thou afraid when one is made rich, when the glory of his house is increased:

For when he dieth, he shall carry nothing away; his glory shall not descend after him;

Though, while he lived, he blessed his soul : (and men will praise thee when thou dost well to thyself :)

He shall go to the generation of his fathers ; they shall never see light.

Man that is in honor, and understandeth not, is like the beasts that perish.

Why boastest thou thyself in mischief, O mighty man? the goodness of God endureth continually.

Thy tongue deviseth mischief, like a sharp razor, working deceitfully.

Thou lovest evil more than good, and lying rather than to speak righteousness.

Thou lovest all-devouring words, thou deceitful tongue.

God shall likewise destroy thee for ever : he shall take thee away, and pluck thee out of thy dwelling-place, and root thee out of the land of the living.

The righteous also shall see, and fear, and shall laugh at him :

Lo, this is the man that made not God his strength ; but trusted in the abundance of his riches, and strengthened himself in his wickedness.

But I trust in the mercy of God for ever and ever.

I will praise thee for ever, because thou hast done it : and I will wait on thy name ; for it is good.

BENEDICTION I.

FIFTH SUNDAY AFTER EPIPHANY.

COLLECT.

O LORD, we beseech thee to keep thy Church and household continually in thy true religion ; that they, who do lean only upon the hope of thy heavenly grace, may evermore be defended by thy mighty power, through Jesus Christ our Lord. *Amen.*

PROPHECIES.

ISAIAH.

FOR Zion's sake will I not hold my peace, and for Jerusalem's sake I will not rest, until the righteousness thereof go forth as brightness, and the salvation thereof as a lamp that burneth.

And the Gentiles shall see thy righteousness, and all kings thy glory: and thou shalt be called by a new name, which the mouth of the Lord shall name.

Thou shalt also be a crown of glory in the hand of the Lord, and a royal diadem in the hand of thy God.

Thou shalt no more be termed Forsaken: neither shall thy land any more be termed Desolate; but thou shalt be called Hephzi-bah,* and thy land Beulah.†

I have set watchmen upon thy walls, O Jerusalem, which shall never hold their peace day nor night: ye that make mention of the Lord, keep not silence;

And give him no rest, till he establish, and till he make Jerusalem a praise in the earth.

Go through, go through the gates; prepare ye the way of the people; cast up, cast up the highway; gather out the stones; lift up a standard for the people.

Behold, the Lord hath proclaimed unto the end of the world, Say ye, Behold, thy salvation cometh; behold, his reward is with him, and his work before him.

And they shall call them, The holy people, The redeemed of the Lord: and thou shalt be called, Sought out, A city not forsaken.

The Spirit of the Lord God is upon me; because the Lord hath anointed me to preach good tidings unto the meek: he hath

---

* My-delight-is-in-thee.　　　　† The Wedded.

sent me to bind up the broken-hearted, to proclaim liberty to the captives, and the opening of the prison to them that are bound;

To proclaim the acceptable year of the Lord, and the day of vengeance of our God; to comfort all that mourn;

To appoint unto them that mourn, to give unto them beauty for ashes, the oil of joy for mourning, the garment of praise for the spirit of heaviness: that they might be called Trees of Righteousness, The Planting of the Lord, that he might be glorified.

And they shall build the old wastes, they shall raise up the former desolations, and they shall repair the waste cities, the desolations of many generations.

And strangers shall stand and feed your flocks, and the sons of the alien shall be your ploughmen, and your vine-dressers.

But ye shall be named the priests of the Lord; men shall call you the ministers of our God:

For your shame you shall have double, and for confusion they shall rejoice in their portion: everlasting joy shall be unto you.

For I the Lord love judgment, I hate robbery for burnt-offering; and I will direct their work in truth; and I will make an everlasting covenant with them.

All that see them shall acknowledge them, that they are the seed which the Lord hath blessed.

I will greatly rejoice in the Lord, my soul shall be joyful in my God: for he hath clothed me with the garments of salvation, he hath covered me with the robe of righteousness, as a bridegroom decketh himself with ornaments, and as a bride adorneth herself with her jewels.

For as the earth bringeth forth her bud, and as the garden causeth the things that are sown in it to spring forth; so the Lord God will cause righteousness and praise to spring forth before all the nations.

Now unto the King eternal, immortal, invisible, the only wise God,

Be honor and glory, through Jesus Christ, for ever and ever.

5 *

PSALMS.

In thee, O Lord, do I put my trust; let me never be put to confusion.

Deliver me in thy righteousness, and cause me to escape: incline thine ear unto me, and save me.

Be thou my strong habitation, whereunto I may continually resort: thou hast given commandment to save me; for thou art my rock and my fortress.

Deliver me, O my God, out of the hand of the wicked, out of the hand of the unrighteous and cruel man.

For thou art my hope, O Lord God: thou art my trust from my youth.

Let my mouth be filled with thy praise and with thy honor all the day.

Cast me not off in the time of old age; forsake me not when my strength faileth.

For mine enemies speak against me; and they that lay wait for my soul take counsel together,

Saying, God hath forsaken him: persecute and take him; for there is none to deliver him.

O God, be not far from me: O my God, make haste for my help.

I will hope continually, and will yet praise thee more and more.

My mouth shall show forth thy righteousness and thy salvation all the day; for I know not the numbers thereof.

I will go in the strength of the Lord God: I will make mention of thy righteousness, even of thine only.

O God, thou hast taught me from my youth: and hitherto have I declared thy wondrous works.

When I am old and gray-headed, O God, forsake me not, until I have showed thy strength unto this generation, and thy power to every one that is to come.

Thy righteousness also, O God, is very high, who hast done great things: O God, who is like unto thee?

Thou, which hast showed me great and sore troubles, shalt quicken me again, and shalt bring me up again from the depths of the earth.

I will also praise thee, even thy truth, O my God: unto thee will I sing, O thou Holy One of Israel.

My lips shall greatly rejoice when I sing unto thee; and my soul, which thou hast redeemed.

My tongue also shall talk of thy righteousness all the day long.

O God, why hast thou cast us off for ever? why doth thine anger smoke against the sheep of thy pasture?

Remember thy congregation, which thou hast purchased of old; the rod of thine inheritance, which thou hast redeemed.

Lift up thy feet unto the perpetual desolations; even all that the enemy hath done wickedly in the sanctuary.

Why withdrawest thou thy hand, even thy right hand? pluck it out of thy bosom.

For God is my King of old, working salvation in the midst of the earth.

Thou didst divide the sea by thy strength: thou brakest the heads of the dragons in the waters.

Thou didst cleave the fountain and the flood: thou driedst up mighty rivers.

The day is thine, the night also is thine: thou hast prepared the light and the sun.

Thou hast set all the borders of the earth: thou hast made summer and winter.

Remember this, that the enemy hath reproached, O Lord, and that the foolish people have blasphemed thy name.

O deliver not the soul of thy turtle-dove unto the multitude of the wicked: forget not the congregation of thy poor for ever.

Have respect unto the covenant: for the dark places of the earth are full of the habitations of cruelty.

O let not the oppressed return ashamed : let the poor and needy praise thy name.

Arise, O God, plead thine own cause.

BENEDICTION VI.

SIXTH SUNDAY AFTER EPIPHANY.

COLLECT.

O GOD, whose blessed Son was manifested, that he might make us the sons of God, and heirs of eternal life ; grant us, we beseech thee, that, having this hope, we may purify ourselves even as he is pure ; that when he shall appear again with power and great glory, we may be made like unto him in his glorious kingdom ; where we may ascribe blessing, and honor, and glory, and power, to Him who sitteth upon the throne, and to the Lamb for ever and ever.

PROPHECIES.

ISAIAH.

I am sought of them that asked not for me ; I am found of them that sought me not ; I said, Behold me, behold me, unto a nation that was not called by my name.

I have spread out my hands all the day unto a rebellious people, which walketh in a way that was not good, after their own thoughts ;

A people that provoketh me to anger continually to my face ; that sacrificeth in gardens and burneth incense upon altars ;

Which say, Stand by thyself, come not near to me ; for I am holier than thou.

Behold, it is written before me, I will not keep silence, but will recompense, even recompense into their bosom,

Your iniquities, and the iniquities of your fathers together, saith the Lord, which have burnt incense upon the mountains, and blasphemed me upon the hills: therefore will I measure their former work into their bosom.

Because, when I called, ye did not answer; when I spake, ye did not hear; but did evil before mine eyes, and did choose that wherein I delighted not.

Therefore, thus saith the Lord God, Behold, my servants shall eat, but ye shall be hungry: behold, my servants shall drink, but ye shall be thirsty; behold, my servants shall rejoice, but ye shall be ashamed.

Behold, my servants shall sing for joy of heart, but ye shall cry for sorrow of heart, and for vexation of spirit.

And ye shall leave your name for a curse unto my chosen: for the Lord God shall slay thee, and call his servants by another name.

That he who blesseth himself in the earth, shall bless himself in the God of truth; and he that sweareth in the earth, shall swear by the God of truth; because the former troubles are forgotten, and because they are hid from mine eyes.

For behold, I create new heavens and a new earth; and the former shall not be remembered, nor come into mind.

But be ye glad and rejoice for ever in that which I create: for, behold, I create Jerusalem a rejoicing, and her people a joy.

And I will rejoice in my people: and the voice of weeping shall be no more heard in thee, nor the voice of crying.

There shall be no more thence the infant of days, nor an old man that hath not filled his days: for the child shall die an hundred years old; but the sinner being an hundred years old shall be accursed.

And they shall build houses, and inhabit them; and they shall plant vineyards, and eat the fruit of them.

They shall not build and another inhabit; and they shall not plant and another eat: for as the days of a tree are the days of my people, and mine elect shall long enjoy the work of their hands.

They shall not labor in vain, nor bring forth for trouble: for they are the seed of the blessed of the Lord, and their offspring with them.

And it shall come to pass, that, before they call, I will answer: and while they are yet speaking, I will hear.

The wolf and the lamb shall feed together. They shall not hurt nor destroy in all my holy mountain, saith the Lord.

Praise ye the Lord.
The Lord's name be praised.

PSALMS.

MAKE haste, O God, to deliver me: make haste to help me, O Lord.

Let all those that seek thee rejoice and be glad in thee: and let such as love thy salvation say continually, Let God be magnified.

But I am poor and needy; make haste unto me, O God: thou art my help and my deliverer; O Lord, make no tarrying.

Consider mine affliction, and deliver me; for I do not forget thy law.

Plead my cause, and deliver me: quicken me according to thy word.

Salvation is far from the wicked: for they seek not thy statutes.

Great are thy tender mercies, O Lord; quicken me according to thy judgments.

Many are mine enemies; yet do I not decline from thy testimonies.

I beheld the transgressors, and was grieved; because they kept not thy word.

Thy word is true from the beginning : and every one of thy righteous judgments endureth for ever.

I rejoice at thy word, as one that findeth great spoil.

I hate and abhor lying ; but thy law do I love.

Seven times a day do I praise thee : because of thy righteous judgments.

Great peace have they which love thy law : and nothing shall offend them.

Lord, I have hoped for thy salvation, and done thy commandments.

My soul hath kept thy testimonies ; and I love them exceedingly.

Let my cry come near before thee, O Lord : give me understanding according to thy word.

Let my supplication come before thee : deliver me according to thy word.

My lips shall utter praise, when thou hast taught me thy statutes.

My tongue shall speak of thy word : for all thy commandments are righteousness.

Let thine hand help me : for I have chosen thy precepts.

I have longed for thy salvation, O Lord ; and thy law is my delight.

Let my soul live, and it shall praise thee ; and let thy judgments help me.

I have gone astray like a lost sheep : seek thy servant ; for I do not forget thy commandments.

In my distress I cried unto the Lord, and he heard me.

Deliver my soul, O Lord, from lying lips, and from a deceitful tongue.

BENEDICTION V.

SEPTUAGESIMA SUNDAY.

COLLECT.

GRANT unto us, O merciful Father, resolution and constancy to persevere in the path of our duty to the end of our lives. Let no prospect of danger deter us from doing that which is right, nor any enticement of evil example tempt us to forfeit our hope of immortality. Preserve us, we humbly beseech thee, from every evil way, and conduct us in the paths of innocence and virtue to eternal life ; which we ask in the name and as disciples of Jesus Christ our Lord. *Amen.*

PROPHECIES.

JEREMIAH.

WHY is this people slidden back by a perpetual backsliding ? they hold fast deceit, they refuse to return.

I hearkened and heard, but they spake not aright : no man repented him of his wickedness, saying, What have I done? every one turned to his course, as the horse rusheth into the battle.

Yea, the stork in the heaven knoweth her appointed times ; and the turtle, and the crane, and the swallow, observe the time of their coming : but my people know not the judgment of the Lord.

How do ye say, We are wise, and the law of the Lord is with us ? Lo, certainly in vain made he it ; the pen of the scribes is in vain.

The wise men are ashamed, they are dismayed and taken : lo, they have rejected the word of the Lord ; and what wisdom is in them ?

For they have healed the hurt of the daughter of my people slightly, saying, Peace, peace ; when there is no peace.

Were they ashamed when they had committed abomination? nay, they were not at all ashamed, neither could they blush: therefore shall they fall among them that fall; in the time of their visitation they shall be cast down, saith the Lord.

The harvest is past, the summer is ended, and we are not saved.

For the hurt of the daughter of my people am I hurt; astonishment hath taken hold on me.

Is there no balm in Gilead? is there no physician there? why then is not the health of the daughter of my people recovered?

Hear the word of the Lord, O people that enter in by these gates;

Thus saith the Lord, Execute ye judgment and righteousness, and deliver the spoiled out of the hand of the oppressor: and do no wrong, do no violence to the stranger, the fatherless, nor the widow, neither shed innocent blood in this place.

But if ye will not hear these words, I swear by myself, saith the Lord, that this house shall become a desolation.

And many nations shall pass by, and they shall say every man to his neighbor, Wherefore hath the Lord done thus?

Then they shall answer, Because they have forsaken the covenant of the Lord their God, and worshipped other gods, and served them.

Weep ye not for the dead, neither bemoan him; but weep sore for him that goeth away.

Woe unto him that buildeth his house by unrighteousness, and his chambers by wrong; that useth his neighbor's service without wages, and giveth him not for his work;

That saith, I will build me a wide house, and large chambers, and cutteth him out windows; and it is ceiled with cedar, and painted with vermilion!

Shalt thou reign because thou closest thyself in cedar? Did not thy father eat and drink, and do judgment and justice, and then it was well with him?

6

He judged the cause of the poor and needy; then, it was well with him: was not this to know me? saith the Lord.

But thine eyes and thy heart are not but for thy covetousness, and for oppression, and for violence, to do it.

I spake unto thee in thy prosperity; but thou saidst, I will not hear: this hath been thy manner from thy youth, that thou obeyest not my voice.

Surely then shalt thou be ashamed and confounded for all thy wickedness.

O earth, hear the word of the Lord.

O Lord, open thou our ears!

That we may hear meekly thy word, and receive it with pure affection.

PSALMS.

O GOD, my heart is fixed: I will sing and give praise.

I will praise thee, O Lord, among the people: and I will sing praises unto thee among the nations.

For thy mercy is great above the heavens, and thy truth reacheth unto the clouds.

Be thou exalted, O God, above the heavens; and thy glory above all the earth:

That thy beloved may be delivered, save with thy right hand, and answer me.

God hath spoken in his holiness; I will rejoice;

Give us help from trouble: for vain is the help of man.

Through God we shall do valiantly; for he it is that shall tread down our enemies.

Hold not thy peace, O God of my praise;

For the mouth of the wicked and the mouth of the deceitful are opened: they have spoken with a lying tongue.

They compassed me about also with words of hatred; and fought against me without a cause.

For my love they are my adversaries: but I give myself unto prayer.

Help me, O Lord my God : O save me according to thy mercy ;

That they may know that this is thy hand ; that thou, Lord, hast done it.

I will greatly praise the Lord with my mouth ; yea, I will praise him among the multitude.

For he shall stand at the right hand of the poor, to save him from those that condemn his soul.

BENEDICTION VII.

SEXAGESIMA SUNDAY.

COLLECT.

O LORD God, who seest that we put not our trust in anything which we do ; mercifully grant that by thy power we may be defended against all adversity, through Jesus Christ our Lord. *Amen.*

PROPHECIES.

JEREMIAH AND LAMENTATIONS.

THE sin of Judah is written with a pen of iron, and with the point of a diamond : it is graven upon the table of their heart.

Thus saith the Lord : Cursed be the man that trusteth in man, and maketh flesh his arm, and whose heart departeth from the Lord.

For he shall be like the heath in the desert, and shall not see when good cometh ; but shall inhabit the parched places in the wilderness, in a salt land and not inhabited.

Blessed is the man that trusteth in the Lord, and whose hope the Lord is :

For he shall be as a tree planted by the waters, and that spreadeth out her roots by the river, and shall not see when heat cometh, but her leaf shall be green; and shall not be careful in the year of drought, neither shall cease from yielding fruit.

The heart is deceitful above all things, and desperately wicked: who can know it?

I the Lord search the heart, I try the reins, even to give every man according to his ways, and according to the fruit of his doings.

As the partridge sitteth on eggs, and hatcheth them not; so he that getteth riches, and not by right, shall leave them in the midst of his days, and at his end shall be a fool.

A glorious high throne from the beginning is the place of our sanctuary.

O Lord, the Hope of Israel, all that forsake thee shall be ashamed, and they that depart from me shall be written in the earth, because they have forsaken the Lord, the fountain of living waters.

Heal me, O Lord, and I shall be healed; save me, and I shall be saved: for thou art my praise.

Be not a terror unto me: thou art my hope in the day of evil.

Thus said the Lord unto me, Go and stand in the gate of the children of the people, and in all the gates of Jerusalem;

Hear ye the word of the Lord, all that enter in by these gates.

Thus saith the Lord: Take heed to yourselves, and bear no burden on the Sabbath-day;

Neither carry forth a burden out of your houses on the Sabbath-day, neither do ye any work; but hallow ye the Sabbath-day, as I commanded your fathers.

And it shall come to pass, if ye diligently hearken unto me, saith the Lord, to bring in no burden through the gates of this city on the Sabbath-day, but hallow the Sabbath-day, to do no work therein;

Then shall there enter into the gates of this city kings and princes sitting upon the throne of David, riding in chariots and on horses; and this city shall remain for ever.

And they shall come from the plain, and from the mountains, and from the south, bringing sacrifices of praise unto the house of the Lord.

But if ye will not hearken unto me to hallow the Sabbath-day and not to bear a burden, then will I kindle a fire, and it shall not be quenched.

How is the gold become dim; how is the most fine gold changed! the stones of the sanctuary are poured out in the top of every street.

The precious sons of Zion, comparable to fine gold, how are they esteemed as earthen pitchers, the work of the hands of the potter!

The crown is fallen from our head: woe unto us that we have sinned!

For this our heart is faint; for these things our eyes are dim.

Thou, O Lord, remainest for ever; thy throne from generation to generation.

Turn thou us unto thee, O Lord, and we shall be turned; renew our days as of old.

O Lord, open thou our lips;
And our mouth shall show forth thy praise.

PSALMS.

O GIVE thanks unto the Lord; call upon his name; make known his deeds among the people.

Sing unto him, sing psalms unto him: talk ye of all his wondrous works.

Glory ye in his holy name: let the heart of them rejoice that seek the Lord.

Seek the Lord, and his strength; seek his face evermore.

Remember his marvellous works that he hath done; his wonders, and the judgments of his mouth;

6 *

He is the Lord our God ; his judgments are in all the earth.

He hath remembered his covenant for ever, the word which he commanded to a thousand generations :

Which covenant he made with Abraham, and his oath unto Isaac ;

And confirmed the same unto Jacob for a law, and to Israel for an everlasting covenant ;

When they were but a few men in number ; yea, very few, and strangers.

When they went from one nation to another, from one kingdom to another people,

He suffered no man to do them wrong ; yea, he reproved kings for their sakes ;

Saying, Touch not mine anointed, and do my prophets no harm.

Moreover, he called for a famine upon the land ; he brake the whole staff of bread.

He sent a man before them, even Joseph, who was sold for a servant ;

Whose feet they hurt with fetters : he was laid in iron ;

Until the time that his word came ; the word of the Lord tried him.

The king sent and loosed him ; even the ruler of the people, and let him go free.

He made him lord of his house, and ruler of all his substance ;

To bind his princes at his pleasure, and teach his senators wisdom.

And he increased his people greatly, and made them stronger than their enemies.

He sent Moses his servant, and Aaron whom he had chosen.

They showed his signs among them, and wonders in the land o Ham.

He sent darkness, and made it dark ; and they rebelled not against his work.

He turned their waters into blood, and slew their fish.

The land brought forth frogs in abundance, in the chambers of their kings.

He spake, and there came divers sorts of flies, and lice in all their coasts.

He gave them hail for rain, and flaming fire in their land.

He smote their vines also, and their fig-trees; and brake the trees of their coasts.

He spake, and the locusts came, and caterpillars, and that without number,

And did eat up all the herbs in their land, and devoured the fruit of their ground.

He smote also all the first-born in their land, the chief of all their strength.

He brought them forth also with silver and gold; and there was not one feeble person among their tribes.

Egypt was glad when they departed; for the fear of them fell upon them.

He spread a cloud for a covering, and fire to give light in the night.

The people asked, and he brought quails, and satisfied them with the bread of heaven.

He opened the rock, and the waters gushed out; they ran in the dry places like a river.

For he remembered his holy promise, and Abraham his servant.

And he brought forth his people with joy, and his chosen with gladness;

And gave them the lands of the heathen: and they inherited the labor of the people;

That they might observe his statutes, and keep his laws. Praise ye the Lord.

BENEDICTION VI.

QUINQUAGESIMA SUNDAY.

COLLECT.

O LORD, who hast taught us that all our doings without charity are nothing worth ; send thy Holy Spirit and pour into our hearts that most excellent gift of charity, the very bond of peace, and of all virtues ; without which whosoever liveth is counted dead before thee.   Grant this, O Lord, for thy mercy's sake in Jesus Christ our Saviour.   *Amen.*

PROPHECIES.

LAMENTATIONS.

The Lord hath led me, and brought me into darkness, but not into light.

He hath set me in dark places, as they that be dead of old.

He hath hedged me about, that I cannot get out ; he hath made my chain heavy.

He hath enclosed my ways with hewn stone, he hath made my paths crooked.

And thou hast removed my soul far off from peace ; I forgot prosperity.

And I said, My strength and my hope is perished from the Lord ;

Remembering mine affliction and my misery, the wormwood and the gall.

My soul hath them still in remembrance, and is humbled in me.

This I recall to my mind, therefore have I hope.

It is of the Lord's mercies that we are not consumed, because his compassions fail not.

They are new every morning : great is thy faithfulness.

The Lord is my portion, saith my soul ; therefore will I hope in him.

The Lord is good unto them that wait for him, to the soul that seeketh him.

It is good that a man should both hope and quietly wait for the salvation of the Lord.

It is good for a man that he bear the yoke in his youth.

He sitteth alone and keepeth silence, because he hath borne it upon him.

He putteth his mouth in the dust, if so be there may be hope.

He giveth his cheek to him that smiteth him ; he is filled full with reproach.

For the Lord will not cast off for ever ;

But though he cause grief, yet will he have compassion according to the multitude of his mercies.

For he doth not afflict willingly, nor grieve the children of men.

To crush under his feet all the prisoners of the earth,

To turn aside the right of a man before the face of the Most High,

To subvert a man in his cause, the Lord approveth not.

Who is he that saith, and it cometh to pass, when the Lord commandeth it not?

Wherefore doth a living man complain, a man for the punishment of his sins?

Let us search and try our ways, and turn again to the Lord.

Let us lift up our heart with our hands unto God in the heavens.

Thou hast heard my voice; hide not thine ear at my breathing, at my cry.

Thou drewest near in the day that I called upon thee ; thou saidst, Fear not.

O Lord, thou hast pleaded the causes of my soul; thou hast redeemed my life.

O Lord, thou hast seen my wrong ; judge thou my cause.

Now unto the King eternal, immortal, invisible, the only wise God,

Be honor and glory, through Jesus Christ, for ever and ever.

PSALMS.

GIVE ear to my prayer, O God; and hide not thyself from my supplication.

Attend unto me, and hear me,

Because of the oppression of the wicked: for they cast iniquity upon me.

My heart is sore pained within me; and the terrors of death are fallen upon me.

And I said, O that I had wings like a dove! for then would I fly away, and be at rest.

Lo, then would I wander far off, and remain in the wilderness.

I would hasten my escape from the windy storm and tempest,

For it was not an enemy that reproached me; then I could have borne it; neither was it he that hated me, that did magnify himself against me; then I would have hid myself from him;

But it was thou, mine equal, my guide, and mine acquaintance.

We took sweet counsel together, and walked unto the house of God in company.

As for me, I will call upon God; and the Lord shall save me.

Evening, and morning, and at noon, will I pray, and cry aloud; and he shall hear my voice.

Cast thy burden upon the Lord, and he shall sustain thee: he shall never suffer the righteous to be moved.

What time I am afraid I will trust in thee. In God I have put my trust; I will not fear what flesh can do unto me.

Thy vows are upon me, O God. I will render praises unto thee.

For thou hast delivered my soul from death; wilt not thou deliver my feet from falling, that I may walk before God in the light of the living?

Be merciful unto me, O God, be merciful unto me: for my soul trusteth in thee: yea, in the shadow of thy wings will I make my refuge, until these calamities be overpast.

I will cry unto God most high; unto God that performeth all things for me.

He shall send from heaven and save me. God shall send forth his mercy and his truth.

Be thou exalted, O God, above the heavens; let thy glory be above all the earth.

My heart is fixed, O God, my heart is fixed; I will sing and give praise.

For thy mercy is great unto the heavens, and thy truth unto the clouds.

Be thou exalted, O God, above the heavens: let thy glory be above all the earth.

BENEDICTION IV.

FIRST SUNDAY IN LENT.

COLLECT.

O GOD, whose Son, Jesus Christ our Lord, for our sake did fast forty days and forty nights; give us grace to use such abstinence, that, our flesh being subdued to the spirit, we may ever obey thy godly motions in righteousness and true holiness, to thy honor and glory. Almighty and everlasting

God, who hatest nothing which thou hast made, and dost forgive the sins of all those who are penitent; create and make in us new and contrite hearts; that we, worthily lamenting our sins, and acknowledging our wretchedness, may obtain of thee, the God of all mercy, perfect remission and forgiveness; through Jesus Christ our Lord. *Amen.*

PROPHECIES.

JOEL AND JEREMIAH.

SANCTIFY ye a fast, call a solemn assembly, gather the elders, and all the inhabitants of the land, into the house of the Lord your God, and cry unto the Lord,

Alas for the day! for the day of the Lord is at hand, and as a destruction from the Almighty shall it come.

Stand in the gate of the Lord's house, and proclaim there this word, and say, Hear the word of the Lord, all ye that enter in at these gates to worship the Lord.

Thus saith the Lord of hosts, Amend your ways and your doings, and I will cause you to dwell in this place.

Trust ye not in lying words, saying, The temple of the Lord, The temple of the Lord, The temple of the Lord, are these.

For if ye thoroughly amend your ways and your doings; if you thoroughly execute judgment between a man and his neighbor;

If ye oppress not the stranger, the fatherless, and the widow, and shed not innocent blood in this place, neither walk after other gods to your hurt:

Then will I cause you to dwell in this place, in the land that I gave to your fathers, for ever and ever.

Behold, ye trust in lying words, that cannot profit.

Will ye steal, murder, and commit adultery, and swear falsely, and walk after other gods whom ye know not;

And come and stand before me in this house, which is called by my name, and say, We are delivered to do all these abominations?

Is this house which is called by my name become a den of robbers in your eyes? behold, I, even I, have seen it, saith the Lord.

But go ye now unto my place, which was in Shiloh, where I set my name at the first, and see what I did to it for the wickedness of my people.

And now, because ye have done all these works, saith the Lord, and I spake unto you, rising up early and speaking, but ye heard not; and I called you, but ye answered not;

Therefore will I do unto this house, which is called by my name, wherein ye trust, and unto the place which I gave to you and to your fathers, as I have done to Shiloh.

Do they provoke me to anger? saith the Lord: do they not provoke themselves, to the confusion of their own faces?

But this thing commanded I them, saying, Obey my voice, and I will be your God, and ye shall be my people; and walk ye in all the ways that I have commanded you, that it may be well unto you.

But they hearkened not, nor inclined their ear, but walked in the counsels and in the imagination of their evil heart, and went backward, and not forward.

Therefore thou shalt speak all these words unto them; but they will not hearken unto thee: thou shalt also call unto them; but they will not answer thee.

But thou shalt say unto them, This is a nation that obeyeth not the voice of the Lord their God, nor receiveth correction: truth is perished, and is cut off from their mouth.

Then will I cause to cease the voice of mirth, and the voice of gladness, the voice of the bridegroom, and the voice of the bride; for the land shall be desolate.

Thus saith the Lord, Let not the wise man glory in his wisdom, neither let the mighty man glory in his might, let not the rich man glory in his riches.

But let him that glorieth glory in this, that he understandeth and knoweth me, that I am the Lord which exercise lov-

7

ing-kindness, judgment, and righteousness in the earth ; for in these things I delight, saith the Lord.

Praise ye the Lord.
The Lord's name be praised !

PSALMS.

HAVE mercy upon me, O God, according to thy loving-kindness : according unto the multitude of thy tender mercies blot out my transgression.

Wash me thoroughly from mine iniquity, and cleanse me from my sin.

For I acknowledge my transgressions : and my sin is ever before me.

Against thee, thee only, have I sinned, and done this evil in thy sight : that thou mightest be justified when thou speakest, and be clear when thou judgest.

Behold, I was shapen in iniquity ; and in sin did my mother conceive me.

Behold, thou desirest truth in the inward parts : and in the hidden part thou shalt make me to know wisdom.

Purge me with hyssop, and I shall be clean : wash me, and I shall be whiter than snow.

Make me to hear joy and gladness ; that the bones which thou hast broken may rejoice.

Hide thy face from my sins, and blot out all mine iniquities.

Create in me a clean heart, O God ; and renew a right spirit within me.

Cast me not away from thy presence ; and take not thy Holy Spirit from me.

Restore unto me the joy of thy salvation ; and uphold me with thy free spirit :

Then will I teach transgressors thy ways ; and sinners shall be converted unto thee.

Deliver me from blood-guiltiness, O God, thou God of my

salvation; and my tongue shall sing aloud of thy righteousness.

O Lord, open thou my lips ; and my mouth shall show forth thy praise.

For thou desirest not sacrifice, else would I give it; thou delightest not in burnt-offering.

The sacrifices of God are a broken spirit : a broken and a contrite heart, O God, thou wilt not despise.

Do good in thy good pleasure unto Zion : build thou the walls of Jerusalem.

Then shalt thou be pleased with the sacrifices of righteousness.

The fool hath said in his heart, There is no God. Corrupt are they, and have done abominable iniquity: there is none that doeth good.

God looked down from heaven upon the children of men, to see if there were any that did understand, that did seek God.

Every one of them is gone back; they are altogether become filthy : there is none that doeth good, no, not one.

Have the workers of iniquity no knowledge ? who eat up my people as they eat bread : they have not called upon God.

There were they in great fear, where no fear was : for God hath scattered the bones of him that encampeth against thee.

Save me, O God, by thy name, and judge me by thy strength.

Hear my prayer, O God ; give ear to the words of my mouth.

Behold, God is mine helper : the Lord is with them that uphold my soul.

I will praise thy name, O Lord, for it is good.

BENEDICTION I.

SECOND SUNDAY IN LENT.

COLLECT.

ALMIGHTY God, who seest that we have no power of ourselves to help ourselves; keep us both outwardly in our bodies, and inwardly in our souls; that we may be defended from all adversities which may happen to the body, and from all evil thoughts which may assault and hurt the soul, through Jesus Christ our Lord. *Amen.*

PROPHECIES.

EZEKIEL.

AND the word of the Lord came unto me, saying,

Son of man, these men have set up their idols in their heart, and put the stumbling-block of their iniquity before their face: should I be inquired of at all by them?

Therefore speak unto them, and say unto them, Thus saith the Lord God: Every man of the house of Israel that setteth up his idols in his heart, and putteth the stumbling-block of his iniquity before his face, and cometh to the prophet, I the Lord will answer him that cometh according to the multitude of his idols;

Therefore say unto the house of Israel, Thus saith the Lord God, Repent, and turn yourselves from your idols; and turn away your faces from all your abominations.

For every one of the house of Israel, or of the stranger that sojourneth in Israel, which separateth himself from me, and setteth up his idols in his heart, and putteth the stumbling-block of his iniquity before his face, and cometh to a prophet to inquire of him concerning me; I the Lord will answer him by myself.

And they shall bear the punishment of their iniquity: the

punishment of the prophet shall be even as the punishment of him that seeketh unto him;

That the house of Israel may go no more astray from me, neither be polluted any more with all their transgressions; but that they may be my people, and I may be their God, saith the Lord God.

The word of the Lord came again to me, saying,

Son of man, when the land sinneth against me by trespassing grievously, then will I stretch out mine hand upon it, and will break the staff of the bread thereof, and will send famine upon it, and will cut off man and beast from it:

Though these three men, Noah, Daniel, and Job, were in it, they should deliver but their own souls by their righteousness, saith the Lord God.

If I cause noisome beasts to pass through the land, and they spoil it, so that it be desolate, that no man may pass through because of the beasts:

Though these three men were in it, as I live, saith the Lord God, they shall deliver neither sons nor daughters; they only shall be delivered, but the land shall be desolate.

Or if I bring a sword upon that land, and say, Sword, go through the land; so that I cut off man and beast from it:

Though these three men were in it, as I live, saith the Lord God, they shall deliver neither sons nor daughters, but they only shall be delivered themselves.

Or if I send a pestilence into that land, and pour out my fury upon it in blood, to cut off from it man and beast:

Though Noah, Daniel, and Job were in it, as I live, saith the Lord God, they shall deliver neither son nor daughter; they shall but deliver their own souls by their righteousness.

For thus saith the Lord God, How much more when I send my four sore judgments, the sword, and the famine, and the noisome beast, and the pestilence, to cut off from it man and beast!

Yet, behold, therein shall be left a remnant that shall be

7 *

brought forth, both sons and daughters; behold, they shall come forth unto you, and ye shall see their way and their doings: and ye shall be comforted concerning the evil that I have brought upon you.

And they shall comfort you, when ye see their ways and their doings : and ye shall know that I have not done without cause all that I have done in it, saith the Lord God.

Moreover, he said unto me, Son of man, all my words that I shall speak unto thee receive in thine heart, and hear with thine ears.

And go, get thee unto thy people, and speak unto them, and tell them, Thus saith the Lord God, whether they will hear, or whether they will forbear.

Then the spirit took me up, and I heard behind me a voice of a great rushing, saying, Blessed be the glory of the Lord from his place.

I heard also the noise of the wings of living creatures that touched one another, and the noise of wheels over against them, and a noise of a great rushing.

So the spirit lifted me up, and took me away, and I went in bitterness, in the heat of my spirit : but the hand of the Lord was strong upon me.

And it came to pass, at the end of seven days, that the word of the Lord came unto me, saying,

Son of man, I have made thee a watchman unto the house of Israel : therefore hear the word at my mouth, and give them warning from me.

When I say unto the wicked, Thou shalt surely die; and thou givest him not warning, nor speakest to warn the wicked from his wicked way, to save his life ; the same wicked man shall die in his iniquity : but his blood will I require at thine hand.

Yet if thou warn the wicked, and he turn not from his wickedness, nor from his wicked way, he shall die in his iniquity : but thou hast delivered thy soul.

Again, when a righteous man doth turn from his righteousness, and commit iniquity, and I lay a stumbling-block before him, he shall die : because thou hast not given him warning, he shall die in his sin, and his righteousness which he hath done shall not be remembered ; but his blood will I require at thine hand.

Nevertheless, if thou warn the righteous man, that the righteous sin not, and he doth not sin, he shall surely live, because he is warned : also thou hast delivered thy soul.

O Lord, open thou our ears !

That we may hear meekly thy word and receive it with pure affection.

PSALMS.

O GOD, thou hast cast us off, thou hast scattered us, thou hast been displeased ; O turn thyself to us again.

Thou hast made the earth to tremble ; thou hast broken it : heal the breaches thereof ; for it shaketh.

Thou hast showed thy people hard things ; thou hast made us to drink the wine of astonishment.

Thou hast given a banner to them that feared thee, that it may be displayed because of the truth.

That thy beloved may be delivered, save with thy right hand, and hear me.

God hath spoken in his holiness : I will rejoice.

Who will bring me into the strong city ?

Wilt not thou, O God, which hadst cast us off? and thou, O God, which didst not go out with our armies ?

Give us help from trouble : for vain is the help of man.

Through God we shall do valiantly, for he it is that shall tread down our enemies.

Hear my cry, O God ; attend unto my prayer.

From the end of the earth will I cry unto thee, when my heart is overwhelmed : lead me to the Rock that is higher than I.

For thou hast been a shelter for me, and a strong tower from the enemy.

I will abide in thy tabernacle for ever; I will trust in the covert of thy wings.

For thou, O God, hast heard my vows: thou hast given me the heritage of those that fear thy name.

I shall abide before God for ever: O prepare mercy and truth, which may preserve me.

So will I sing praise unto thy name for ever, that I may daily perform my vows.

O Lord, rebuke me not in thy wrath, nor chasten me in thy hot displeasure!

For thine arrows have deeply pierced me, and thy hand hath been heavy upon me.

There is no soundness in my flesh, because of thine anger; nor rest in my bones, because of my sin.

For my iniquities have gone over my head; like a heavy burden, they are more than I can bear.

O Lord, thou knowest all my desire, and my groaning is not hidden from thee!

My heart panteth; my strength faileth me; the very light of my eyes is gone from me.

I am like one who heareth nothing, and in whose mouth is no reply.

But in thee, O Lord, do I trust; thou wilt hear, O Lord, my God!

For I have prayed, Let them not rejoice over me; let them not exult at the slipping of my feet!

For I confess my iniquity, and am troubled on account of my sin.

Forsake me not, O Lord!   O my God, be not far from me!

Make haste to mine aid, O Lord, my salvation!

Truly my soul waiteth upon God: from him cometh my salvation.

He only is my rock and my salvation; he is my defence: I shall not be greatly moved.

How long will ye imagine mischief against a man? ye shall be slain all of you: as a bowing wall shall ye be, and as a tottering fence.

They only consult to cast him down from his excellency; they delight in lies: they bless with their mouth, but they curse inwardly.

My soul, wait thou only upon God: for my expectation is from him.

He only is my rock and my salvation: he is my defence: I shall not be moved.

In God is my salvation and my glory: the rock of my strength, and my refuge, is in God.

Trust in him at all times, ye people; pour out your heart before him: God is a refuge for us.

Surely men of low degree are vanity, and men of high degree are a lie: to be laid in the balance, they are altogether lighter than vanity.

Trust not in oppression, become not vain in robbery: if riches increase, set not your heart upon them.

God hath spoken once; twice have I heard this, that power belongeth unto God.

Also unto thee, O Lord, belongeth mercy: for thou renderest to every man according to his work.

BENEDICTION II.

THIRD SUNDAY IN LENT.

COLLECT.

WE beseech thee, Almighty God, look upon the hearty desires of thy humble servants, and stretch forth the right hand of thy majesty, to be our defence against all our enemies, through Jesus Christ our Lord. *Amen.*

PROPHECIES.

EZEKIEL.

FOR in mine holy mountain, saith the Lord God, there shall all of them in the land serve me : there will I accept them, and there will I require your offerings, with all your holy things.

I will accept you when I bring you out from the people, and gather you out of the countries wherein ye have been scattered ; and I will be sanctified in you.

And ye shall know that I am the Lord, when I shall bring you into the country for the which I lifted up mine hand to give it to your fathers.

And there shall ye remember your ways, and all your doings, wherein ye have been defiled ; and ye shall loathe yourselves in your own sight, for all your evils that ye have committed.

And ye shall know that I am the Lord, when I have wrought with you for my name's sake, not according to your wicked ways, nor according to your corrupt doings, O ye house of Israel, saith the Lord God.

Moreover, the word of the Lord came unto me, saying,

Son of man, set thy face toward the south, and drop thy word toward the south, and prophesy against the forest of the south field ;

And say to the forest of the south, Hear the word of the Lord, Thus saith the Lord God, Behold, I will kindle a fire in thee, and it shall devour every green tree in thee, and every dry tree : the flaming flame shall not be quenched.

And all flesh shall see that I the Lord have kindled it : it shall not be quenched.

The soul that sinneth, it shall die.   The son shall not bear the iniquity of the father, neither shall the father bear the iniquity of the son ; the righteousness of the righteous shall be upon him, and the wickedness of the wicked shall be upon him.

But if the wicked will turn from all his sins that he hath

committed, and keep all my statutes, and do that which is lawful and right, he shall surely live, he shall not die.

All his transgressions that he hath committed, they shall not be mentioned unto him: in his righteousness that he hath done, he shall live.

Have I any pleasure at all that the wicked should die? saith the Lord God; and not that he should return from his ways, and live?

But when the righteous turneth away from his righteousness, and committeth iniquity, and doeth according to all the abominations that the wicked man doeth, shall he live? All his righteousness that he hath done shall not be mentioned: in his trespass that he hath trespassed, and in his sin that he hath sinned, in them shall he die.

Yet ye say, The way of the Lord is not equal. Hear now, O house of Israel. Is not my way equal? are not your ways unequal?

When a righteous man turneth away from his righteousness, and committeth iniquity, and dieth in them; for his iniquity that he hath done, shall he die.

Again, when the wicked man turneth away from his wickedness that he hath committed, and doeth that which is lawful and right, he shall save his soul alive.

Because he considereth, and turneth away from all his transgressions that he hath committed, he shall surely live, he shall not die.

Yet saith the house of Israel, The way of the Lord is not equal. O house of Israel, are not my ways equal? are not your ways unequal?

Therefore I will judge you, every one according to his ways, saith the Lord God. Repent, and turn yourselves from all your transgressions; so iniquity shall not be your ruin.

Cast away from you all your transgressions, whereby ye have transgressed, and make you a new heart and a new spirit: for why will ye die?

For I have no pleasure in the death of him that dieth, saith the Lord God ; wherefore turn yourselves, and live ye.

O Lord, open thou our lips !
And our mouth shall show forth thy praise.

PSALMS.

O LORD, rebuke me not in thine anger, neither chasten me in thy hot displeasure.

Have mercy upon me, O Lord ; for I am weak : O Lord, heal me ; for my bones are vexed.

My soul is also sore vexed : but thou, O Lord, how long ?

Return, O Lord, deliver my soul : O save me for thy mercies' sake.

For in death there is no remembrance of thee : in the grave who shall give thee thanks ?

Depart from me, all ye workers of iniquity : for the Lord hath heard the voice of my weeping.

The Lord hath heard my supplication ; the Lord will receive my prayer.

O Lord my God, in thee do I put my trust ; save me from all them that persecute me, and deliver me ;

Lest he tear my soul like a lion, rending it in pieces, while there is none to deliver.

O Lord my God, if I have done this ; if there be iniquity in my hands ;

If I have rewarded evil unto him that was at peace with me ;

Let the enemy persecute my soul, and take it ; yea, let him tread down my life upon the earth, and lay mine honor in the dust.

Arise, O Lord ; lift up thyself, and awake for me to the judgment that thou hast commanded.

So shall the congregation of the people compass thee about : for their sakes, therefore, return thou on high.

The Lord shall judge the people : judge me, O Lord, according to my righteousness, and according to mine integrity that is in me.

O, let the wickedness of the wicked come to an end ; but establish the just : for the righteous God trieth the hearts and reins.

My defence is of God, which saveth the upright in heart.

God judgeth the righteous, and God is angry with the wicked every day.

I will praise the Lord according to his righteousness ; and will sing praise to the name of the Lord most high.

O Lord, our Lord, how excellent is thy name in all the earth ! who hast set thy glory above the heavens.

Out of the mouth of babes and sucklings hast thou ordained strength, because of thine enemies ; that thou mightest still the enemy and the avenger.

When I consider thy heavens, the work of thy fingers ; the moon and the stars, which thou hast ordained :

What is man, that thou art mindful of him ? and the son of man, that thou visitest him ?

For thou hast made him a little lower than the angels, and hast crowned him with glory and honor.

Thou madest him to have dominion over the works of thy hands : thou hast put all things under his feet.

All sheep and oxen, yea, and the beasts of the field.

The fowl of the air, and the fish of the sea, and whatsoever passeth through the paths of the sea.

O Lord, our Lord, how excellent is thy name in all the earth !

I will praise thee, O Lord, with my whole heart ; I will show forth all thy marvellous works.

I will be glad and rejoice in thee : I will sing praise to thy name, O thou Most High.

For thou hast maintained my right and my cause ; thou satest in the throne judging right.

BENEDICTION XII.
8

FOURTH SUNDAY IN LENT.

COLLECT.

GRANT, we beseech thee, Almighty God, that we, who for our evil deeds do worthily deserve to be punished, by the comfort of thy grace may mercifully be relieved, through our Lord and Saviour Jesus Christ. *Amen.*

PROPHECIES.

MICAH.

HEAR, all ye people; hearken, O earth, and all that therein is: and let the Lord God be witness against you, the Lord from his holy temple.

For, behold, the Lord cometh forth out of his place, and will come down, and tread upon the high places of the earth.

And the mountains shall be molten, and the valleys shall be cleft, as wax before the fire, and as the waters that are poured down a steep place.

Hear ye now what the Lord saith: Arise, contend thou before the mountains, and let the hills hear thy voice.

Hear ye, O mountains, the Lord's controversy, and ye strong foundations of the earth: for the Lord hath a controversy with his people, and he will plead with Israel.

O my people, what have I done unto thee? and wherein have I wearied thee? testify against me.

For I brought thee up out of the land of Egypt, and redeemed thee out of the house of servants; and I sent before thee Moses, Aaron, and Miriam.

Wherewith shall I come before the Lord, and bow myself before the high God? shall I come before him with burnt-offerings, with calves of a year old?

Shall I give my first-born for my transgression, the fruit of my body for the sin of my soul?

He hath showed thee, O man, what is good ; and what doth the Lord require of thee, but to do justly, and to love mercy, and to walk humbly with thy God?

The Lord's voice crieth unto the city, and the man of wisdom shall see thy name : hear ye the rod, and who hath appointed it.

Are there yet the treasures of wickedness in the house of the wicked, and the scant measure that is abominable ?

Shall I count them pure with the wicked balances, and with the bag of deceitful weights ?

For the rich men thereof are full of violence, and the inhabitants thereof have spoken lies, and their tongue is deceitful in their mouth.

Therefore also will I make thee sick in smiting thee, in making thee desolate because of thy sins.

Thou shalt eat, but not be satisfied ; and thy casting down shall be in the midst of thee ; and that which thou deliverest will I give up to the sword.

Woe to them that devise iniquity and work evil upon their beds! when the morning is light, they practise it, because it is in the power of their hand.

And they covet fields, and take them by violence : and houses, and take them away : so they oppress a man and his house, even a man and his heritage.

In that day shall one take up a parable against you, and lament with a doleful lamentation, and say, We be utterly spoiled ; he hath changed the portion of my people : how hath he removed it from me ! turning away, he hath divided our fields.

Is the spirit of the Lord straitened? are these his doings? do not my words do good to him that walketh uprightly?

Arise ye, and depart ; for this is not your rest.

Now unto the King eternal, immortal, invisible, the only wise God,

Be honor and glory, through Jesus Christ, for ever and ever.

PSALMS.

WHY standest thou afar off, O Lord? why hidest thou thy-self in times of trouble?

The wicked in his pride doth persecute the poor: let them be taken in the devices that they have imagined.

For the wicked boasteth of his heart's desire, and blesseth the covetous, whom the Lord abhorreth.

The wicked, through the pride of his countenance, will not seek after God: God is not in all his thoughts.

His ways are always grievous; thy judgments are far above, out of his sight: as for all his enemies, he puffeth at them.

He hath said in his heart, I shall not be moved; for I shall never be in adversity.

His mouth is full of cursing and deceit and fraud; under his tongue is mischief and vanity.

He sitteth in the lurking-places of the villages; his eyes are privily set against the poor.

He lieth in wait secretly, as a lion in his den: he lieth in wait to catch the poor: he doth catch the poor, when he draweth him into his net.

He croucheth, and humbleth himself, that the poor may fall by his strong ones.

He hath said in his heart, God hath forgotten: he hideth his face; he will never see it.

Arise, O Lord; O God, lift up thine hand: forget not the humble.

Wherefore doth the wicked contemn God? he hath said in his heart, Thou wilt not require it.

Thou hast seen it; for thou beholdest mischief and spite, to requite it with thy hand: the poor committeth himself unto thee; thou art the helper of the fatherless.

The Lord is King for ever and ever.

Lord, thou hast heard the desire of the humble: thou wilt prepare their heart, thou wilt cause thine ear to hear;

To judge the fatherless and the oppressed, that the man of the earth may no more oppress.

Help, Lord; for the godly man ceaseth; for the faithful fail from among the children of men.

They speak vanity every one with his neighbor: with flattering lips, and with a double heart, do they speak.

The Lord shall cut off all flattering lips, and the tongue that speaketh proud things;

Who have said, With our tongue will we prevail; our lips are our own: who is lord over us?

For the oppression of the poor, for the sighing of the needy, now will I arise, saith the Lord; I will set him in safety from him that puffeth at him.

The words of the Lord are pure words; as silver tried in a furnace of earth, purified seven times.

Thou shalt keep them, O Lord, thou shalt preserve them from this generation for ever.

The wicked walk on every side, when the vilest men are exalted.

In the Lord put I my trust: how say ye to my soul, Flee as a bird to your mountain?

For, lo, the wicked bend their bow, they make ready their arrow upon the string, that they may privily shoot at the upright in heart.

If the foundations be destroyed, what can the righteous do?

The Lord is in his holy temple, the Lord's throne is in heaven: his eyes behold, his eyelids try, the children of men.

The Lord trieth the righteous: but the wicked, and him that loveth violence, his soul hateth.

Upon the wicked he shall rain snares, fire and brimstone, and an horrible tempest: this shall be the portion of their cup.

For the righteous Lord loveth righteousness; his countenance doth behold the upright.

BENEDICTION XIII.

8 *

FIFTH SUNDAY IN LENT.

COLLECT.

WE beseech thee, O Father, who delightest in mercy, and art not willing that any should perish, to grant unto us the pardon of all our sins, and a joyful hope of thine approbation; and to assist us in forsaking all our evil ways, and returning to the path of thy commandments; that, when our days on earth shall be finished, we may obtain everlasting life, through Jesus Christ our Lord. *Amen.*

PROPHECIES.

HAGGAI AND ZECHARIAH.

YET now be strong, all ye people of the land, saith the Lord, and work: for I am with you, saith the Lord of hosts.

According to the word that I covenanted with you, so my spirit remaineth among you: fear ye not.

For thus saith the Lord of hosts, Yet once, it is a little while, and I will shake the heavens, and the earth, and the sea, and the dry land;

And I will shake all nations, and the desire of all nations shall come: and I will fill this house with glory, saith the Lord of hosts.

The silver is mine, and the gold is mine, saith the Lord of hosts.

The glory of this latter house shall be greater than of the former, saith the Lord of hosts: and in this place will I give peace, saith the Lord of hosts.

Therefore say thou unto them, Thus saith the Lord of hosts, Turn ye unto me, and I will turn unto you.

Be ye not as your fathers, unto whom the former prophets have cried, saying, Thus saith the Lord of hosts, Turn ye now

*from your evil ways, and from your evil doings : but they did
not hear, nor hearken unto me, saith the Lord.*

Your fathers, where are they? and the prophets, do they
live for ever?

*But my words and my statutes, which I commanded my
servants the prophets, did they not take hold of your fathers?
and they returned and said, Like as the Lord of hosts thought
to do unto us, according to our ways, and according to our
doings, so hath he dealt with us.*

Then I turned, and lifted up mine eyes, and looked, and
behold a flying roll.

*And he said unto me, What seest thou? and I answered, I
see a flying roll.*

Then said he unto me, This is the curse that goeth forth
over the face of the whole earth: for every one that stealeth
shall be cut off as on this side according to it; and every
one that sweareth shall be cut off as on that side according
to it.

*I will bring it forth, saith the Lord of hosts, and it shall
enter into the house of the thief, and into the house of him that
sweareth falsely by my name : and it shall remain in the midst
of his house, and shall consume it with the timber thereof and
the stones thereof.*

And speak unto him, saying, Thus speaketh the Lord of
hosts, saying, Behold the man whose name is The Branch:
and he shall grow up out of his place, and he shall build the
temple of the Lord:

*Even he shall build the temple of the Lord ; and he shall
bear the glory, and shall sit and rule upon his throne ; and he
shall be a priest upon his throne: and the counsel of peace
shall be between them both.*

And they that are far off shall come and build the temple
of the Lord ; and ye shall know that the Lord of hosts hath
sent me unto you. And this shall come to pass, if ye will
diligently obey the voice of the Lord your God.

In that day there shall be a fountain opened for sin and for uncleanness.

And it shall come to pass in that day, saith the Lord of hosts, that I will cut off the names of the idols out of the land, and they shall no more be remembered; and also I will cause the prophets and the unclean spirit to pass out of the land.

Awake, O sword, against my shepherd, and against the man that is my fellow, saith the Lord of hosts; smite the shepherd, and the sheep shall be scattered; and I will turn mine hand upon the little ones.

And it shall come to pass in that day, that the light shall not be clear nor dark.

But it shall be one day, which shall be known to the Lord, not day, nor night; but it shall come to pass, that at evening time it shall be light.

And it shall be in that day, that living waters shall go out from Jerusalem; half of them toward the former sea, and half of them toward the hinder sea; in summer and in winter shall it be.

And the Lord shall be king over all the earth: in that day shall there be one Lord, and his name one.

Praise ye the Lord.
The Lord's name be praised.

PSALMS.

HEAR the right, O Lord, attend unto my cry; give ear unto my prayer, that goeth not out of feigned lips.

Let my sentence come forth from thy presence; let thine eyes behold the things that are equal.

Thou hast proved mine heart; thou hast visited me in the night; I am purposed that my mouth shall not transgress.

By the word of thy lips I have kept me from the paths of the destroyer.

Hold up my goings in thy paths, that my footsteps slip not.

I have called upon thee ; for thou wilt hear me, O God ; incline thine ear unto me, and hear my speech.

Show thy marvellous loving-kindness, O thou that savest by thy right hand them which put their trust in thee from those that rise up against them.

Keep me as the apple of the eye ; hide me under the shadow of thy wings.

As for me, I will behold thy face in righteousness : I shall be satisfied, when I awake, with thy likeness.

Consider and hear me, O Lord my God ; lighten mine eyes, lest I sleep the sleep of death ;

Lest mine enemy say, I have prevailed against him : and those that trouble me rejoice when I am moved.

But I have trusted in thy mercy ; my heart shall rejoice in thy salvation.

I will sing unto the Lord, because he hath dealt bountifully with me.

Lord, who shall abide in thy tabernacle ? who shall dwell in thy holy hill ?

He that walketh uprightly, and worketh righteousness, and speaketh the truth in his heart.

He that backbiteth not with his tongue, nor doeth evil to his neighbor, nor taketh up a reproach against his neighbor.

In whose eyes a vile person is contemned ; but he honoreth them that fear the Lord. He that sweareth to his own hurt, and changeth not.

He that putteth not out his money to usury, nor taketh reward against the innocent. He that doeth these things shall never be moved.

Preserve me, O God : for in thee do I put my trust.

O my soul, thou hast said unto the Lord, Thou art my Lord : my goodness extendeth not to thee ;

But to the saints that are in the earth, and to the excellent, in whom is all my delight.

Their sorrows shall be multiplied that hasten after another god: their drink-offerings of blood will I not offer, nor take up their names into my lips.

The Lord is the portion of mine inheritance, and of my cup : thou maintainest my lot.

The lines are fallen unto me in pleasant places ; yea, I have a goodly heritage.

I will bless the Lord, who hath given me counsel ; my reins also instruct me in the night-seasons.

I have set the Lord always before me : because he is at my right hand, I shall not be moved.

Therefore my heart is glad, and my glory rejoiceth ; my flesh also shall rest in hope :

For thou wilt not leave my soul in hell ; neither wilt thou suffer thine Holy One to see corruption.

Thou wilt show me the path of life: in thy presence is fullness of joy ; at thy right hand there are pleasures for evermore.

BENEDICTION XI.

SUNDAY BEFORE EASTER.

COLLECT.

ALMIGHTY and everlasting God, who, of thy tender love toward mankind, hast sent thy Son, our Saviour Jesus Christ, to take upon him our flesh, and to suffer death upon the cross, that all mankind should follow the example of his great humility ; mercifully grant that we may both follow the example of his patience, and also be made partakers of his resurrection, through the same Jesus Christ our Lord. *Amen.*

PROPHECIES.

ISAIAH.

BEHOLD, my servant shall deal prudently, he shall be exalted and extolled, and be very high.

As many were astonished at thee ; (his visage was so marred more than any man, and his form more than the sons of men ;)

So shall he sprinkle many nations ; the kings shall shut their mouths at him : for that which had not been told them shall they see, and that which they had not heard shall they consider.

Who hath believed our report ? and to whom is the arm of the Lord revealed ?

For he shall grow up before him as a tender plant, and as a root out of a dry ground ; he hath no form nor comeliness ; and when we shall see him, there is no beauty that we should desire him.

He is despised and rejected of men ; a man of sorrows, and acquainted with grief : and we hid as it were our faces from him ; he was despised, and we esteemed him not.

Surely he hath borne our griefs, and carried our sorrows : yet we did esteem him stricken, smitten of God, and afflicted.

But he was wounded for our transgressions, he was bruised for our iniquities : the chastisement of our peace was upon him ; and with his stripes we are healed.

All we, like sheep, have gone astray ; we have turned every one to his own way ; and the Lord hath laid on him the iniquity of us all.

He was oppressed, and he was afflicted ; yet he opened not his mouth : he was brought as a lamb to the slaughter, and as a sheep before her shearers is dumb, so he opened not his mouth.

. He was taken from prison and from judgment : and who shall declare his generation ? for he was cut off out of the land of the living : for the transgression of my people was he stricken.

And he made his grave with the wicked, and with the rich in his death; because he had done no violence, neither was any deceit in his mouth.

Yet it pleased the Lord to bruise him; he hath put him to grief: when thou shalt make his soul an offering for sin, he shall see his seed, he shall prolong his days, and the pleasure of the Lord shall prosper in his hand.

He shall see of the travail of his soul, and shall be satisfied: by his knowledge shall my righteous servant justify many; for he shall bear their iniquities.

Therefore will I divide him a portion with the great, and he shall divide the spoil with the strong; because he hath poured out his soul unto death: and he was numbered with the transgressors: and he bare the sin of many, and made intercession for the transgressors.

O Lord, open thou our ears,

That we may hear meekly thy word, and receive it with pure affection.

PSALMS.

GOD be merciful unto us, and bless us; and cause his face to shine upon us.

That thy way may be known upon earth, thy saving health among all nations.

Let the people praise thee, O God; let all the people praise thee.

O let the nations be glad, and sing for joy; for thou shalt judge the people righteously, and govern the nations upon earth.

Let the people praise thee, O God; let all the people praise thee.

Then shall the earth yield her increase; and God, even our own God, shall bless us.

God shall bless us; and all the ends of the earth shall fear him.

Let God arise, let his enemies be scattered ; let them also that hate him flee before him.

As smoke is driven away, so drive them away : as wax melteth before the fire, so let the wicked perish in the presence of God.

But let the righteous be glad : let them rejoice before God ; yea, let them exceedingly rejoice.

Sing unto God, sing praises unto his name : extol him that rideth upon the heavens by his name, and rejoice before him.

A father of the fatherless, and a judge of the widows, is God in his holy habitation.

God setteth the solitary in families : he bringeth out those which are bound with chains ; but the rebellious dwell in a dry land.

O God, when thou wentest forth before thy people, when thou didst march through the wilderness ;

The earth shook, the heavens also dropped at the presence of God : even Sinai itself was moved at the presence of God, the God of Israel.

Thou, O God, didst send a plentiful rain, whereby thou didst confirm thine inheritance, when it was weary.

Thy congregation hath dwelt therein : thou, O God, hast prepared of thy goodness for the poor.

The Lord gave the word ; great was the company of those that published it.

Kings of armies did flee apace ; and she that tarried at home divided the spoil.

Why leap ye, ye high hills ? this is the hill which God desireth to dwell in ; yea, the Lord will dwell in it for ever.

The chariots of God are twenty thousand, even thousands, of angels : the Lord is among them, as in Sinai, in the holy place.

Thou hast ascended on high, thou hast led captivity captive : thou hast received gifts for men ; yea, for the rebellious also, that the Lord God might dwell among them.

9

Blessed be the Lord who daily loadeth us with benefits, even the God of our salvation.

He that is our God is the God of salvation; and unto God the Lord belong the issues from death.

But God shall wound the head of his enemies, and such an one as goeth on still in his trespasses.

The Lord said, I will bring again; I will bring my people again from the depths of the sea.

They have seen thy goings, O God; even the goings of my God, my King, in the sanctuary.

Bless ye God in the congregations, even the Lord, from the fountain of Israel.

Thy God hath commanded thy strength: strengthen, O God, that which thou hast wrought for us.

Sing unto God, ye kingdoms of the earth; O sing praises unto the Lord;

To him that rideth upon the heavens of heavens, which were of old; lo, he doth send out his voice, and that a mighty voice.

Ascribe ye strength unto God: his excellency is over Israel, and his strength is in the clouds.

O God, thou art terrible out of thy holy places: the God of Israel is he that giveth strength and power unto his people. Blessed be God.

BENEDICTION VII.

EASTER DAY.

COLLECT.

O MERCIFUL God, by whose power thy Son Jesus Christ hath overcome death, and opened unto us the gates of everlasting life; grant that we thy servants, having this hope, may purify ourselves even as he is pure; and, by continually mortifying our corrupt affections, may pass the grave and gate of death, to our joyful resurrection; which we ask as disciples of him, who died, and was buried, and rose again for us, thy Son Jesus Christ our Lord. *Amen.*

PROPHECIES.

ISAIAH AND MALACHI.

BUT now thus saith the Lord that created thee, O Jacob, and he that formed thee, O Israel, Fear not; for I have redeemed thee, I have called thee by thy name; thou art mine.

When thou passest through the waters, I will be with thee; and through the rivers, they shall not overflow thee: when thou walkest through the fire, thou shall not be burnt; neither shall the flame kindle upon thee.

For I am the Lord thy God, the Holy One of Israel, thy Saviour.

Since thou wast precious in my sight, thou hast been honorable, and I have loved thee: therefore will I give men for thee, and people for thy life.

Fear not; for I am with thee: I will bring thy seed from the east, and gather thee from the west;

I will say to the north, Give up; and to the south, Keep not back: bring my sons from far, and my daughters from the ends of the earth;

Even every one that is called by my name: for I have created him for my glory, I have formed him; yea, I have made him.

Bring forth the blind people that have eyes, and the deaf that have ears.

Let all the nations be gathered together, and let the people be assembled: who among them can declare this, and show us former things? let them bring forth their witnesses, that they may be justified: or let them hear, and say, It is truth.

Ye are my witnesses, saith the Lord, and my servant whom

I have chosen ; that ye may know and believe me, and under-
stand that I am he: before me there was no God formed,
neither shall there be after me.

I, even I, am the Lord ; and beside me there is no Saviour.

Behold, I will send my messenger, and he shall prepare the
way before me : and the Lord, whom ye seek, shall suddenly
come to his temple, even the messenger of the covenant, whom
ye delight in : behold, he shall come, saith the Lord of hosts.

But who may abide the day of his coming ? and who shall
stand when he appeareth ? for he is like a refiner's fire, and
like fuller's soap.

And he shall sit as a refiner and purifier of silver ; and he
shall purify the sons of Levi, and purge them as gold and silver,
that they may offer unto the Lord an offering in righteousness.

And I will come near to you to judgment ; and I will be a
swift witness against the sorcerers, and against the adulterers,
and against false swearers, and against those that oppress the
hireling in his wages, the widow, and the fatherless, and that
turn aside the stranger from his right, and fear not me, saith
the Lord of hosts.

For I am the Lord, I change not ; therefore ye sons of Jacob
are not consumed.

Even from the days of your fathers ye are gone away from
mine ordinances, and have not kept them. Return unto me,
and I will return unto you, saith the Lord of hosts. But ye
said, Wherein shall we return ?

Will a man rob God ? Yet ye have robbed me. But ye say,
Wherein have we robbed thee ? In tithes and offerings.

Bring ye all the tithes into the store-house, that there may
be meat in mine house, and prove me now herewith, saith the
Lord of hosts, if I will not open you the windows of heaven,
and pour you out a blessing, that there shall not be room
enough to receive it.

And I will rebuke the devourer for your sakes, and he shall
not destroy the fruits of your ground ; neither shall your vine

cast her fruit before the time in the field, saith the Lord of hosts.

And all nations shall call you blessed : for ye shall be a delightsome land, saith the Lord of hosts.

Your words have been stout against me, saith the Lord : yet ye say, What have we spoken so much against thee ?

Ye have said, It is vain to serve God ; and what profit is it that we have kept his ordinance, and that we have walked mournfully before the Lord of hosts ?

And now we call the proud happy ; yea, they that work wickedness are set up ; yea, they that tempt God are even delivered.

Then they that feared the Lord spake often one to another ; and the Lord hearkened, and heard it : and a book of remembrance was written before him for them that feared the Lord, and that thought upon his name.

And they shall be mine, saith the Lord of hosts, in that day when I make up my jewels ; and I will spare them, as a man spareth his own son that serveth him.

Then shall ye return, and discern between the righteous and the wicked : between him that serveth God, and him that serveth him not.

For, behold, the day cometh, that shall burn as an oven ; and all the proud, yea, and all that do wickedly, shall be stubble : and the day that cometh shall burn them up, saith the Lord of hosts, that it shall leave them neither root nor branch.

But unto you that fear my name shall the Sun of righteousness arise with healing in his wings ;

O Lord, open thou our lips !
And our mouth shall show forth thy praise.

PSALMS.

Praise ye the Lord. Sing unto the Lord a new song, and his praise in the congregation of saints.

9 *

Let Israel rejoice in him that made him : let the children of Zion be joyful in their King.

For the Lord taketh pleasure in his people : he will beautify the meek with salvation.

Let the saints be joyful in glory : let them sing aloud.

This honor have all his saints.   Praise ye the Lord.

O give thanks unto the Lord ; for he is good ; because his mercy endureth for ever.

Let them now that fear the Lord say, that his mercy endureth for ever.

I called upon the Lord in distress : the Lord answered me, and set me in a large place.

The Lord is on my side ; I will not fear : what can man do unto me ?

The Lord taketh my part with them that help me :

It is better to trust in the Lord, than to put confidence in man :

It is better to trust in the Lord, than to put confidence in princes.

The Lord is my strength and song, and is become my salvation.

The voice of rejoicing and salvation is in the tabernacles of the righteous : the right hand of the Lord doeth valiantly.

The right hand of the Lord is exalted ; the right hand of the Lord doeth valiantly.

I shall not die, but live, and declare the works of the Lord.

The Lord hath chastened me sore : but he hath not given me over unto death.

BENEDICTION XIII.

FIRST SUNDAY AFTER EASTER.

COLLECT.

ALMIGHTY Father, who hast given thine only Son to die for our sins, and to rise again for our justification; grant us so to put away the leaven of malice and wickedness, that we may alway serve thee in pureness of living and truth, through the merits and mediation of the same, thy Son Jesus Christ our Lord. *Amen.*

PROPHECIES.

ISAIAH.

HEARKEN unto me, my called; I am the first, I also am the last.

Mine hand also hath laid the foundation of the earth, and my right hand hath spanned the heavens: when I call unto them, they stand up together.

All ye, assemble yourselves, and hear; which among them hath declared these things?

Come ye near unto me, hear ye this; I have not spoken in secret from the beginning: and now the Lord God, and his spirit, hath sent me.

Thus saith the Lord, thy Redeemer, the Holy One of Israel; I am the Lord thy God, which teacheth thee to profit, which leadeth thee by the way that thou shouldest go.

O that thou hadst hearkened to my commandments! then had thy peace been as a river, and thy righteousness as the waves of the sea.

The spirit of the Lord God is upon me; because the Lord hath anointed me to preach good tidings unto the meek: he hath sent me to bind up the broken-hearted, to proclaim liberty to the captives, and the opening of the prison to them that are bound;

To proclaim the acceptable year of the Lord, and the day of vengeance of our God ; to comfort all that mourn ;

To appoint unto them that mourn, to give unto them beauty for ashes, the oil of joy for mourning, the garment of praise for the spirit of heaviness ; that they might be called Trees of Righteousness, The planting of the Lord, that he might be glorified.

And they shall build the old wastes, they shall raise up the former desolations, and they shall repair the waste cities, the desolations of many generations.

And strangers shall stand and feed your flocks, and the sons of the alien shall be your ploughmen, and your vine-dressers.

But ye shall be named the priests of the Lord ; men shall call you the ministers of our God : ye shall eat the riches of the Gentiles, and in their glory shall you boast yourselves.

For your shame you shall have double, and for confusion they shall rejoice in their portion : therefore in their land they shall possess the double ; everlasting joy shall be unto them.

For I the Lord love judgment, I hate robbery for burnt-offering ; and I will direct their work in truth, and I will make an everlasting covenant with them.

And their seed shall be known among the Gentiles, and their offspring among the people : all that see them shall acknowledge them, that they are the seed which the Lord hath blessed.

I will greatly rejoice in the Lord, my soul shall be joyful in my God : for he hath clothed me with the garments of salvation, he hath covered me with the robe of righteousness, as a bridegroom decketh himself with ornaments, and as a bride adorneth herself with her jewels.

For as the earth bringeth forth her bud, and as the garden causeth the things that are sown in it to spring forth ; so the Lord God will cause righteousness and praise to spring forth before all the nations.

Now unto the King eternal, immortal, invisible, the only wise God,

Be honor and glory, through Jesus Christ, for ever and ever.

PSALMS.

PRAISE ye the Lord : for it is good to sing praises unto our God ; for it is pleasant ; and praise is comely.

The Lord doth build up Jerusalem ; he gathereth together the outcasts of Israel.

He healeth the broken in heart, and bindeth up their wounds.

He telleth the number of the stars ; he calleth them all by their names.

Great is our Lord, and of great power : his understanding is infinite.

The Lord lifteth up the meek : he casteth the wicked down to the ground.

Sing unto the Lord with thanksgiving ; sing praise upon the harp unto our God ;

Who covereth the heaven with clouds, who prepareth rain for the earth, who maketh grass to grow upon the mountains.

He giveth to the beast his food, and to the young ravens which cry.

He delighteth not in the strength of the horse ; he taketh not pleasure in the swiftness of a man.

The Lord taketh pleasure in them that fear him, in those that hope in his mercy.

Praise the Lord, O Jerusalem : praise thy God, O Zion.

For he hath strengthened the bars of thy gates ; he hath blessed thy children within thee.

He maketh peace in thy borders, and filleth thee with the finest of the wheat.

He sendeth forth his commandment upon earth : his word runneth very swiftly.

He giveth snow like wool: he scattereth the hoar-frost like ashes.

He casteth forth his ice like morsels: who can stand before his cold?

He sendeth out his word, and melteth them : he causeth his wind to blow, and the waters flow.

He showeth his word unto Jacob, his statutes and his judgments unto Israel.

He hath not dealt so with any nation ; and as for his judgments, they have not known them.   Praise ye the Lord.

BENEDICTION VI.

SECOND SUNDAY AFTER EASTER.

COLLECT.

ALMIGHTY God, who hast given thine only Son to be unto us both a sacrifice for sin and also an example of godly life, give us grace, that we may always most thankfully receive this inestimable benefit, and daily endeavor ourselves to follow the blessed steps of his most holy life, through the same Jesus Christ our Lord.   *Amen.*

PROPHECIES.

HOSEA AND DANIEL.

COME, and let us return unto the Lord ; for he hath torn, and he will heal us ; he hath smitten, and he will bind us up.

After two days will he revive us ; in the third day he will raise us up, and we shall live in his sight.

Then shall we know, if we follow on to know the Lord : his going forth is prepared as the morning ; and he shall come unto us as the rain, as the latter and former rain unto the earth.

For your goodness is as a morning cloud, and as the early dew it goeth away.

For I desired mercy, and not sacrifice ; and the knowledge of God more than burnt-offerings.

And I set my face unto the Lord God, to seek by prayer and supplications. _

And I prayed unto the Lord my God, and made my confession, and said, O Lord, the great and dreadful God, keeping the covenant and mercy to them that love him, and to them that keep his commandments ;

We have sinned, and have committed iniquity, and have done wickedly, and have rebelled, even by departing from thy precepts, and from thy judgments :

Neither have we hearkened unto thy servants the prophets, which spake in thy name to our fathers, and to all the people of the land.

O Lord, righteousness belongeth unto thee ; but unto us confusion of face, as at this day : unto all that are near, and that are far off, through all the countries whither thou hast driven them, because of their trespass that they have trespassed against thee.

O Lord, to us belongeth confusion of face, because we have sinned against thee.

To the Lord our God belong mercies and forgivenesses, though we have rebelled against him.

Neither have we obeyed the voice of the Lord our God, to walk in his laws which he set before us by his servants the prophets.

And he hath confirmed his words, which he spake against us, and against our judges that judged us, by bringing upon us a great evil.

As it is written in the law of Moses, all this evil is come upon us : yet made we not our prayer before the Lord our

God, that we might turn from our iniquities, and understand thy truth.

Therefore hath the Lord watched upon the evil, and brought it upon us : for the Lord our God is righteous in all his works which he doeth : for we obeyed not his voice.

And now, O Lord our God, that hast brought thy people forth with a mighty hand ; we have sinned, we have done wickedly.

Now, therefore, O our God, hear the prayer of thy servant, and his supplications, and cause thy face to shine upon our sanctuary that is desolate, for the Lord's sake.

O my God, incline thine ear, and hear ; open thine eyes, and behold our desolations, not for our righteousness, but for thy great mercies.

O Lord, hear ; O Lord, forgive ; O Lord, hearken, and do ; defer not, for thine own sake, O my God.

And at that time thy people shall be delivered, every one that shall be found written in the book.

And many of them that sleep in the dust of the earth shall awake, some to everlasting life, and some to shame and everlasting contempt.

And they that be wise shall shine as the brightness of the firmament ; and they that turn many to righteousness, as the stars for ever and ever.

But shut up the words, and seal the book, even to the time of the end : many shall run to and fro, and knowledge shall be increased.

And one said, How long shall it be to the end of these wonders ?

And I heard the man when he held up his right hand and his left hand unto heaven, and sware by him that liveth for ever, that it shall be for a time, times, and an half ; and when he shall have accomplished to scatter the power of the holy people, all these things shall be finished.

Many shall be purified, and made white, and tried ; but

the wicked shall do wickedly : and none of the wicked shall understand ; but the wise shall understand.

And from the time that the daily sacrifice shall be taken away, and the abomination that maketh desolate set up, there shall be a thousand two hundred and ninety days.

But go thou thy way till the end be, for thou shalt rest, and stand in thy lot at the end of the days.

Praise ye the Lord !
The Lord's name be praised.

PSALMS.

SAVE me, O God, by thy name, and judge me by thy strength.

Hear my prayer, O God ; give ear to the words of my mouth.

Behold, God is my helper : the Lord is with them that up-hold my soul.

I will praise thy name, O Lord, for it is good. Give ear to my prayer, O God ; and hide not thyself from my supplication.

Attend unto me, and hear me :

Because of the voice of the enemy, because of the oppression of the wicked : for they cast iniquity upon me, and in wrath they hate me.

My heart is sore pained within me ; and the terrors of death are fallen upon me.

And I said, O that I had wings like a dove! for then would I fly away, and be at rest.

Lo, then would I wander far off, and remain in the wilderness.

I would hasten my escape from the windy storm and tempest.

For it was not an enemy that reproached me ; then could I have borne it : neither was it he that hated me that did magnify himself against me ; then I would have hid myself from him ;

10

But it was thou, a man mine equal, my guide, and mine ac-quaintance.

We took sweet counsel together, and walked unto the house of God in company.

As for me, I will call upon God: and the Lord shall save me.

Evening, and morning, and at noon, will I pray, and cry aloud; and he shall hear my voice.

Cast thy burden upon the Lord, and he shall sustain thee: he shall never suffer the righteous to be moved.

BENEDICTION I.

THIRD SUNDAY AFTER EASTER.

COLLECT.

ALMIGHTY God, who showest to those who are in error the light of thy truth, to the intent that they may return into the way of righteousness; grant unto all those who are admitted into the fellowship of Christ's religion, that they may avoid those things that are contrary to their profession, and follow all such things as are agreeable to the same, through Jesus Christ our Lord. *Amen.*

PROPHECIES.

JOEL, MICAH, ZEPHANIAH, AND AMOS.

I WILL also gather all nations, and will bring them, and will plead with them for my people and for my heritage.

Assemble yourselves, and come, and gather yourselves together round about: thither cause thy mighty ones to come down, O Lord.

Put ye in the sickle; for the harvest is ripe: come, get you down; for the press is full.

Multitudes, multitudes in the valley of decision : for the day of the Lord is near in the valley of decision.

The sun and the moon shall be darkened, and the stars shall withdraw their shining.

The Lord also shall utter his voice ; and the heavens and the earth shall shake : but the Lord will be the hope of his people, and the strength of the children of Israel.

So shall ye know that I am the Lord your God, dwelling in my holy mountain.

But in the last days it shall come to pass, that the mountain of the house of the Lord shall be established in the top of the mountains, and it shall be exalted above the hills ; and people shall flow unto it.

And many nations shall come, and say, Come, and let us go up to the mountain of the Lord, and to the house of God, and he will teach us of his ways, and we will walk in his paths ; for the law shall go forth of Zion, and the word of the Lord from Jerusalem.

And he shall judge among many people, and rebuke strong nations afar off ; and they shall beat their swords into plough-shares, and their spears into pruning-hooks : nation shall not lift up a sword against nation, neither shall they learn war any more.

But they shall sit every man under his vine and under his fig-tree ; and none shall make them afraid : for the mouth of the Lord of hosts hath spoken it.

For all people will walk every one in the name of his god, and we will walk in the name of the Lord our God for ever and ever.

Hold thy peace at the presence of the Lord God ; for the day of the Lord is at hand : for the Lord hath prepared a sacrifice, he hath bid his guests.

In the same day also will I punish all those that fill their masters' houses with violence and deceit.

And it shall come to pass at that time, that I will search

Jerusalem with candles, and punish the men that say in their heart, The Lord will not do good, neither will he do evil.

Therefore their goods shall become a booty, and their houses a desolation: they shall also build houses, but not inhabit them; and they shall plant vineyards, but not drink the wine thereof.

The great day of the Lord is near, it is near and hasteth greatly, even the voice of the day of the Lord.

For thus saith the Lord, Seek ye me, and ye shall live.

Ye who turn judgment to wormwood, and leave off righteousness in the earth,

Seek him that maketh the seven stars and Orion, and turneth the shadow of death into the morning, and maketh the day dark with night: that calleth for the waters of the sea, and poureth them out upon the face of the earth: The Lord is his name:

For I know your manifold transgressions and your mighty sins: they afflict the just, they take a bribe, and they turn aside the poor in the gate from their right.

Therefore the prudent shall keep silence in that time; for it is an evil time.

Seek good, and not evil, that ye may live; and so the Lord, the God of hosts, shall be with you, as ye have spoken.

Hate the evil, and love the good, and establish judgment in the gate: it may be that the Lord God of hosts will be gracious unto the remnant of Joseph.

Let judgment run down as waters, and righteousness as a mighty stream.

Hear this, O ye that swallow up the needy, even to make the poor of the land to fail.

Saying, When will the new moon be gone, that we may sell corn? and the sabbath, that we may set forth wheat, making the ephah small, and the shekel great, and falsifying the balances by deceit?

The Lord hath sworn by the excellency of Jacob, Surely I will never forget any of their works.

Though they dig into hell, thence shall mine hand take them; though they climb up to heaven, thence will I bring them down.

And the Lord God of hosts is he that toucheth the land, and it shall melt, and all they that dwell therein shall mourn.

It is he that buildeth his stories in the heaven, and hath founded his troop in the earth; he that calleth for the waters of the sea, and poureth them out upon the face of the earth; The Lord is his name.

In that day will I raise up the tabernacle that is fallen, and close up the breaches thereof; and I will raise up his ruins, and I will build it as in the days of old.

Behold, the days come, saith the Lord, that the ploughman shall overtake the reaper, and the treader of grapes him that soweth seed.

And I will bring again the captivity of my people, and they shall build the waste cities, and inhabit them; they shall also make gardens, and eat the fruit of them.

And I will plant them upon their land, and they shall no more be pulled up out of their land which I have given them, saith the Lord thy God.

O Lord, open thou our ears!

That we may hear meekly thy word, and receive it with pure affection.

PSALMS.

BLESSED is the man that walketh not in the counsel of the ungodly, nor standeth in the way of sinners, nor sitteth in the seat of the scornful:

But his delight is in the law of the Lord; and in his law doth he meditate day and night.

And he shall be like a tree planted by the rivers of water, that bringeth forth his fruit in his season: his leaf also shall not wither; and whatsoever he doeth shall prosper.

10 *

The ungodly are not so: but are like the chaff which the wind driveth away.

Therefore the ungodly shall not stand in the judgment, nor sinners in the congregation of the righteous.

For the Lord knoweth the way of the righteous: but the way of the ungodly shall perish.

Lord, how are they increased that trouble me? many are they that rise up against me.

But thou, O Lord, art a shield for me; my glory, and the lifter up of mine head.

I cried unto the Lord with my voice, and he heard me out of his holy hill.

I laid me down and slept; I awaked: for the Lord sustained me.

I will not be afraid of ten thousands of people, that have set themselves against me round about.

Arise, O Lord; save me, O my God.

Salvation belongeth unto the Lord: thy blessing is upon thy people.

Hear me when I call, O God of my righteousness: thou hast enlarged me when I was in distress; have mercy upon me, and hear my prayer.

O ye sons of men, how long will ye turn glory into shame? how long will ye love vanity?

But know that the Lord hath set apart him that is godly for himself.

Stand in awe, and sin not: commune with your own heart upon your bed, and be still.

Offer the sacrifices of righteousness, and put your trust in the Lord.

There be many that say, Who will show us any good? Lord, lift thou up the light of thy countenance upon us.

Thou hast put gladness in my heart, more than in the time that corn and wine increased.

I will both lay me down in peace, and sleep: for thou, Lord, only makest me dwell in safety.

Give ear to my words, O Lord; consider my meditation.

Hearken unto the voice of my cry, my King, and my God: for unto thee will I pray.

My voice shalt thou hear in the morning, O Lord; in the morning will I direct my prayer unto thee, and will look up.

For thou art not a God that hath pleasure in wickedness; neither shall evil dwell with thee.

The foolish shall not stand in thy sight: thou hatest all workers of iniquity.

Thou shalt destroy them that speak leasing: the Lord will abhor the bloody and deceitful man.

But as for me, I will come into thy house in the multitude of thy mercy: and in thy fear will I worship toward thy holy temple.

Lead me, O Lord, in thy righteousness: make thy way straight before my face.

Let all those that put their trust in thee rejoice: let them ever shout for joy, because thou defendest them: let them also that love thy name be joyful in thee.

For thou, Lord, wilt bless the righteous: with favor wilt thou compass him as with a shield.

BENEDICTION XV.

FOURTH SUNDAY AFTER EASTER.

COLLECT.

O ALMIGHTY God, who alone canst order the unruly wills and affections of sinful men, grant unto thy people, that they may love the thing which thou commandest, and desire that which thou dost promise; that so, among the sundry and manifold changes of the world, our hearts may surely there be fixed, where true joys are to be found, through Jesus Christ our Lord. *Amen.*

PROPHECIES.

NAHUM AND MICAH.

THE Lord is slow to anger, and great in power, and will not at all acquit the wicked: the Lord hath his way in the whirlwind and in the storm, and the clouds are the dust of his feet.

He rebuketh the sea, and maketh it dry, and drieth up all the rivers.

The mountains quake at him, and the hills melt, and the earth is burnt at his presence, yea, the world, and all that dwell therein.

Who can stand before his indignation? and who can abide in the fierceness of his anger? his fury is poured out like fire, and the rocks are thrown down by him.

The Lord is good, a strong hold in the day of trouble; and he knoweth them that trust in him.

There is one come out of thee that imagineth evil against the Lord, a wicked counsellor.

Thus saith the Lord, Though they be quiet, and likewise many, yet thus shall they be cut down, when he shall pass through. Though I have afflicted thee, I will afflict thee no more.

For now will I break his yoke from off thee, and will burst thy bonds in sunder.

Behold upon the mountains the feet of him that bringeth good tidings, that publisheth peace! Keep thy solemn feasts, perform thy vows: for the wicked shall no more pass through thee.

Thou, Bethlehem, though thou be little among the thousands of Judah, yet out of thee shall he come forth unto me that is to be the ruler in Israel ; whose goings forth have been from of old, from everlasting.

And he shall stand and feed in the strength of the Lord, in the majesty of the name of the Lord his God ; and they shall abide : for now shall he be great unto the ends of the earth.

O Lord, open thou our lips !
And our mouth shall show forth thy praise.

PSALMS.

I WILL love thee, O Lord, my strength.

The Lord is my rock, and my fortress, and my deliverer ; my God, my strength, in whom I will trust ; my buckler, and my salvation, and my high tower.

I will call upon the Lord, who is worthy to be praised.

In my distress I called upon the Lord, and cried unto my God : he heard my voice out of his temple, and my cry came before him, even into his ears.

Then the earth shook and trembled ; the foundations also of the hills moved and were shaken, because he was wroth.

He bowed the heavens also, and came down : and darkness was under his feet.

And he rode upon a cherub, and did fly ; yea, he did fly upon the wings of the wind.

He made darkness his secret place ; his pavilion round about him was dark waters and thick clouds of the skies.

At the brightness that was before him his thick clouds passed ; hail-stones and coals of fire.

The Lord also thundered in the heavens, and the Highest gave his voice ; hail-stones and coals of fire.

Yea, he sent out his arrows, and scattered them ; and he shot out lightnings, and discomfited them.

Then the channels of waters were seen, and the foundations of the world were discovered at thy rebuke, O Lord, at the blast of the breath of thy nostrils.

He sent from above, he took me, he drew me out of many waters.

With the merciful thou wilt show thyself merciful ; with an upright man thou wilt show thyself upright ;

With the pure thou wilt show thyself pure ; and with the froward thou wilt show thyself froward.

For thou wilt save the afflicted people ; but wilt bring down high looks.

For thou wilt light my candle : the Lord my God will enlighten my darkness.

BENEDICTION II.

FIFTH SUNDAY AFTER EASTER.

COLLECT.

O LORD, from whom all good things do come, grant to us thy humble servants, that by thy holy inspiration we may think those things that are good, and by thy merciful guiding may perform the same, through our Lord Jesus Christ. *Amen.*

PROPHECIES.

ZECHARIAH.

THUS saith the Lord, I am returned unto Zion ; and Jerusalem shall be called, A city of truth ; and the mountain of the Lord of hosts, The holy mountain.

Thus saith the Lord of hosts, There shall yet old men and old women dwell in the streets of Jerusalem, and every man with his staff in his hand for very age.

And the streets of the city shall be full of boys and girls playing in the streets thereof.

If it be marvellous in the eyes of the remnant of this people in these days, should it also be marvellous in mine eyes? saith the Lord of hosts.

Thus saith the Lord of hosts, Behold, I will save my people from the east country, and from the west country;

And I will bring them, and they shall dwell in the midst of Jerusalem; and they shall be my people, and I will be their God, in truth and in righteousness.

Thus saith the Lord of hosts, Let your hands be strong, ye that hear in these days these words by the mouth of the prophets, which were in the day that the foundation of the house of the Lord of hosts was laid, that the temple might be built.

For before these days there was no hire for man, nor any hire for beast; neither was there any peace to him that went out or came in, because of the affliction: for I set all men every one against his neighbor.

But now I will not be unto the residue of this people as in the former days, saith the Lord of hosts.

For the seed shall be prosperous; the vine shall give her fruit, and the ground shall give her increase, and the heavens shall give their dew; and I will cause the remnant of this people to possess all these things.

And it shall come to pass, that as ye were a curse among the heathen, so will I save you, and ye shall be a blessing: fear not, but let your hands be strong.

For thus saith the Lord of hosts, As I thought to punish you, when your fathers provoked me to wrath, saith the Lord of hosts, and I repented not;

So again have I thought in these days to do well unto Jerusalem, and to the house of Judah: fear ye not.

These are the things that ye shall do, Speak ye every man the truth to his neighbor; execute the judgment of truth and peace in your gates:

And let none of you imagine evil in your hearts against his

neighbor; and love no false oath : for all these are things that I hate, saith the Lord.

And the word of the Lord of hosts came unto me, saying,

Thus saith the Lord of hosts, It shall yet come to pass, that there shall come people, and the inhabitants of many cities.

And the inhabitants of one city shall go to another, saying, Let us go speedily to pray before the Lord, and to seek the Lord of hosts ; I will go also.

Yea, many people and strong nations shall come to seek the Lord of hosts, and to pray before the Lord.

Now unto the King eternal, immortal, invisible, the only wise God ;

Be honor and glory, through Jesus Christ, for ever and ever.

PSALMS.

O GOD, thou art my God; early will I seek thee : my soul thirsteth for thee, my flesh longeth for thee in a dry and thirsty land, where no water is ;

To see thy power and thy glory, so as I have seen thee in the sanctuary.

Because thy loving-kindness is better than life, my lips shall praise thee.

Thus will I bless thee while I live ; I will lift up my hands in thy name.

My soul shall be satisfied ; and my mouth shall praise thee with joyful lips ;

When I remember thee upon my bed, and meditate on thee in the night-watches.

Because thou hast been my help : therefore in the shadow of thy wings will I rejoice.

My soul followeth hard after thee: thy right hand upholdeth me.

The king shall rejoice in God ; every one that sweareth by him shall glory : but the mouth of them that speak lies shall be stopped.

Hear my voice, O God, in my prayer: preserve my life from fear of the enemy.

Hide me from the secret counsel of the wicked; from the insurrection of the workers of iniquity;

They encourage themselves in an evil matter: they commune of laying snares privily; they say, Who shall see them?

So they shall make their own tongue to fall upon themselves: all that see them shall flee away.

And all men shall fear, and shall declare the work of God; for they shall wisely consider of his doing.

The righteous shall be glad in the Lord, and shall trust in him, and all the upright in heart shall glory.

Praise waiteth for thee, O God, in Zion: and unto thee shall the vow be performed.

O thou that hearest prayer, unto thee shall all flesh come.

Iniquities prevail against me: as for our transgressions, thou shalt purge them away.

Blessed is the man whom thou choosest, and causest to approach unto thee, that he may dwell in thy courts: we shall be satisfied with the goodness of thy house, even of thy holy temple.

By terrible things in righteousness wilt thou answer us, O God of our salvation; who art the confidence of all the ends of the earth, and of them that are afar off upon the sea:

Which by his strength setteth fast the mountains; being girded with power:

Which stilleth the noise of the seas, the noise of their waves, and the tumult of the people.

They also that dwell in the uttermost parts are afraid at thy tokens: thou makest the outgoings of the morning and evening to rejoice.

Thou visitest the earth, and waterest it: thou greatly enrichest it with the river of God, which is full of water: thou preparest them corn, when thou hast so provided for it.

Thou waterest the ridges thereof abundantly; thou settlest

11

the furrows thereof; thou makest it soft with showers; thou blessest the springing thereof:

Thou crownest the year with thy goodness; and thy paths drop fatness.

They drop upon the pastures of the wilderness; and the little hills rejoice on every side.

The pastures are clothed with flocks; the valleys also are covered over with corn; they shout for joy, they also sing.

BENEDICTION III.

SUNDAY AFTER ASCENSION.

COLLECT.

O GOD, the King of glory, who hast exalted thine only Son Jesus Christ with great triumph unto thy kingdom in heaven; we beseech thee leave us not comfortless; but send to us thine Holy Spirit to comfort us, and exalt us unto the same place whither our Saviour Christ is gone before, who liveth to make intercession for us at the right hand of God for ever and ever. *Amen.*

PROPHECIES.

ZECHARIAH AND JOEL.

THE just Lord will not do iniquity: every morning doth he bring his judgment to light, he faileth not; but the unjust knoweth no shame.

I said, Surely thou wilt fear me, thou wilt receive instruction: so their dwelling should not be cut off: but they rose early, and corrupted all their doings.

The remnant of Israel shall not do iniquity, nor speak lies;

neither shall a deceitful tongue be found in their mouth : for they shall feed and lie down, and none shall make them afraid.

Sing, O daughter of Zion : shout, O Israel, be glad and rejoice with all the heart, O daughter of Jerusalem.

The Lord hath taken away thy judgments, he hath cast out thine enemy : the King of Israel, even the Lord, is in the midst of thee : thou shalt not see evil any more.

In that day it shall be said to Jerusalem, Fear thou not ; and to Zion, Let not thine hands be slack.

The Lord thy God in the midst of thee is mighty ; he will save, he will rejoice over thee with joy ; he will rest in his love ; he will joy over thee with singing.

I will gather them that are sorrowful for the solemn assembly who are of thee, to whom the reproach of it was a burden.

Behold, at that time I will undo all that afflict them ; and I will get them praise and fame in every land where they have been put to shame.

At that time will I bring you again, even in the time that I gather you : for I will make you a name and a praise among all people of the earth, when I turn back your captivity before your eyes, saith the Lord.

Therefore also now, saith the Lord, turn ye even to me with all your heart, and with fasting, and with weeping, and with mourning ;

And rend your heart, and not your garments, and turn unto the Lord your God : for he is gracious and merciful, slow to anger, and of great kindness, and repenteth him of the evil.

Who knoweth if he will return and repent, and leave a blessing behind him ?

Blow the trumpet in Zion, sanctify a fast, call a solemn assembly :

Gather the people, sanctify the congregation, assemble the elders, gather the children.

Let the priests, the ministers of the Lord, weep between the porch and the altar, and let them say, Spare thy people, O Lord, and give not thine heritage to reproach, that the heathen should rule over them : wherefore should they say among the people, Where is their God?

Then will the Lord pity his people.

Fear not, O land; be glad and rejoice: for the Lord will do great things.

Be not afraid, ye beasts of the field : for the pastures of the wilderness do spring, for the tree beareth her fruit, the fig-tree and the vine do yield their strength.

Be glad then, and rejoice in the Lord your God: for he hath given you the former rain moderately, and he will cause to come down for you the rain, the former rain, and the latter rain in the first month.

And I will restore to you the years that the locust hath eaten, the canker-worm, and the caterpiller, and the palmer-worm, my great army which I sent among you.

And ye shall eat in plenty, and be satisfied, and praise the name of the Lord your God, that hath dealt wondrously with you : and my people shall never be ashamed.

And ye shall know that I am in the midst of Israel, and that I am the Lord your God, and none else : and my people shall never be ashamed.

And it shall come to pass afterward, that I will pour out my spirit upon all flesh ; and your sons and your daughters shall prophesy, your old men shall dream dreams, your young men shall see visions.

And also upon the servants and upon the handmaids in those days will I pour out my Spirit.

And I will show wonders in the heavens and in the earth, blood, and fire, and pillars of smoke.

The sun shall be turned into darkness, and the moon into blood, before the great and the terrible day of the Lord come.

Praise ye the Lord!
The Lord's name be praised.

PSALMS.

I WILL sing of the mercies of the Lord for ever : with my mouth will I make known thy faithfulness to all generations.

For I have said, Mercy shall be built up for ever : thy faithfulness shalt thou establish in the very heavens.

And the heavens shall praise thy wonders, O Lord ; thy faithfulness also in the congregation of the saints.

For who in the heaven can be compared unto the Lord ? who among the sons of the mighty can be likened unto the Lord ?

God is greatly to be feared in the assembly of the saints, and to be had in reverence of all them that are about him.

O Lord God of hosts, who is a strong Lord like unto thee ? or to thy faithfulness round about thee ?

Thou rulest the raging of the sea : when the waves thereof arise, thou stillest them.

Thou hast scattered thine enemies with thy strong arm.

The heavens are thine, the earth also is thine : as for the world, and the fulness thereof, thou hast founded them.

The north and the south, thou hast created them.

Thou hast a mighty arm : strong is thy hand, and high is thy right hand.

Justice and judgment are the habitation of thy throne : mercy and truth shall go before thy face.

Blessed is the people that know the joyful sound ; they shall walk, O Lord, in the light of thy countenance.

In thy name shall they rejoice all the day : and in thy righteousness shall they be exalted.

For thou art the glory of their strength ; and in thy favor we shall be exalted.

For the Lord is our defence ; and the Holy One of Israel is our King.

Then thou spakest in vision to thy Holy One, and saidst, I have laid help upon one that is mighty ; I have exalted one chosen out of the people :

11 *

With whom my hand shall be established; mine arm also shall strengthen him.

The enemy shall not exact upon him; nor the son of wickedness afflict him.

And I will beat down his foes before his face, and plague them that hate him.

But my faithfulness and my mercy shall be with him; and in my name shall he be exalted.

I will set his hand also in the sea, and his right hand in the rivers.

He shall cry unto me, Thou art my Father, my God, and the Rock of my salvation.

Also I will make him my first-born, higher than the kings of the earth.

My mercy will I keep for him for evermore, and my covenant shall stand fast with him.

His seed also will I make to endure for ever, and his throne as the days of heaven.

If his children forsake my law, and walk not in my judgments;

If they break my statutes, and keep not my commandments;

Then will I visit their transgression with the rod, and their iniquity with stripes.

Nevertheless my loving-kindness will I not utterly take from him, nor suffer my faithfulness to fail.

My covenant will I not break, nor alter the thing that is gone out of my lips.

What man is he that liveth, and shall not see death? shall he deliver his soul from the hand of the grave?

Remember, Lord, the reproach of thy servants; how I do bear in my bosom the reproach of all the mighty people;

Wherewith thine enemies have reproached, O Lord; wherewith they have reproached the footsteps of thine anointed.

Blessed be the Lord for evermore.   Amen, and amen.

BENEDICTION V.

WHITSUNDAY.

COLLECT.

GOD, who as at this time didst teach the hearts of thy faithful people, by sending to them the light of thy Holy Spirit, grant us by the same Spirit to have a right judgment in all things, and evermore to rejoice in his holy comfort, through Christ Jesus our Saviour; in whose name we ascribe unto thee all honor and glory now and for ever. *Amen.*

PROPHECIES.

PROVERBS.

DOTH not wisdom cry? and understanding put forth her voice?

She standeth in the top of high places, by the way in the places of the paths;

She crieth at the gates, at the entry of the city, at the coming in at the doors;

Unto you, O men, I call; and my voice is to the sons of man.

O ye simple, understand wisdom, and ye fools, be ye of an understanding heart.

Hear; for I will speak of excellent things; and the opening of my lips shall be right things.

For my mouth shall speak truth; and wickedness is an abomination to my lips.

All the words of my mouth are in righteousness; there is nothing froward or perverse in them.

They are all plain to him that understandeth, and right to them that find knowledge.

Receive my instruction, and not silver; and knowledge rather than choice gold.

For wisdom is better than rubies; and all the things that may be desired are not to be compared to it.

I, wisdom, dwell with prudence, and find out knowledge of witty inventions.

The fear of the Lord is to hate evil: pride, and arrogancy, and the evil way, and the froward mouth, do I hate.

Counsel is mine, and sound wisdom: I am understanding; I have strength.

By me kings reign, and princes decree justice.

By me princes rule, and nobles, even all the judges of the earth.

I love them that love me; and those that seek me early shall find me.

Riches and honor are with me; yea, durable riches and righteousness.

My fruit is better than gold, yea, than fine gold; and my revenue than choice silver.

I lead in the way of righteousness in the midst of the paths of judgment:

That I may cause those that love me to inherit substance; and I will fill their treasures.

The Lord possessed me in the beginning of his way, before his works of old.

I was set up from everlasting, from the beginning, or ever the earth was.

When there were no depths, I was brought forth; when there were no fountains abounding with water.

Before the mountains were settled, before the hills, was I brought forth.

While as yet he had not made the earth, nor the fields, nor the highest part of the dust of the world.

When he prepared the heavens, I was there: when he set a compass upon the face of the depth;

When he established the clouds above; when he strengthened the fountains of the deep;

When he gave to the sea his decree, that the waters should not pass his commandment; when he appointed the foundations of the earth:

Then I was by him, as one brought up with him; and I was daily his delight, rejoicing always before him;

Rejoicing in the habitable part of his earth; and my delights were with the sons of men.

Now therefore hearken unto me, O ye children; for blessed are they that keep my ways.

Hear instruction, and be wise, and refuse it not.

Blessed is the man that heareth me, watching daily at my gates, waiting at the posts of my doors.

For whoso findeth me findeth life, and shall obtain favor of the Lord.

But he that sinneth against me wrongeth his own soul: all they that hate me love death.

O Lord, open thou our ears!

That we may hear meekly thy word, and receive it with pure affection.

PSALMS.

THE Lord is my light and my salvation; whom shall I fear? the Lord is the strength of my life; of whom shall I be afraid?

Though an host should encamp against me, my heart shall not fear: though war should rise against me, in this will I be confident.

One thing have I desired of the Lord, that will I seek after; that I may dwell in the house of the Lord all the days of my life, to behold the beauty of the Lord, and to inquire in his temple.

For in the time of trouble he shall hide me in his pavilion: in the secret of his tabernacle shall he hide me; he shall set me up upon a rock.

Therefore will I offer in his tabernacle sacrifices of joy; I will sing, yea, I will sing praises unto the Lord.

Hear, O Lord, when I cry with my voice: have mercy also upon me, and answer me.

When thou saidst, Seek ye my face; my heart said unto thee, Thy face, Lord, will I seek.

Hide not thy face far from me; put not thy servant away in anger: thou hast been my help; leave me not, neither forsake me, O God of my salvation.

When my father and my mother forsake me, then the Lord will take me up.

Teach me thy way, O Lord, and lead me in a plain path.

I had fainted, unless I had believed to see the goodness of the Lord in the land of the living.

Wait on the Lord; be of good courage, and he shall strengthen thine heart: wait, I say, on the Lord.

Rejoice in the Lord, O ye righteous; for praise is comely for the upright.

Sing unto him a new song; play skilfully with a loud noise.

For the word of the Lord is right; and all his works are done in truth.

He loveth righteousness and judgment: the earth is full of the goodness of the Lord.

By the word of the Lord were the heavens made: and all the host of them by the breath of his mouth.

He gathereth the waters of the sea together as an heap: he layeth up the depth in storehouses.

Let all the earth fear the Lord; let all the inhabitants of the world stand in awe of him:

For he spake, and it was done; he commanded, and it stood fast.

The Lord bringeth the counsel of the heathen to naught; he maketh the devices of the people of none effect.

The counsel of the Lord standeth for ever, the thoughts of his heart to all generations.

Blessed is the nation whose God is the Lord; and the people whom he hath chosen for his own inheritance.

The Lord looketh from heaven ; he beholdeth all the sons of men.

From the place of his habitation he looketh upon all the inhabitants of the earth.

He fashioneth their hearts alike ; he considereth all their works.

There is no king saved by the multitude of an host : a mighty man is not delivered by much strength.

An horse is a vain thing for safety : neither shall he deliver any by his great strength.

Behold, the eye of the Lord is upon them that fear him, upon them that hope in his mercy ; ·

To deliver their soul from death, and to keep them alive in famine.

Our soul waiteth for the Lord ; he is our help and our shield.

For our heart shall rejoice in him ; because we have trusted in his holy name.

Let thy mercy, O Lord, be upon us, according as we hope in thee.

BENEDICTION VI.

FIRST SUNDAY AFTER WHITSUNDAY.

COLLECT.

ALMIGHTY and everlasting God, who hast given us thy servants grace, by the confession of a true faith, to acknowledge the glory of thy eternal Godhead ; we beseech thee that thou wouldest keep us steadfast in this faith, and evermore defend us from all adversities, who livest and reignest one God, world without end.   *Amen.*

PROPHECIES.

PROVERBS.

A GOOD name is rather to be chosen than great riches, and loving favor rather than silver and gold.

The rich and poor meet together: the Lord is the maker of them all.

A prudent man foreseeth the evil, and hideth himself; but the simple pass on and are punished.

By humility, and the fear of the Lord, are riches, and honor, and life.

Thorns and snares are in the way of the froward: he that doth keep his soul shall be far from them.

Train up a child in the way he should go; and when he is old, he will not depart from it.

The rich ruleth over the poor, and the borrower is servant to the lender.

He that soweth iniquity shall reap vanity; and the rod of his anger shall fail.

He that hath a bountiful eye shall be blessed; for he giveth of his bread to the poor.

Cast out the scorner, and contention shall go out; yea, strife and reproach shall cease.

He that loveth pureness of heart, for the grace of his lips the king shall be his friend.

The eyes of the Lord preserve knowledge; and he overthroweth the words of the transgressor.

The slothful man saith, There is a lion without, I shall be slain in the streets.

Foolishness is bound in the heart of a child; but the rod of correction shall drive it far from him.

He that oppresseth the poor to increase his riches, and he that giveth to the rich, shall surely come to want.

Bow down thine ear, and hear the words of the wise, and apply thine heart unto my knowledge:

7

For it is a pleasant thing if thou keep them within thee; they shall withal be fitted in thy lips.

Have not I written to thee excellent things in counsels and knowledge,

That I might make thee know the certainty of the words of truth, that thou mightest answer the words of truth to them that send unto thee?

Rob not the poor, because he is poor; neither oppress the afflicted in the gate;

For the Lord will plead their cause; and spoil the soul of those that spoiled them.

Be not thou one of them that strike hands, or of them that are sureties for debts.

If thou hast nothing to pay, why should he take away thy bed from under thee?

Remove not the ancient landmark which thy fathers have set.

Seest thou a man diligent in his business? he shall stand before kings; he shall not stand before mean men.

O Lord, open thou our lips!

And our mouth shall show forth thy praise.

PSALMS.

NOT unto us, O Lord, not unto us, but unto thy name give glory, for thy mercy and for thy truth's sake.

Wherefore should the heathen say, Where is now thy God?

But our God is in the heavens: he hath done whatsoever he pleased.

Their idols are silver and gold, the work of men's hands.

They have mouths, but they speak not; eyes have they, but they see not;

They have ears, but they hear not; noses have they, but they smell not;

They have hands, but they handle not; feet have they, but they walk not; neither speak they through their throat.

12

They that make them are like unto them ; so is every one that trusteth in them.

O, trust thou in the Lord ; he is your help and your shield.

Ye that fear the Lord, trust in the Lord : he is your help and your shield.

The Lord hath been mindful of us : he will bless us.

He will bless them that fear the Lord, both small and great.

The Lord shall increase you more and more, you and your children.

Ye are blessed of the Lord, which made heaven and earth.

The heaven, even the heavens, are the Lord's : but the earth hath he given to the children of men.

The dead praise not the Lord, neither any that go down into silence.

But we will bless the Lord from this time forth and for evermore. Praise the Lord.

I love the Lord, because he hath heard my voice and my supplications.

Because he hath inclined his ear unto me, therefore will I call upon him as long as I live.

The sorrows of death compassed me, and the pains of hell gat hold upon me : I found trouble and sorrow.

Then called I upon the name of the Lord : O Lord, I beseech thee, deliver my soul.

Gracious is the Lord, and righteous : yea, our God is merciful.

The Lord preserveth the simple : I was brought low, and he helped me.

Return unto thy rest, O my soul ; for the Lord hath dealt bountifully with thee.

For thou hast delivered my soul from death, mine eyes from tears, and my feet from falling.

I will walk before the Lord in the land of the living.

I believed, therefore have I spoken : I was greatly afflicted.

I said in my haste, All men are liars.

What shall I render unto the Lord for all his benefits towards me?

I will take the cup of salvation, and call upon the name of the Lord.

I will pay my vows unto the Lord now in the presence of all his people.

Precious in the sight of the Lord is the death of his saints.

I will offer to thee the sacrifice of thanksgiving, and will call upon the name of the Lord.

I will pay my vows unto the Lord now in the presence of all his people,

In the courts of the Lord's house. Praise ye the Lord.

O praise the Lord, all ye nations : praise him, all ye people.

For his merciful kindness is great towards us : and the truth of the Lord endureth for ever. Praise ye the Lord.

BENEDICTION XII.

SECOND SUNDAY AFTER WHITSUNDAY.

COLLECT.

O GOD, the strength of those who put their trust in thee, mercifully accept our prayers ; and because, through the weakness of our mortal nature, we can do no good thing without thee, grant us the help of thy grace, that in keeping thy commandments we may please thee both in will and deed, through Jesus Christ our Lord. *Amen.*

PROPHECIES.

PROVERBS.

Labor not to be rich ; cease from thine own wisdom.

Wilt thou set thine eyes upon that which is not? for riches

*certainly make themselves wings; they fly away, as an eagle
toward heaven.*

Eat thou not the bread of him that hath an evil eye, neither desire thou his dainty meats:

*For as he thinketh in his heart, so is he: Eat and drink,
saith he to thee; but his heart is not with thee.*

Remove not the old landmark: and enter not into the
fields of the fatherless.

*For their Redeemer is mighty; he shall plead their cause
with thee.*

Apply thine heart unto instruction, and thine ears to the
words of knowledge.

*Let not thine heart envy sinners: but be thou in the fear of
the Lord all the day long.*

For surely there is an end; and thine expectation shall not
be cut off.

*Hear thou, my son, and be wise, and guide thine heart in the
way.*

Be not amongst wine-bibbers; amongst riotous eaters of
flesh;

*For the drunkard and the glutton shall come to poverty; and
drowsiness shall clothe a man with rags.*

Hearken unto thy father that begat thee, and despise not
thy mother when she is old.

*Buy the truth, and sell it not; also wisdom, and instruction,
and understanding.*

The father of the righteous shall greatly rejoice; and he
that begetteth a wise child shall have joy of him.

*Who hath woe? who hath sorrow? who hath contentions?
who hath babbling? who hath wounds without cause? who hath
redness of eyes?*

They that tarry long at the wine, they that go to seek
mixed wine.

*Look not thou upon the wine when it is red, when it giveth
his color in the cup, when it moveth itself aright:*

At the last it biteth like a serpent, and stingeth like an adder.

Yea, thou shalt be as he that lieth down in the midst of the sea, or as he that lieth upon the top of a mast.

Who hath ascended up into heaven, or descended? who hath gathered the wind in his fists? who hath bound the waters in a garment? who hath established all the ends of the earth? what is his name, and what is his son's name, if thou canst tell?

Every word of God is pure : he is a shield unto them that put their trust in him.

Add thou not unto his words, lest he reprove thee, and thou be found a liar.

Two things have I required of thee ; deny me them not before I die :

Remove far from me vanity and lies ; give me neither poverty nor riches ; feed me with food convenient for me :

Lest I be full, and deny thee, and say, Who is the Lord? or lest I be poor, and steal, and take the name of my God in vain.

There is a generation that curseth their father, and doth not bless their mother.

There is a generation that are pure in their own eyes, and yet is not washed from their filthiness.

There is a generation, O how lofty are their eyes! and their eyelids are lifted up.

There is a generation whose teeth are as swords, to devour the poor from off the earth, and the needy from among men.

Now unto the King eternal, immortal, invisible, the only wise God ;

Be honor and glory, through Jesus Christ, for ever and ever.

PSALMS.

PRAISE ye the Lord.   Praise the Lord, O my soul.

While I live will I praise the Lord : I will sing praises unto my God while I have any being.

Put not your trust in princes, nor in the son of man, in whom there is no help.

His breath goeth forth, he returneth to the earth ; in that very day his thoughts perish.

Happy is he that hath God for his help, whose hope is in the Lord his God ;

Which made heaven and earth, the sea, and all that therein is ; which keepeth truth for ever ;

Which executeth judgment for the oppressed ; which giveth food to the hungry.   The Lord looseth the prisoners :

The Lord openeth the eyes of the blind : the Lord raiseth them that are bowed down : the Lord loveth the righteous :

The Lord preserveth the strangers ; he relieveth the fatherless and widow ; but the way of the wicked he turneth upside down.

The Lord shall reign for ever, even thy God, O Zion, unto all generations.   Praise ye the Lord.

BENEDICTION XI.

THIRD SUNDAY AFTER WHITSUNDAY.

COLLECT.

O LORD, who never failest to help and govern those whom thou dost bring up in thy steadfast fear and love ; keep us, we beseech thee, under the protection of thy good providence, and make us to have a perpetual fear and love of thy holy name, through Jesus Christ our Lord.   *Amen.*

PROPHECIES.

JOB.

Now a thing was secretly brought to me, and mine ear received a little thereof.

In thoughts from the visions of the night, when deep sleep falleth on men,

Fear came upon me, and trembling, which made all my bones to shake.

Then a spirit passed before my face ;

It stood still, but I could not discern the form thereof : an image was before mine eyes ; there was silence, and I heard a voice, saying,

Shall mortal man be more just than God ? shall a man be more pure than his Maker ?

Behold, he put no trust in his servants ; and his angels he charged with folly :

How much less in them that dwell in houses of clay, whose foundation is in the dust, which are crushed before the moth ?

They are destroyed from morning to evening : they perish for ever, without any regarding it.

Doth not their excellency which is in them go away ? they die, even without wisdom.

Call now, if there be any that will answer thee ; and to which of the saints wilt thou turn ?

For wrath killeth the foolish man, and envy slayeth the silly one.

I have seen the foolish taking root : but suddenly I cursed his habitation.

His children are far from safety, and they are crushed in the gate, neither is there any to deliver them.

Although affliction cometh not forth of the dust, neither doth trouble spring out of the ground ;

Yet man is born unto trouble, as the sparks fly upward.

I would seek unto God, and unto God would I commit my cause;

Which doeth great things and unsearchable; marvellous things without number :

Who giveth rain upon the earth, and sendeth waters upon the fields :

To set up on high those that be low; that those which mourn may be exalted to safety.

He disappointeth the devices of the crafty, so that their hands cannot perform their enterprise.

He taketh the wise in their own craftiness; and the counsel of the froward is carried headlong.

They meet with darkness in the day-time, and grope in the noonday as in the night.

But he saveth the poor from the sword, from their mouth, and from the hand of the mighty.

So the poor hath hope, and iniquity stoppeth her mouth.

Behold, happy is the man whom God correcteth; therefore despise not thou the chastening of the Almighty :

For he maketh sore, and bindeth up; he woundeth, and his hands make whole.

He shall deliver thee in six troubles; yea, in seven there shall no evil touch thee.

In famine he shall redeem thee from death; and in war from the power of the sword.

Thou shalt be hid from the scourge of the tongue; neither shalt thou be afraid of destruction when it cometh.

At destruction and famine thou shalt laugh : neither shalt thou be afraid of the beasts of the earth.

For thou shalt be in league with the stones of the field; and the beasts of the field shall be at peace with thee.

And thou shalt know that thy tabernacle shall be in peace ; and thou shalt visit thy habitation, and shalt not sin.

Thou shalt come to thy grave in a full age, like as a shock of corn cometh in his season.

Lo this, we have searched it, so it is ; hear it, and know thou it for thy good.

Praise ye the Lord!
The Lord's name be praised.

PSALMS.

GIVE unto the Lord, O ye mighty, give unto the Lord glory and strength.

Give unto the Lord the glory due unto his name ; worship the Lord in the beauty of holiness.

The voice of the Lord is upon the waters : the God of glory thundereth : the Lord is upon many waters.

The voice of the Lord is powerful ; the voice of the Lord is full of majesty.

The voice of the Lord breaketh the cedars ; yea, the Lord breaketh the cedars of Lebanon.

He maketh them also to skip like a calf ; Lebanon and Sirion like a young unicorn.

The voice of the Lord divideth the flames of fire.

The voice of the Lord shaketh the wilderness ; the Lord shaketh the wilderness of Kadesh.

The voice of the Lord discovereth the forests : and in his temple doth every one speak of his glory.

The Lord sitteth upon the flood ; yea, the Lord sitteth King for ever.

The Lord will give strength unto his people ; the Lord will bless his people with peace.

I will extol thee, O Lord ; for thou hast lifted me up.

O Lord my God, I cried unto thee, and thou hast healed me.

O Lord, thou hast brought up my soul from the grave : thou hast kept me alive, that I should not go down to the pit.

Sing unto the Lord, O ye saints of his, and give thanks at the remembrance of his holiness.

For his anger endureth but a moment : in his favor is life ; weeping may endure for a night, but joy cometh in the morning.

And in my prosperity I said, I shall never be moved.

Lord, by thy favor thou hast made my mountain to stand strong : thou didst hide thy face, and I was troubled.

I cried to thee, O Lord ; and unto the Lord I made supplication.

What profit is there in my blood, when I go down to the pit ? Shall the dust praise thee ? shall it declare thy truth ?

Hear, O Lord, and have mercy upon me : Lord, be thou my helper.

To the end that my glory may sing praise to thee, and not be silent.   O Lord my God, I will give thanks unto thee for ever.

In thee, O Lord, do I put my trust ; let me never be ashamed : deliver me in thy righteousness.

Bow down thine ear to me : deliver me speedily : be thou my strong rock, for an house of defence to save me.

For thou art my rock and my fortress : therefore, for thy name's sake, lead me and guide me.

Into thine hand I commit my spirit : thou hast redeemed me, O Lord God of truth.

I have hated them that regard lying vanities : but I trust in the Lord.

I will be glad and rejoice in thy mercy : for thou hast considered my trouble ; thou hast known my soul in adversities,

And hast not shut me up into the hand of the enemy : thou hast set my feet in a large room.

My times are in thy hand : deliver me from the hand of mine enemies, and from them that persecute me.

Make thy face to shine upon thy servant : save me for thy mercies' sake.

Let me not be ashamed, O Lord : for I have called upon thee : let the wicked be ashamed.

Let the lying lips be put to silence, which speak grievous things proudly and contemptuously against the righteous.

O how great is thy goodness, which thou hast laid up for them that fear thee; which thou hast wrought for them that trust in thee before the sons of men!

Thou shalt hide them in the secret of thy presence from the pride of man; thou shalt keep them secretly in a pavilion from the strife of tongues.

Blessed be the Lord; for he hath showed me his marvellous kindness.

For I said in my haste, I am cut off from before thine eyes: nevertheless thou heardest the voice of my supplications, when I cried unto thee.

· O love the Lord, all ye his saints; for the Lord preserveth the faithful, and plentifully rewardeth the proud doer.

Be of good courage, and he shall strengthen your heart, all ye that hope in the Lord.

BENEDICTION X.

FOURTH SUNDAY AFTER WHITSUNDAY.

COLLECT.

O LORD, we beseech thee mercifully to hear us, and grant that we, truly seeking thine aid, may by thy mighty power be defended, and by thy gracious mercy be comforted in all dangers and adversities, through Jesus Christ our Lord. *Amen.*

PROPHECIES.

JOB.

BEHOLD, God is mighty, and despiseth not any: he is mighty in strength and wisdom.

He preserveth not the life of the wicked : but giveth right to the poor.

He withdraweth not his eyes from the righteous : yea, he doth establish them for ever, and they are exalted.

And if they be bound in fetters, and be holden in cords of affliction ;

Then he showeth them their work, and their transgressions.

He openeth also their ear to discipline, and commandeth that they return from iniquity.

If they obey and serve him, they shall spend their days in prosperity, and their years in pleasures :

But if they obey not, they shall die without knowledge.

But the hypocrites in heart heap up wrath.

He delivereth the poor in his affliction, and openeth their ears in oppression.

Will he esteem thy riches : no, not gold, nor all the forces of strength.

Behold, God exalteth by his power : who teacheth like him ?

Remember that thou magnify his work, which men behold.

Every man may see it ; man may behold it afar off.

Behold, God is great, and we know him not ; neither can the number of his years be searched out.

For he maketh small the drops of water : they pour down rain according to the vapor thereof,

Which the clouds do drop and distil upon man abundantly.

Also can any understand the spreadings of the clouds, or the noise of his tabernacle ?

Behold, he spreadeth his light upon it, and covereth the bottom of the sea.

For by them judgeth he the people ; he giveth meat in abundance.

With clouds he covereth the light ; and commandeth it not to shine, by the cloud that cometh betwixt.

The noise thereof showeth concerning it, the cattle also concerning the vapor.

At this also my heart trembleth, and is moved out of his place.

Hear attentively the noise of his voice, and the sound that goeth out of his mouth.

He directeth it under the whole heaven, and his lightning unto the ends of the earth.

After it a voice roareth : he thundereth with the voice of his excellency.

God thundereth marvellously with his voice ; great things doeth he, which we cannot comprehend.

For he saith to the snow, Be thou on the earth ; likewise to the small rain, and to the great rain of his strength.

He sealeth up the hand of every man, that all men may know his work.

Then the beasts go into dens, and remain in their places.

Out of the south cometh the whirlwind ; and cold out of the north.

By the breath of God frost is given ; and the breadth of the waters is straitened.

Also by watering he wearieth the thick cloud ; he scattereth his bright cloud.

And it is turned round about by his counsels ; that they may do whatsoever he commandeth them upon the face of the world in the earth.

He causeth it to come, whether for correction, or for his land, or for mercy.

Hearken unto this : stand still, and consider the wondrous works of God.

Dost thou know when God disposed them, and caused the light of his cloud to shine ?

Dost thou know the balancings of the clouds, the wondrous works of him which is perfect in knowledge ?

How thy garments are warm, when he quieteth the earth by the south wind ?

Hast thou with him spread out the sky, which is strong, and as a molten looking-glass?

Teach us what we shall say unto him; for we cannot order our speech by reason of darkness.

And now men see not the bright light which is in the clouds; but the wind passeth, and cleanseth them.

Fair weather cometh out of the north: with God is terrible majesty.

Touching the Almighty, we cannot find him out: he is excellent in power, and in judgment, and in plenty of justice.

O Lord, open thou our ears!

That we may hear meekly thy word, and receive it with pure affection.

PSALMS.

WHY standest thou afar off, O Lord? why hidest thou thyself in times of trouble?

The wicked in his pride doth persecute the poor: let them be taken in the devices that they have imagined.

For the wicked boasteth of his heart's desire, and blesseth the covetous, whom the Lord abhorreth.

The wicked, through the pride of his countenance, will not seek after God: God is not in all his thoughts.

His ways are always grievous: thy judgments are far above out of his sight: as for all his enemies, he puffeth at them.

He hath said in his heart, I shall not be moved; for I shall never be in adversity.

His mouth is full of cursing and deceit and fraud; under his tongue is mischief and vanity.

He sitteth in the lurking-places of the villages: in the secret places doth he murder the innocent: his eyes are privily set against the poor.

He lieth in wait secretly, as a lion in his den: he lieth in wait to catch the poor: he doth catch the poor when he draweth him into his net.

He croucheth, and humbleth himself, that the poor may fall by his strong ones.

He hath said in his heart, God hath forgotten: he hideth his face; he will never see it.

Arise, O Lord; O God, lift up thine hand; forget not the humble.

Wherefore doth the wicked contemn God? he hath said in his heart, thou wilt not require it.

Thou hast seen it: for thou beholdest mischief and spite to requite it with thy hand: the poor committeth himself unto thee: thou art the helper of the fatherless.

Break thou the arm of the wicked and the evil man: seek out his wickedness till thou find none.

The Lord is King for ever and ever: the heathen are perished out of his land.

Lord, thou hast heard the desire of the humble: thou wilt prepare their heart, thou wilt cause thine ear to hear:

To judge the fatherless and the oppressed, that the man of the earth may no more oppress.

Help, Lord: for the godly man ceaseth; for the faithful fail from among the children of men.

They speak vanity every one with his neighbor: with flattering lips and with a double heart do they speak.

The Lord shall cut off all flattering lips, and the tongue that speaketh proud things:

Who have said, With our tongue will we prevail; our lips are our own: who is lord over us?

For the oppression of the poor, for the sighing of the needy, now will I arise, saith the Lord; I will set him in safety from him that puffeth at him.

The words of the Lord are pure words: as silver tried in a furnace of earth, purified seven times.

Thou shalt keep them, O Lord, thou shalt preserve them from this generation for ever.

The wicked walk on every side, when the vilest men are exalted.

In the Lord put I my trust: how say ye to my soul, Flee, as a bird to your mountain ?

For lo, the wicked bend their bow, they make ready their arrow upon the string, that they may privily shoot at the upright in heart.

If the foundations be destroyed, what can the righteous do?

The Lord is in his holy temple, the Lord's throne is in heaven: his eyes behold, his eyelids try the children of men.

The Lord trieth the righteous: but the wicked and him that loveth violence his soul hateth.

Upon the wicked he shall rain snares, fire and brimstone, and an horrible tempest: this shall be the portion of their cup.

For the righteous Lord loveth righteousness; his countenance doth behold the upright.

BENEDICTION VII.

FIFTH SUNDAY AFTER WHITSUNDAY.

COLLECT.

O GOD, the protector of all who trust in thee, without whom nothing is strong, nothing is holy ; increase and multiply upon us thy mercy, that, thou being our ruler and guide, we may so pass through things temporal, that we finally lose not the things eternal. Grant this, O Heavenly Father, through Jesus Christ our Lord. *Amen.*

PROPHECIES.

PROVERBS.

BETTER is the poor that walketh in his integrity, than he that is perverse in his lips, and is a fool.

Also, that the soul be without knowledge, it is not good; and he that hasteth with his feet sinneth.

The foolishness of man perverteth his way: and his heart fretteth against the Lord.

A false witness shall not be unpunished; and he that speaketh lies shall not escape.

He that getteth wisdom loveth his own soul: he that keepeth understanding shall find good.

A false witness shall not be unpunished; and he that speaketh lies shall perish.

Delight is not seemly for a fool; much less for a servant to have rule over princes.

The discretion of a man deferreth his anger; and it is his glory to pass over a transgression.

Slothfulness casteth into a deep sleep; and an idle soul shall suffer hunger.

He that keepeth the commandment keepeth his own soul; but he that despiseth his ways shall die.

He that hath pity upon the poor lendeth unto the Lord; and that which he hath given will he pay him again.

A man of great wrath shall suffer punishment; for if thou deliver him, yet thou must do it again.

Hear counsel, and receive instruction, that thou mayest be wise in thy latter end.

There are many devices in a man's heart; nevertheless, the counsel of the Lord, that shall stand.

The fear of the Lord tendeth to life; and he that hath it shall abide satisfied; he shall not be visited with evil.

A slothful man hideth his hand in his bosom, and will not so much as bring it to his mouth again.

He that wasteth his father, and chaseth away his mother, is a son that causeth shame, and bringeth reproach.

Cease, my son, to hear the instruction that causeth to err from the words of knowledge.

13 *

Wine is a mocker, strong drink is raging, and whosoever is deceived thereby is not wise.

It is an honor for a man to cease from strife ; but every fool will be meddling.

The sluggard will not plough by reason of the cold ; therefore shall he beg in harvest, and have nothing.

Counsel in the heart of man is like deep water : but a man of understanding will draw it out.

Most men will proclaim every one his own goodness : but a faithful man who can find ?

The just man walketh in his integrity ; his children are blessed after him.

Who can say, I have made my heart clean, I am pure from my sin ?

Divers weights, and divers measures, both of them are alike abomination to the Lord.

Even a child is known by his doings, whether his work be pure, and whether it be right.

The hearing ear, and the seeing eye, the Lord hath made even both of them.

Love not sleep, lest thou come to poverty ; open thine eyes, and thou shalt be satisfied with bread.

It is naught, it is naught, saith the buyer : but when he is gone his way, then he boasteth.

There is gold, and a multitude of rubies : but the lips of knowledge are a precious jewel.

Bread of deceit is sweet to a man ; but afterwards his mouth shall be filled with gravel.

He that goeth about as a talebearer revealeth secrets ; therefore meddle not with him that flattereth with his lips.

Whoso curseth his father or his mother, his lamp shall be put out in obscure darkness.

An inheritance may be gotten hastily at the beginning ; but the end thereof shall not be blessed.

Say not thou, I will recompense evil: but wait on the Lord, and he shall save thee.

O Lord, open thou our lips!
And our mouth shall show forth thy praise.

PSALMS.

WE have heard with our ears, O God, our fathers have told us, what work thou didst in their days, in the times of old;

How thou didst drive out the heathen with thy hand, and plantedst them; how thou didst afflict the people, and cast them out.

For they got not the land in possession by their own sword, neither did their own arm save them; but thy right hand, and thine arm, and the light of thy countenance, because thou hadst a favor unto them.

In God we boast all the day long, and praise thy name for ever.

But thou hast cast off, and put us to shame; and goest not forth with our armies.

Thou hast given us like sheep appointed for meat; and hast scattered us among the heathen.

Thou sellest thy people for naught, and dost not increase thy wealth by their price.

Thou makest us a reproach to our neighbors, a scorn and derision to them that are round about us.

Thou makest us a byword among the heathen, a shaking of the head among the people.

My confusion is continually before me, and the shame of my face hath covered me,

For the voice of him that reproacheth and blasphemeth; by reason of the enemy and avenger.

If we have forgotten the name of our God, or stretched out our hands to a strange god;

Shall not God search this out? for he knoweth the secrets of the heart.

Yea, for thy sake are we killed all the day long ; we are counted as sheep for the slaughter.

Awake, why sleepest thou, O Lord ? arise, cast us not off for ever.

Wherefore hidest thou thy face, and forgettest our affliction and our oppression ?

Arise for our help, and redeem us, for thy mercies' sake.

God is our refuge and strength, a very present help in trouble :

Therefore will not we fear, though the earth be removed, and though the mountains be carried into the midst of the sea ;

Though the waters thereof roar and be troubled, though the mountains shake with the swelling thereof.

There is a river, the streams whereof shall make glad the city of God, the holy place of the tabernacles of the Most High.

God is in the midst of her : she shall not be moved : God shall help her, and that right early.

The heathen raged, the kingdoms were moved : he uttered his voice, the earth melted.

The Lord of hosts is with us ; the God of Jacob is our refuge.

Come, behold the works of the Lord, what desolations he hath made in the earth.

He maketh wars to cease unto the end of the earth ; he breaketh the bow, and cutteth the spear in sunder ; he burneth the chariot in the fire.

Be still, and know that I am God ; I will be exalted among the heathen, I will be exalted in the earth.

BENEDICTION II.

SIXTH SUNDAY AFTER WHITSUNDAY.

COLLECT.

GRANT, O Lord, we beseech thee, that the course of this world may be so peaceably ordered by thy governance, that thy Church may joyfully serve thee in all godly quietness, through Jesus Christ our Lord.   *Amen.*

PROPHECIES.

JOB.

O THAT I knew where I might find God! that I might come even to his seat!

I would order my cause before him, and fill my mouth with arguments.

I would know the words which he would answer me, and understand what he would say unto me.

Will he plead against me with his great power?   No; but he would put strength in me.

Behold, I go forward, but he is not there; and backward, but I cannot perceive him:

On the left hand, where he doth work, but I cannot behold him: he hideth himself on the right hand, that I cannot see him:

But he knoweth the way that I take: when he hath tried me, I shall come forth as gold.

My foot hath held his steps, his way have I kept, and not declined.

Neither have I gone back from the commandment of his lips; I have esteemed the words of his mouth more than my necessary food.

But he is in one mind, and who can turn him? and what his soul desireth, even that he doeth.

Therefore am I troubled at his presence: when I consider, I am afraid of him.

For God maketh my heart soft, and the Almighty troubleth me :

Dominion and fear are with him, he maketh peace in his high places.

Is there any number of his armies? and upon whom doth not his light arise?

How then can man be justified with God? or how can he be clean that is born of a woman?

Behold even to the moon, and it shineth not ; yea, the stars are not pure in his sight.

Hell is naked before him, and destruction hath no covering.

He stretcheth out the north over the empty place, and hangeth the earth upon nothing.

He bindeth up the waters in his thick clouds ; and the cloud is not rent under them.

He holdeth back the face of his throne, and spreadeth his cloud upon it.

He hath compassed the waters with bounds, until the day and night come to an end.

The pillars of heaven tremble, and are astonished at his reproof.

He divideth the sea with his power, and by his understanding he smiteth through the proud.

By his Spirit he hath garnished the heavens ; his hand hath formed the crooked serpent.

Lo, these are parts of his ways ; but how little a portion is heard of him ? but the thunder of his power who can understand ?

Now unto the King eternal, immortal, invisible, the only wise God ;

Be honor and glory, through Jesus Christ, for ever and ever.

PSALMS.

H<small>E</small> that dwelleth in the secret place of the Most High shall abide under the shadow of the Almighty.

I will say of the Lord, He is my refuge and my fortress: my God; in him will I trust.

Surely he shall deliver thee from the snare of the fowler, and from the noisome pestilence.

He shall cover thee with his feathers, and under his wings shalt thou trust: his truth shall be thy shield and buckler.

Thou shalt not be afraid for the terror by night; nor for the arrow that flieth by day;

Nor for the pestilence that walketh in darkness; nor for the destruction that wasteth at noonday.

A thousand shall fall at thy side, and ten thousand at thy right hand; but it shall not come nigh thee.

Only with thine eyes shalt thou behold and see the reward of the wicked.

Because thou hast made the Lord which is my refuge, even the Most High, thy habitation,

There shall no evil befall thee, neither shall any plague come nigh thy dwelling.

For he shall give his angels charge over thee, to keep thee in all thy ways.

They shall bear thee up in their hands, lest thou dash thy foot against a stone.

Because he hath set his love upon me, therefore will I deliver him: I will set him on high, because he hath known my name.

He shall call upon me, and I will answer him: I will be with him in trouble; I will deliver him, and honor him.

With long life will I satisfy him, and show him my salvation.

The Lord reigneth; he is clothed with majesty; the Lord is clothed with strength, wherewith he hath girded himself: the world also is established, that it cannot be moved.

Thy throne is established of old : thou art from everlasting.

The floods have lifted up, O Lord, the floods have lifted up their voice ; the floods lift up their waves.

The Lord on high is mightier than the noise of many waters, yea, than the mighty waves of the sea.

Thy testimonies are very sure : holiness becometh thine house, O Lord, for ever.

O Lord God, to whom vengeance belongeth ; O God, show thyself.

Lift up thyself, thou Judge of the earth.

Lord, how long shall the wicked, how long shall the wicked triumph ?

How long shall they utter and speak hard things ? and all the workers of iniquity boast themselves ?

They slay the widow and the stranger, and murder the fatherless.

Yet they say, The Lord shall not see, neither shall God regard it.

Understand, ye brutish among the people : and ye fools, when will ye be wise ?

He that planted the ear, shall he not hear ? he that formed the eye, shall he not see ?

He that teacheth man knowledge, shall not he know ?

The Lord knoweth the thoughts of man, that they are vanity.

Blessed is the man whom thou chastenest, O Lord, and teachest him out of thy law ;

That thou mayest give him rest from the days of adversity.

For the Lord will not cast off his people, neither will he forsake his inheritance.

But judgment shall return unto righteousness : and all the upright in heart shall follow it.

Unless the Lord had been my help, my soul had almost dwelt in silence.

In the multitude of my thoughts within me, thy comforts delight my soul.

Shall the throne of iniquity have fellowship with thee, which frameth mischief by a law?

But the Lord is my defence; and my God is the rock of my refuge.

BENEDICTION IV.

SEVENTH SUNDAY AFTER WHITSUNDAY.

COLLECT.

O GOD, who hast prepared for those who love thee such good things as pass man's understanding, pour into our hearts such love toward thee, that we, loving thee above all things, may obtain thy promises, which exceed all that we can desire, through Jesus Christ our Lord. *Amen.*

PROPHECIES.

PROVERBS.

BE not thou envious against evil men, neither desire to be with them:

For their heart studieth destruction, and their lips talk of mischief.

Through wisdom is an house builded: and by understanding it is established:

And by knowledge shall the chambers be filled with all precious and pleasant riches.

A wise man is strong; yea, a man of knowledge increaseth strength.

If thou faint in the day of adversity, thy strength is small.

Lay not wait, O wicked man, against the dwelling of the righteous; spoil not his resting-place.

Rejoice not when thine enemy falleth; and let not thine heart be glad when he stumbleth;

14

Lest the Lord see it, and it displease him.

Fret not thyself because of evil men, neither be thou envious at the wicked:

For there shall be no reward to the evil man; the candle of the wicked shall be put out.

He that saith unto the wicked, Thou art righteous; him shall the people curse, nations shall abhor him:

But to them that rebuke him shall be delight, and a good blessing shall come upon them.

Prepare thy work without, and make it fit for thyself in the field; and afterwards build thine house.

Be not a witness against thy neighbor without cause; and deceive not with thy lips.

Say not, I will do so to him as he hath done to me: I will render to the man according to his work.

I went by the field of the slothful, and by the vineyard of the man void of understanding;

And lo, it was all grown over with thorns, and nettles had covered the face thereof, and the stone wall thereof was broken down.

Then I saw, and considered it well: I looked upon it, and received instruction.

Yet a little sleep, a little slumber, a little folding of the hands to sleep:

So shall thy poverty come as one that travelleth; and thy want as an armed man.

Go not forth hastily to strive, lest thou know not what to do in the end thereof, when thy neighbor hath put thee to shame.

Debate thy cause with thy neighbor himself; and discover not a secret to another;

Lest he that heareth it put thee to shame, and thine infamy turn not away.

A word fitly spoken is like apples of gold in pictures of silver.

A man that beareth false witness against his neighbor is a maul, and a sword, and a sharp arrow.

Confidence in an unfaithful man in time of trouble is like a broken tooth, and a foot out of joint.

If thine enemy be hungry, give him bread to eat ; and if he be thirsty, give him water to drink :

For thou shalt heap coals of fire upon his head, and the Lord shall reward thee.

He that hath no rule over his own spirit is like a city that is broken down, and without walls.

Praise ye the Lord !
The Lord's name be praised.

PSALMS.

I WILL lift up mine eyes unto the hills, from whence cometh my help.

My help cometh from the Lord, which made heaven and earth.

He will not suffer thy foot to be moved : he that keepeth thee will not slumber.

Behold, he that keepeth Israel shall neither slumber nor sleep.

The Lord is thy keeper; the Lord is thy shade upon thy right hand.

The sun shall not smite . thee by day, nor the moon by night.

The Lord shall preserve thee from all evil : he shall preserve thy soul.

The Lord shall preserve thy going out, and thy coming in, from this time forth, and even for evermore.

I was glad when they said unto me, Let us go into the house of the Lord.

Our feet shall stand within thy gates, O Jerusalem.

Jerusalem is builded as a city that is compact together :

Whither the tribes go up, the tribes of the Lord, unto the testimony of Israel, to give thanks unto the name of the Lord.

For there are set thrones of judgment, the thrones of the house of David.

Pray for the peace of Jerusalem : they shall prosper that love thee.

Peace be within thy walls, and prosperity within thy palaces.

For my brethren and companions' sake, I will now say, Peace be within thee.

Because of the house of the Lord our God I will seek thy good.

Unto thee lift I up mine eyes, O thou that dwellest in the heavens.

Behold, as the eyes of servants look unto the hand of their masters, and as the eyes of a maiden unto the hand of her mistress ; so our eyes wait upon the Lord our God, until that he have mercy upon us.

Have mercy upon us, O Lord, have mercy upon us.

If it had not been the Lord who was on our side ;

If it had not been the Lord who was on our side, when men rose up against us ;

Then they had swallowed us up quick, when their wrath was kindled against us :

Then the waters had overwhelmed us, the stream had gone over our soul :

Our help is in the name of the Lord, who made heaven and earth.

They that trust in the Lord shall be as Mount Zion, which cannot be removed, but abideth for ever.

As the mountains are round about Jerusalem, so the Lord is round about his people from henceforth even for ever.

For the rod of the wicked shall not rest upon the lot of the righteous ; lest the righteous put forth their hands unto iniquity.

Do good, O Lord, unto those that be good, and to them that are upright in their hearts.

As for such as turn aside unto their crooked ways, the Lord shall lead them forth with the workers of iniquity : but peace shall be upon Israel.

They that sow in tears shall reap in joy.

He that goeth forth and weepeth, bearing precious seed, shall doubtless come again with rejoicing, bringing his sheaves with him.

BENEDICTION I.

EIGHTH SUNDAY AFTER WHITSUNDAY.

· COLLECT.

LORD of all power and might, who art the author and giver of all good things, graft in our hearts the love of thy name, increase in us true religion, nourish us with all goodness, and of thy great mercy keep us in the same, through Jesus Christ our Lord.   *Amen.*   ·

PROPHECIES.

ECCLESIASTES.

KEEP thy foot when thou goest to the house of God, and be more ready to hear than to give the sacrifice of fools : for they consider not that they do evil.

Be not rash with thy mouth, and let not thine heart be hasty to utter anything before God : for God is in heaven, and thou upon earth ; therefore let thy words be few.

When thou vowest a vow unto God, defer not to pay it : pay that which thou hast vowed.

. Suffer not thy mouth to cause thy flesh to sin : wherefore should God be angry at thy voice, and destroy the work of thine hands ?

14 *

For in the multitude of dreams and many words there are also divers vanities : but fear thou God.

If thou seest the oppression of the poor, and violent perverting of judgment and justice in a province, marvel not at the matter : for he that is higher than the highest regardeth ; and there be higher than they.

Moreover, the profit of the earth is for all : the king himself is served by the field.

He that loveth silver shall not be satisfied with silver ; nor he that loveth abundance with increase.   This is also vanity.

When goods increase, they are increased that eat them : and what good is there to the owners thereof, saving the beholding of them with their eyes ?

The sleep of a laboring man is sweet, whether he eat little or much : but the abundance of the rich will not suffer him to sleep.

There is a sore evil which I have seen under the sun, namely, riches kept for the owners thereof to their hurt.

But those riches perish by evil travail ; and he begetteth a son, and there is nothing in his hand.

So I returned, and considered all the oppressions that are done under the sun : and, behold, the tears of such as were oppressed, and they had no conforter ; and on the side of their oppressors there was power ; but they had no comforter.

To everything there is a season, and a time to every purpose under the heaven :

I know that whatsoever God doeth, it shall be for ever : nothing can be put to it, nor anything taken from it : and God doeth it that men should fear before him.

That which hath been is now ; and that which is to be hath already been : and God requireth that which is past.

And, moreover, I saw under the sun the place of judgment, that wickedness was there ; and the place of righteousness, that iniquity was there.

I said in mine heart, God shall judge the righteous and the wicked: for there is a time there for every purpose, and for every work.

Then I saw that wisdom excelleth folly, as far as light excelleth darkness.

For God giveth to a man that is good in his sight, wisdom, and knowledge, and joy: but to the sinner he giveth travail, to gather, and to heap up, that he may give to him that is good before God.

O Lord, open thou our ears !

That we may hear meekly thy word, and receive it with pure affection.

PSALMS.

GREAT is the Lord, and greatly to be praised in the city of our God, in the mountain of his holiness.

Beautiful for situation, the joy of the whole earth, is Mount Zion, on the sides of the north, the city of the great King.

We have thought of thy loving-kindness, O God, in the midst of thy temple.

According to thy name, O God, so is thy praise unto the ends of the earth : thy right hand is full of righteousness.

For this God is our God for ever and ever ; he will be our guide even unto death.

Lord, thou hast been favorable unto thy land :

Thou hast forgiven the iniquity of thy people ; hast covered all their sin.

Wilt thou not revive us again, that thy people may rejoice in thee ?

Show us thy mercy, O Lord, and grant us thy salvation.

I will hear what God the Lord will speak : for he will speak peace unto his people, and to his saints ; but let them not turn again to folly.

Surely his salvation is nigh them that fear him ; that glory may dwell in our land.

Mercy and truth are met together ; righteousness and peace have kissed each other.

Truth shall spring out of the earth ; and righteousness shall look down from heaven.

Yea, the Lord shall give that which is good; and our land shall yield her increase.

Righteousness shall go before him, and shall set us in the way of his steps.

Be merciful unto me, O Lord : for I cry unto thee daily.

Rejoice the soul of thy servant : for unto thee, O Lord, do I lift up my soul.

For thou, Lord, art good, and ready to forgive ; and plenteous in mercy unto all them that call upon thee.

Give ear, O Lord, unto my prayer ; and attend to the voice of my supplications.

In the day of my trouble I will call upon thee : for thou wilt answer me.

All nations whom thou hast made shall come and worship before thee, O Lord ; and shall glorify thy name.

For thou art great, and doest wondrous things : thou art God alone.

Teach me thy way, O Lord ; I will walk in thy truth : unite my heart to fear thy name.

I will praise thee, O Lord my God, with all my heart ; and I will glorify thy name for evermore.

Thou, O Lord, art a God full of compassion, and gracious, long-suffering, and plenteous in mercy and truth.

O turn unto me, and have mercy upon me.

Glorious things are spoken of thee, O city of God.

And of Zion it shall be said, This and that man was born in her ; and the Highest himself shall establish her.

The Lord shall count, when he writeth up the people, that this man was born there.

All my springs are in thee.

BENEDICTION II.

NINTH SUNDAY AFTER WHITSUNDAY.

COLLECT.

O GOD, whose never-failing providence ordereth all things both in heaven and earth, we humbly beseech thee to put away from us all hurtful things, and to give us those things which be profitable for us, through Jesus Christ our Lord. *Amen.*

PROPHECIES.

JOB.

CANST thou by searching find out God? canst thou find out the Almighty unto perfection?

It is as high as heaven; what canst thou do? deeper than hell; what canst thou know?

The measure thereof is longer than the earth, and broader than the sea.

If he cut off, and shut up, or gather together, then who can hinder him?

For he knoweth vain men: he seeth wickedness also: will he not then consider it?

If thou prepare thine heart, and stretch out thine hands toward him;

If iniquity be in thy hand, put it far away, and let not wickedness dwell in thy tabernacles.

For then shalt thou lift up thy face without spot; yea, thou shalt be steadfast, and shalt not fear:

And thine age shall be clearer than the noonday; thou shalt shine forth, thou shalt be as the morning.

And thou shalt be secure, because there is hope; yea, thou shalt take thy rest in safety.

Also thou shalt lie down, and none shall make thee afraid;

But the eyes of the wicked shall fail, and they shall not escape, and their hope shall be as the giving up of the ghost.

Who knoweth not in all these, that the hand of the Lord hath wrought this?

In whose hand is the soul of every living thing, and the breath of all mankind.

With the ancient is wisdom; and in length of days understanding.

With him is wisdom and strength, he hath counsel and understanding.

Behold, he breaketh down, and it cannot be built again; he shutteth up, and there can be no opening.

Behold, he withholdeth the waters, and they dry up; also he sendeth them out, and they overturn the earth.

With him is strength and wisdom.

Though he slay me, yet will I trust in him.

He also shall be my salvation.

O Lord, open thou our lips!

And our mouth shall show forth thy praise.

PSALMS.

O GOD, thou knowest my foolishness; and my sins are not hid from thee.

Let not them that wait on thee, O Lord God of hosts, be ashamed, for my sake; let not those that seek thee be confounded.

But as for me, my prayer is unto thee, O Lord, in an acceptable time: O God, in the multitude of thy mercy, hear me, in the truth of thy salvation.

Hear me, O Lord; for thy loving-kindness is good: turn unto me according to the multitude of thy tender mercies.

And hide not thy face from thy servant; hear me speedily.

Draw nigh unto my soul, and redeem it.

I will praise the name of God with a song, and will magnify him with thanksgiving.

The humble shall see this, and be glad: and your heart shall live that seek God.

For the Lord heareth the poor, and despiseth not his prisoners.

Let the heaven and earth praise him, the seas and everything that moveth therein.

Truly God is good to Israel, even to such as are of a clean heart.

But as for me, my feet were almost gone ; my steps had well-nigh slipped.

For I was envious at the foolish, when I saw the prosperity of the wicked.

For there are no bands in their death : but their strength is firm.

They are not in trouble as other men ; neither are they plagued like other men.

Therefore pride compasseth them about as a chain ; violence covereth them as a garment.

They are corrupt, and speak wickedly concerning oppression : they speak loftily.

They set their mouth against the heavens, and their tongue walketh through the earth.

Nevertheless, I am continually with thee ; thou hast holden me by my right hand.

Thou shalt guide me with thy counsel, and afterward receive me to glory.

Whom have I in heaven but thee ? and there is none upon earth that I desire besides thee.

My flesh and my heart faileth : but God is the strength of my heart, and my portion for ever.

For, lo, they that are far from thee shall perish ;

But it is good for me to draw near to God : I have put my trust in the Lord God, that I may declare all thy works.

BENEDICTION VI.

TENTH SUNDAY AFTER WHITSUNDAY.

COLLECT.

GRANT to us, Lord, we beseech thee, the spirit to think and do always such things as be rightful; that we, who cannot do anything that is good without thee, may by thee be enabled to live according to thy will, through Jesus Christ our Lord. *Amen.*

PROPHECIES.

PROVERBS.

THOUGH hand join in hand, the wicked shall not be unpunished : but the seed of the righteous shall be delivered.

There is that scattereth, and yet increaseth ; and there is that withholdeth more than is meet, but it tendeth to poverty.

He that withholdeth corn, the people shall curse him : but blessing shall be upon the head of him that selleth it.

He that diligently seeketh good procureth favor : but he that seeketh mischief, it shall come unto him.

He that trusteth in his riches shall fall : but the righteous shall flourish as a branch.

The fruit of the righteous is a tree of life ; and he that winneth souls is wise.

Behold, the righteous shall be recompensed in the earth : much more the wicked and the sinner.

Whoso loveth instruction loveth knowledge ; but he that hateth reproof is brutish.

A good man obtaineth favor of the Lord : but a man of wicked devices will he condemn.

A man shall not be established by wickedness : but the root of the righteous shall not be moved.

A righteous man regardeth the life of his beast : but the tender mercies of the wicked are cruel.

He that tilleth his land shall be satisfied with bread ; but he that followeth vain persons is void of understanding.

The way of a fool is right in his own eyes : but he that hearkeneth unto counsel is wise.

There is that speaketh like the piercings of a sword : but the tongue of the wise is health.

The lip of truth shall be established for ever : but a lying tongue is but for a moment.

Deceit is in the heart of them that imagine evil : but to the counsellors of peace is joy.

There shall no evil happen to the just : but the wicked shall be filled with mischief.

Lying lips are abomination to the Lord : but they that deal truly are his delight.

The hand of the diligent shall bear rule : but the slothful shall be under tribute.

Heaviness in the heart of man maketh it stoop : but a good word maketh it glad.

In the way of righteousness is life; and in the pathway thereof there is no death.

A wise son heareth his father's instruction : but a scorner heareth not rebuke.

He that keepeth his mouth keepeth his life : but he that openeth wide his lips shall have destruction.

The soul of the sluggard desireth, and hath nothing : but the soul of the diligent shall be made fat.

Righteousness keepeth him that is upright in the way : but wickedness overthroweth the sinner.

There is that maketh himself rich, yet hath nothing : there is that maketh himself poor, yet hath great riches.

The light of the righteous rejoiceth : but the lamp of the wicked shall be put out.

Only by pride cometh contention : but with the well-advised is wisdom.

15

Wealth gotten by vanity shall be diminished: but he that gathereth by labor shall increase.

Hope deferred maketh the heart sick: but when the desire cometh, it is a tree of life.

Whoso despiseth the word shall be destroyed: but he that feareth the commandment shall be rewarded.

Good understanding giveth favor: but the way of transgressors is hard.

Poverty and shame shall be to him that refuseth instruction: but he that regardeth reproof shall be honored.

He that walketh with wise men shall be wise: but a companion of fools shall be destroyed.

Evil pursueth sinners: but to the righteous good shall be repaid.

Now unto the King eternal, immortal, invisible, the only wise God;

Be honor and glory, through Jesus Christ, for ever and ever.

PSALMS.

THE day is thine, the night also is thine: thou hast prepared the light and the sun.

Thou hast set all the borders of the earth: thou hast made summer and winter.

Have respect unto the covenant: for the dark places of the earth are full of the habitations of cruelty.

O let not the oppressed return ashamed: let the poor and needy praise thy name.

Unto thee, O God, do we give thanks, unto thee do we give thanks: for that thy name is near thy wondrous works declare.

For promotion cometh neither from the east, nor from the west, nor from the south:

But God is the judge; he putteth down one, and setteth up another.

Thou didst cause judgment to be heard from heaven ; the earth feared, and was still,

When God arose to judgment, to save all the meek of the earth.

Surely the wrath of man shall praise thee: the remainder of wrath shalt thou restrain.

Vow and pay unto the Lord your God : let all that be round about him bring presents unto him that ought to be feared.

I have considered the days of old, the years of ancient times.

I call to remembrance my song in the night : I commune with mine own heart, and my spirit made diligent search.

Will the Lord cast off for ever ? and will he be favorable no more ?

Is his mercy clean gone for ever ? doth his promise fail for evermore ?

Hath God forgotten to be gracious ? hath he in anger shut up his tender mercies ?

And I said, This is my infirmity : but I will remember the years of the right hand of the Most High.

I will remember the works of the Lord ; surely I will remember thy wonders of old.

I will meditate also of all thy work, and talk of thy doings.

Thy way, O God, is in the sanctuary : who is so great a God as our God !

Thou art the God that doest wonders : thou hast declared thy strength among the people.

Thou hast with thine arm redeemed thy people.

The waters saw thee, O God, the waters saw thee : they were afraid ; the depths also were troubled.

The clouds poured out water ; the skies sent out a sound. thine arrows also went abroad.

The voice of thy thunder was in the heaven: the lightnings lightened the world: the earth trembled and shook.

Thy way is in the sea, and thy path in the great waters, and thy footsteps are not known.

BENEDICTION VII.

ELEVENTH SUNDAY AFTER WHITSUNDAY.

COLLECT.

LET thy merciful ears, O Lord, be open to the prayers of thy humble servants; and that they may obtain their petitions, make them to ask such things as shall please thee, through Jesus Christ our Lord. *Amen.*

PROPHECIES.

PROVERBS.

HE that walketh in his uprightness feareth the Lord: but he that is perverse in his ways despiseth him.

In the mouth of the foolish is a rod of pride : but the lips of the wise shall preserve them.

A scorner seeketh wisdom, and findeth it not: but knowledge is easy unto him that understandeth.

Fools make a mock at sin: but among the righteous there is favor.

The heart knoweth his own bitterness; and a stranger doth not intermeddle with his joy.

The house of the wicked shall be overthrown: but the tabernacle of the upright shall flourish.

There is a way which seemeth right unto a man; but the end thereof are the ways of death.

Even in laughter the heart is sorrowful; and the end of that mirth is heaviness.

The backslider in heart shall be filled with his own ways; and a good man shall be satisfied from himself.

The simple believeth every word: but the prudent man looketh well to his going.

A wise man feareth, and departeth from evil: but the fool rageth, and is confident.

He that is soon angry dealeth foolishly; and a man of wicked devices is hated.

The evil bow before the good; and the wicked at the gates of the righteous.

He that despiseth his neighbor sinneth: but he that hath mercy on the poor, happy is he.

Do they not err that devise evil? but mercy and truth shall be to them that devise good.

In all labor there is profit: but the talk of the lips tendeth only to penury.

The crown of the wise is their riches: but the foolishness of fools is folly.

A true witness delivereth souls: but a deceitful witness speaketh lies.

In the fear of the Lord is strong confidence; and his children shall have a place of refuge.

The fear of the Lord is a fountain of life, to depart from the snares of death.

He that is slow to wrath is of great understanding: but he that is hasty of spirit exalteth folly.

He that oppresseth the poor reproacheth his Maker: but he that honoreth him hath mercy on the poor.

The wicked is driven away in his wickedness: but the righteous hath hope in his death.

Wisdom resteth in the heart of him that hath understanding: but that which is in the midst of fools is made known.

Righteousness exalteth a nation: but sin is a reproach to any people.

15 *

A soft answer turneth away wrath : but grievous words stir up anger.

The tongue of the wise useth knowledge aright : but the mouth of fools poureth out foolishness.

Praise ye the Lord !

The Lord's name be praised.

PSALMS.

GIVE ear, O my people, to my law : incline your ears to the words of my mouth.

We will not hide them from our children, showing to the generation to come the praises of the Lord, and his strength, and his wonderful works that he hath done.

For he established a testimony, and appointed a law, which he commanded our fathers, that they should make them known to their children :

That the generation to come might know them, even the children which should be born, who should arise and declare them to their children ;

That they might set their hope in God, and not forget the works of God, but keep his commandments :

He divided the sea, and caused them to pass through : and he made the waters to stand as an heap.

In the daytime also he led them with a cloud, and all the night with a light of fire.

He clave the rocks in the wilderness, and gave them drink as out of the great depths.

He brought streams also out of the rock, and caused waters to run down like rivers.

And they sinned yet more against him, by provoking the Most High in the wilderness.

And they tempted God in their heart, by asking meat for their lust.

Yea, they spake against God : they said, Can God furnish a table in the wilderness ?

Behold, he smote the rock, that the waters gushed out, and the streams overflowed ; can he give bread also ? can he provide flesh for his people ?

Therefore the Lord heard this, and was wroth : so a fire was kindled against Jacob, and anger also came up against Israel.

Because they believed not in God, and trusted not in his salvation ;

Though he had commanded the clouds from above, and opened the doors of heaven,

And had rained down manna upon them to eat, and had given them of the corn of heaven.

Man did eat angels' food : he sent them meat to the full.

He caused an east wind to blow in the heaven ; and by his power he brought in the south wind.

He rained flesh also upon them as dust, and feathered fowls like as the sand of the sea ;

And he let it fall in the midst of their camp, round about their habitations.

So they did eat, and were well filled : for he gave them their own desire ;

For all this they sinned still, and believed not for his wondrous works.

Therefore their days did he consume in vanity, and their years in trouble.

When he slew them, then they sought him ; and they returned and inquired early after God :

And they remembered that God was their Rock, and the high God their Redeemer.

Nevertheless they did flatter him with their mouth, and they lied unto him with their tongues :

For their heart was not right with him, neither were they steadfast in his covenant.

But he, being full of compassion, forgave their iniquity, and destroyed them not : yea, many a time turned he his anger away, and did not stir up all his wrath :

For he remembered that they were but flesh; a wind that passeth away, and cometh not again.

How oft did they provoke him in the wilderness, and grieve him in the desert!

Yea, they turned back, and tempted God, and limited the Holy One of Israel.

They remembered not his hand, nor the day when he delivered them from the enemy:

And he brought them to the border of his sanctuary, even to this mountain, which his right hand had purchased.

He cast out the heathen also before them, and divided them an inheritance by line, and made the tribes of Israel to dwell in their tents.

Yet they tempted and provoked the most high God, and kept not his testimonies;

But turned back, and dealt unfaithfully like their fathers:

For they provoked him to anger with their high places, and moved him to jealousy with their graven images.

When God heard this, he was wroth, and greatly abhorred Israel:

So that he forsook the tabernacle of Shiloh, the tent which he placed among men;

And delivered his strength into captivity, and his glory into the enemy's hand.

He chose David also his servant, and took him from the sheepfolds:

He brought him to feed Jacob his people, and Israel his inheritance.

So he fed them according to the integrity of his heart; and guided them by the skilfulness of his hands.

Consider and hear me, O Lord my God: lighten mine eyes, lest I sleep the sleep of death;

But I have trusted in thy mercy; my heart shall rejoice in thy salvation.

I will sing unto the Lord, because he hath dealt bountifully with me.

BENEDICTION XII.

TWELFTH SUNDAY AFTER WHITSUNDAY.

COLLECT.

O GOD, who declarest thy almighty power chiefly in show-ing mercy and pity, mercifully grant unto us such a measure of thy grace, that we, running the way of thy com-mandments, may obtain thy gracious promises, and be made partakers of thy heavenly treasure, through Jesus Christ our Lord. *Amen.*

PROPHECIES.

PROVERBS.

THE way of the wicked is an abomination unto the Lord; but he loveth him that followeth after righteousness.

Correction is grievous unto him that forsaketh the way: and he that hateth reproof shall die.

The heart of him that hath understanding seeketh knowl-edge : but the mouth of fools feedeth on foolishness.

Better is a little with the fear of the Lord, than great treas-ure and trouble therewith.

Better is a dinner of herbs where love is, than a stalled ox and hatred therewith.

A wise son maketh a glad father: but a foolish man de-spiseth his mother.

Without counsel purposes are disappointed : but in the multitude of counsellors they are established.

A man hath joy by the answer of his mouth: and a word spoken in due season, how good is it !

The way of life is above to the wise, that he may depart from hell beneath.

The Lord will destroy the house of the proud: but he will establish the border of the widow.

The thoughts of the wicked are an abomination to the Lord ; but the words of the pure are pleasant words.

He that is greedy of gain troubleth his own house ; but he that hateth gifts shall live.

The ear that heareth the reproof of life abideth among the wise.

He that refuseth instruction despiseth his own soul : but he that heareth reproof getteth understanding.

The fear of the Lord is the instruction of wisdom ; and before honor is humility.

All the ways of a man are clean in his own eyes : but the Lord weigheth the spirits.

Commit thy works unto the Lord, and thy thoughts shall be established.

Every one that is proud in heart is an abomination to the Lord : though hand join in hand, he shall not be unpunished.

When a man's ways please the Lord, he maketh even his enemies to be at peace with him.

Better is a little with righteousness, than great revenues without right.

A man's heart deviseth his way : but the Lord directeth his steps.

Pride goeth before destruction, and a haughty spirit before a fall.

Better it is to be of an humble spirit with the lowly, than to divide the spoil with the proud.

He that handleth a matter wisely shall find good : and whoso trusteth in the Lord, happy is he.

O Lord, open thou our ears !

That we may hear meekly thy word, and receive it with pure affection.

PSALMS.

O remember not against us former iniquities : let thy tender mercies speedily prevent us ; for we are brought very low.

Help us, O God of our salvation, for the glory of thy name ; and deliver us, and purge away our sins, for thy name's sake.

Let the sighing of the prisoner come before thee ; according to the greatness of thy power preserve thou those that are appointed to die.

So we, thy people, and sheep of thy pasture, will give thee thanks for ever ; we will show forth thy praise to all generations.

God standeth in the congregation of the mighty : he judgeth among the gods.

How long will ye judge unjustly, and accept the persons of the wicked ?

Defend the poor and fatherless : do justice to the afflicted and needy.

Deliver the poor and needy : rid them out of the hand of the wicked.

They know not, neither will they understand : they walk on in darkness : all the foundations of the earth are out of course.

I have said, Ye are gods ; and all of you are children of the Most High :

But ye shall die like men, and fall like one of the princes.

Arise, O God, judge the earth : for thou shalt inherit all nations.

BENEDICTION II.

THIRTEENTH SUNDAY AFTER WHITSUNDAY.

COLLECT.

ALMIGHTY and everlasting God, who art always more ready to hear than we are to pray, and art wont to give more than either we desire or deserve; pour down upon us the abundance of thy mercy, forgiving us those things whereof our conscience is afraid, and giving us those good things which we are not worthy to ask, but through the mediation of thy Son, Jesus Christ our Lord. *Amen.*

PROPHECIES.

PROVERBS.

BETTER is a dry morsel, and quietness therewith, than an house full of sacrifices with strife.

Whoso mocketh the poor reproacheth his Maker; and he that is glad at calamities shall not be unpunished.

He that covereth a transgression seeketh love; but he that repeateth a matter separateth very friends.

A reproof entereth more into a wise man than an hundred stripes into a fool.

Let a bear robbed of her whelps meet a man, rather than a fool in his folly.

Whoso rewardeth evil for good, evil shall not depart from his house.

He that justifieth the wicked, and he that condemneth the just, even they both are abomination to the Lord.

Wherefore is there a price in the hand of a fool to get wisdom, seeing he hath no heart to it?

A friend loveth at all times, and a brother is born for adversity.

He that hath a froward heart findeth no good; and he that hath a perverse tongue falleth into mischief.

Wisdom is before him that hath understanding : but the eyes of a fool are in the ends of the earth.

He that hath knowledge spareth his words; and a man of understanding is of an excellent spirit.

Through desire a man, having separated himself, seeketh and intermeddleth with all wisdom.

The name of the Lord is a strong tower; the righteous runneth into it, and is safe.

O Lord, open thou our lips !
And our mouth shall show forth thy praise.

PSALMS.

O sing unto the Lord a new song; for he hath done marvellous things : his right hand, and his holy arm, hath gotten him the victory.

The Lord hath made known his salvation: his righteousness hath he openly showed in the sight of the heathen.

He hath remembered his mercy and his truth: all the ends of the earth have seen the salvation of our God.

Make a joyful noise unto the Lord, all the earth; make a loud noise, and rejoice, and sing praise.

Let the sea roar, and the fulness thereof; the world, and they that dwell therein.

Let the floods clap their hands : let the hills be joyful together,

Before the Lord : for he cometh to judge the earth : with righteousness shall he judge the world, and the people with equity.

Make a joyful noise unto the Lord, all ye lands.

Serve the Lord with gladness; come before his presence with singing.

Know ye that the Lord he is God: it is he that hath made us, and not we ourselves : we are his people, and the sheep of his pasture.

16

Enter into his gates with thanksgiving, and into his courts with praise : be thankful unto him, and bless his name.

For the Lord is good, his mercy is everlasting ; and his truth endureth to all generations.

Hear my prayer, O Lord, and let my cry come unto thee.

Hide not thy face from me in the day when I am in trouble ; incline thine ear unto me : in the day when I call, answer me speedily.

My days are like a shadow that declineth ; and I am withered like grass.

But thou, O Lord, shalt endure for ever, and thy remembrance unto all generations.

Thou shalt arise, and have mercy upon Zion : for the time to favor her, yea, the set time, is come.

For thy servants take pleasure in her stones, and favor the dust thereof.

So the heathen shall fear the name of the Lord, and all the kings of the earth thy glory.

This shall be written for the generation to come ; and the people which shall be created shall praise the Lord.

For he hath looked down from the height of his sanctuary ; from heaven did the Lord behold the earth ;

To hear the groaning of the prisoner, to loose those that are appointed to death ;

When the people are gathered together, and the kingdoms, to serve the Lord.

I said, O my God, take me not away in the midst of my days : thy years are throughout all generations.

Of old hast thou laid the foundation of the earth ; and the heavens are the work of thy hands.

They shall perish, but thou shalt endure ; yea, all of them shall wax old like a garment ; as a vesture shalt thou change them, and they shall be changed :

But thou art the same, and thy years shall have no end.

BENEDICTION XIII.

FOURTEENTH SUNDAY AFTER WHITSUNDAY.

COLLECT.

A LMIGHTY and merciful God, of whose only gift it cometh that thy faithful people do unto thee true and laudable service; grant, we beseech thee, that we may so faithfully serve thee in this life, that we fail not finally to attain thy heavenly promises: through the merits of Jesus Christ our Lord. *Amen.*

PROPHECIES.

PROVERBS.

Go to the ant, thou sluggard; consider her ways, and be wise:

Which, having no guide, overseer, or ruler,

Provideth her meat in the summer, and gathereth her food in the harvest.

How long wilt thou sleep, O sluggard? when wilt thou arise out of thy sleep?

Yet a little sleep, a little slumber, a little folding of the hands to sleep:

So shall thy poverty come as one that travelleth, and thy want as an armed man.

A naughty person, a wicked man, walketh with a froward mouth;

Frowardness is in his heart, he deviseth mischief continually: he soweth discord.

Therefore shall his calamity come suddenly; suddenly shall he be broken without remedy.

These six things doth the Lord hate: yea, seven are an abomination unto him:

A proud look, a lying tongue, and hands that shed innocent blood,

An heart that deviseth wicked imaginations, feet that be swift in running to mischief,

A false witness that speaketh lies, and he that soweth discord among brethren.

My son, keep thy father's commandment, and forsake not the law of thy mother:

Bind them continually upon thine heart, and tie them about thy neck.

When thou goest, it shall lead thee; when thou sleepest, it shall keep thee; and when thou awakest, it shall talk with thee.

For the commandment is a lamp, and the law is light; and reproofs of instruction are the way of life,

To keep thee from the evil woman, from the flattery of the tongue of a strange woman.

My son, keep my words, and lay up my commandments with thee.

Keep my commandments, and live; and my law as the apple of thine eye.

Bind them upon thy fingers, write them upon the table of thine heart.

Now unto the king eternal, immortal, invisible, the only wise God;

Be honor and glory, through Jesus Christ, for ever and ever.

PSALMS.

BLESSED are the undefiled in the way, who walk in the law of the Lord.

Blessed are they that keep his testimonies, and that seek him with the whole heart.

They also do no iniquity: they walk in his ways.

Thou hast commanded us to keep thy precepts diligently.

O that my ways were directed to keep thy statutes!

Then shall I not be ashamed, when I have respect unto all thy commandments.

I will praise thee with uprightness of heart, when I shall have learned thy righteous judgments.

I will keep thy statutes : O forsake me not utterly.

Wherewith shall a young man cleanse his way? By taking heed thereto according to thy word.

O let me not wander from thy commandments.

Thy word have I hid in mine heart, that I might not sin against thee.

Blessed art thou, O Lord : teach me thy statutes.

I have rejoiced in the way of thy testimonies, as much as in all riches.

I will meditate in thy precepts, and have respect unto thy ways.

I will delight myself in thy statutes : I will not forget thy word.

Deal bountifully with thy servant, that I may live, and keep thy word.

I am a stranger in the earth : hide not thy commandments from me.

My soul cleaveth unto the dust : quicken thou me according to thy word.

Teach me thy statutes.

Make me to understand the way of thy precepts: so shall I talk of thy wondrous works.

Remove from me the way of lying, and grant me thy law graciously.

I will run the way of thy commandments, when thou shalt enlarge my heart.

Let thy mercies come also unto me, O Lord; even thy salvation.

So shall I have wherewith to answer him that reproacheth me : for I trust in thy word.

And take not the word of truth utterly out of my mouth ; for I have hoped in thy judgments.

So shall I keep thy law continually for ever and ever.

16 *

And I will walk at liberty, for I seek thy precepts.

I will speak of thy testimonies also, and will not be ashamed.

And I will delight myself in thy commandments, which I have loved.

My hands also will I lift up unto thy commandments, which I have loved ; and I will meditate in thy statutes.

BENEDICTION XII.

FIFTEENTH SUNDAY AFTER WHITSUNDAY.

COLLECT.

ALMIGHTY and everlasting God, give unto us the increase of faith, hope, and charity ; and that we may obtain that which thou dost promise, make us to love that which thou dost command, through Jesus Christ our Lord. *Amen.*

PROPHECIES.

PROVERBS.

HEAR, ye children, the instruction of a father, and attend to know understanding.

For I give you good doctrine, forsake ye not my law.

Let thine heart retain my words : keep my commandments, and live.

Get wisdom, get understanding: forget it not ; neither decline from the words of my mouth.

Forsake her not, and she shall preserve thee : love her, and she shall keep thee.

Wisdom is the principal thing ; therefore get wisdom : and with all thy getting, get understanding.

Exalt her, and she shall promote thee : she shall bring thee to honor, when thou dost embrace her.

She shall give to thine head an ornament of grace : a crown of glory shall she deliver to thee.

Hear, O my son, and receive my sayings ; and the years of thy life shall be many.

I have taught thee in the way of wisdom ; I have led thee in right paths.

When thou goest, thy steps shall not be straitened ; and when thou runnest, thou shalt not stumble.

Take fast hold of instruction ; let her not go : keep her ; for she is thy life.

My son, forget not my law ; but let thine heart keep my commandments ;

For length of days, and long life, and peace shall they add to thee.

Let not mercy and truth forsake thee : bind them about thy neck ; write them upon the table of thine heart :

So shalt thou find favor and good understanding in the sight of God and man.

Trust in the Lord with all thine heart ; and lean not unto thine own understanding.

In all thy ways acknowledge him, and he shall direct thy paths.

Be not wise in thine own eyes : fear the Lord, and depart from evil.

Honor the Lord with thy substance, and with the first-fruits of all thine increase :

So shall thy barns be filled with plenty, and thy presses shall burst out with new wine.

My son, despise not the chastening of the Lord ; neither be weary of his correction :

For whom the Lord loveth, he correcteth ; even as a father the son in whom he delighteth.

Happy is the man that findeth wisdom, and the man that getteth understanding.

For the merchandise of it is better than the merchandise of silver, and the gain thereof than fine gold.

She is more precious than rubies : and all the things thou canst desire are not to be compared unto her.

Length of days is in her right hand ; and in her left hand riches and honor.

Her ways are ways of pleasantness, and all her paths are peace.

She is a tree of life to them that lay hold upon her : and happy is every one that retaineth her.

The Lord by wisdom hath founded the earth ; by understanding hath he established the heavens.

By his knowledge the depths are broken up, and the clouds drop down the dew.

My son, let not them depart from thine eyes : keep sound wisdom and discretion :

So shall they be life unto thy soul, and grace to thy neck.

Then shalt thou walk in thy way safely, and thy foot shall not stumble.

When thou liest down, thou shalt not be afraid : yea, thou shalt lie down, and thy sleep shall be sweet.

Praise ye the Lord !
The Lord's name be praised.

PSALMS.

O LORD, thou hast searched me, and known me.

Thou knowest my down-sitting and mine up-rising, thou understandest my thought afar off.

Thou compassest my path and my lying down, and art acquainted with all my ways.

For there is not a word in my tongue, but lo, O Lord, thou knowest it altogether.

Thou hast beset me behind and before, and laid thine hand upon me.

Such knowledge is too wonderful for me ; it is high, I cannot attain unto it.

Whither shall I go from thy spirit ? or whither shall I flee from thy presence ?

If I ascend up into heaven, thou art there : if I make my bed in hell, behold, thou art there.

If I take the wings of the morning, and dwell in the uttermost parts of the sea ;

Even there shall thy hand lead me, and thy right hand shall hold me.

If I say, Surely the darkness shall cover me ; even the night shall be light about me.

Yea, the darkness hideth not from thee ; but the night shineth as the day: the darkness and the light are both alike to thee.

I will praise thee ; for I am fearfully and wonderfully made : marvellous are thy works ; and that my soul knoweth right well.

My substance was not hid from thee, when I was made in secret, and curiously wrought.

Thine eyes did see my substance, yet being unperfect ; and in thy book all my members were written, which in continuance were fashioned.

How precious also are thy thoughts unto me, O God ! how great is the sum of them !

If I should count them, they are more in number than the sand : when I awake, I am still with thee.

Search me, O God, and know my heart : try me, and know my thoughts.

And see if there be any wicked way in me, and lead me in the way everlasting.

BENEDICTION XIV.

SIXTEENTH SUNDAY AFTER WHITSUNDAY.

COLLECT.

KEEP, we beseech thee, O Lord, thy Church with thy perpetual mercy; and because the frailty of man without thee cannot but fall, keep us ever by thy help from all things hurtful, and lead us to all things profitable to our salvation, through Jesus Christ our Lord. *Amen.*

PROPHECIES.

JOB.

CAN a man be profitable unto God, as he that is wise may be profitable unto himself?

Is it any pleasure to the Almighty that thou art righteous? or is it gain to him that thou makest thy ways perfect?

Will he reprove thee for fear of thee? will he enter with thee into judgment?

Is not God in the height of heaven? and behold the height of the stars, how high they are!

And thou sayest, How doth God know? can he judge through the dark cloud?

Thick clouds are a covering to him; and he walketh in the circuit of heaven.

Hast thou marked the old way which wicked men have trodden?

Which were cut down out of time, whose foundation was overflown with a flood:

Which said unto God, Depart from us: and what can the Almighty do for them?

Acquaint now thyself with him, and be at peace; thereby good shall come unto thee.

Receive, I pray thee, the law from his mouth, and lay up his words in thine heart.

If thou return to the Almighty, thou shalt be built up, thou shalt put away iniquity far from thy tabernacles.

Yea, the Almighty shall be thy defence.

For then shalt thou have thy delight in the Almighty, and shalt lift up thy face unto God.

Thou shalt make thy prayer unto him, and he shall hear thee, and thou shalt pay thy vows.

Thou shalt also decree a thing, and it shall be established unto thee: and the light shall shine upon thy ways.

When men are cast down, then thou shalt say, There is lifting up; and he shall save the humble person.

Man that is born of a woman is of few days, and full of trouble.

He cometh forth like a flower, and is cut down: he fleeth also as a shadow, and continueth not.

Seeing his days are determined, the number of his months are with thee, thou hast appointed his bounds that he cannot pass;

Turn from him, that he may rest, till he shall accomplish, as an hireling, his day.

If a man die, shall he live again? all the days of my appointed time will I wait, till my change come.

For I know that my Redeemer liveth, and that he shall stand at the latter day upon the earth:

And though after my skin worms destroy this body, yet in my flesh shall I see God:

Whom I shall see for myself, and mine eyes shall behold, and not another; though my reins be consumed within me.

O Lord, open thou our ears!

That we may hear meekly thy word, and receive it with pure affection.

PSALMS.

PRAISE ye the Lord. O give thanks unto the Lord, for he is good: for his mercy endureth for ever.

Who can utter the mighty acts of the Lord? who can show forth all his praise?

Blessed are they that keep judgment, and he that doeth righteousness at all times.

Remember me, O Lord, with the favor that thou bearest unto thy people: O visit me with thy salvation;

That I may see the good of thy chosen, that I may rejoice in the gladness of thy nation, that I may glory with thine inheritance.

We have sinned with our fathers, we have committed iniquity, we have done wickedly.

Our fathers understood not thy wonders in Egypt; they remembered not the multitude of thy mercies; but provoked thee at the sea, even at the Red Sea.

Nevertheless he saved them for his name's sake, that he might make his mighty power to be known.

He rebuked the Red Sea also, and it was dried up: so he led them through the depths, as through the wilderness.

And he saved them from the hand of him that hated them, and redeemed them from the hand of the enemy.

And the waters covered their enemies: there was not one of them left.

Then believed they his words; they sang his praise.

They soon forgat his works, they waited not for his counsel:

But lusted exceedingly in the wilderness, and tempted God in the desert.

And he gave them their request; but sent leanness into their soul.

Many times did he deliver them: but they provoked him with their counsel: and were brought low for their iniquity.

Nevertheless he regarded their affliction, when he heard their cry:

And he remembered for them his covenant, according to the multitude of his mercies.

He made them also to be pitied of all those that carried them captives.

Save us, O Lord our God, and gather us from among the heathen, to give thanks unto thy holy name, and to triumph in thy praise.

Blessed be the Lord God of Israel from everlasting to everlasting: and let all the people say, Amen.   Praise ye the Lord.

BENEDICTION VIII.

SEVENTEENTH SUNDAY AFTER WHIT-SUNDAY.

COLLECT.

O LORD, we beseech thee, let thy continual pity cleanse and defend thy Church; and because it cannot continue in safety without thy succor, preserve it evermore by thy help and goodness, through Jesus Christ our Lord.   *Amen.*

PROPHECIES.

PROVERBS.

To do justice and judgment is more acceptable to the Lord than sacrifice.

An high look, and a proud heart, and the ploughing of the wicked, is sin.

The thoughts of the diligent tend only to plenteousness; but of every one that is hasty, only to want.

The getting of treasures by a lying tongue is a vanity tossed to and fro of them that seek death.

The way of man is froward and strange : but as for the pure, his work is right.

The soul of the wicked desireth evil: his neighbor findeth no favor in his eyes.

When the scorner is punished, the simple is made wise : and when the wise is instructed, he receiveth knowledge.

The righteous man wisely considereth the house of the wicked : but God overthroweth the wicked for their wickedness.

Whoso stoppeth his ears at the cry of the poor, he also shall cry himself, but shall not be heard.

It is joy to the just to do judgment : but destruction shall be to the workers of iniquity.

The man that wandereth out of the way of understanding shall remain in the congregation of the dead.

He that followeth after righteousness and mercy, findeth life, righteousness, and honor.

Whoso keepeth his mouth and his tongue, keepeth his soul from troubles.

Proud and haughty scorner is his name, who dealeth in proud wrath.

The desire of the slothful killeth him ; for his hands refuse to labor.

He coveteth greedily all the day long : but the righteous giveth and spareth not.

A wicked man hardeneth his face : but as for the upright, he directeth his way.

There is no wisdom, nor understanding, nor counsel, against the Lord.

O Lord, open thou our lips !
And our mouth shall show forth thy praise.

PSALMS.

THE mighty God, even the Lord, hath spoken, and called the earth from the rising of the sun unto the going down thereof.

Out of Zion, the perfection of beauty, God hath shined.

Our God shall come, and shall not keep silence : a fire shall devour before him, and it shall be very tempestuous round about him.

He shall call to the heavens from above, and to the earth, that he may judge his people.

Gather my saints together unto me ; those that have made a covenant with me.

And the heavens shall declare his righteousness : for God is judge himself.

Hear, O my people, and I will speak ; O Israel, and I will testify against thee : I am God, even thy God.

For every beast of the forest is mine, and the cattle upon a thousand hills.

I know all the fowls of the mountains : and the wild beasts of the field are mine,

If I were hungry I would not tell thee : for the world is mine, and the fulness thereof.

Offer unto God thanksgiving ; and pay thy vows unto the Most High.

And call upon me in the day of trouble : and I will deliver thee, and thou shalt glorify me.

But unto the wicked God saith, What hast thou to do to declare my statutes, or that thou shouldest take my covenant in thy mouth ?

Seeing thou hatest instruction, and castest my words behind thee.

When thou sawest a thief, then thou consentedst with him, and hast been partaker with adulterers.

Thou givest thy mouth to evil, and thy tongue frameth deceit.

Thou sittest and speakest against thy brother : thou slanderest thine own mother's son.

These things hast thou done, and I kept silence ; thou thoughtest that I was altogether such an one as thyself: but I will reprove thee, and set them in order before thine eyes.

Now consider this, ye that forget Good, lest I tear you in pieces, and there be none to deliver.

Whoso offereth praise glorifieth me : and to him that ordereth his conversation aright will I show the salvation of God.

BENEDICTION IV.

EIGHTEENTH SUNDAY AFTER WHITSUNDAY.

COLLECT.

LORD, we pray thee that thy grace may be always with us, to enlighten and purify, to defend and preserve us ; and make us continually to be given to all good works, through Jesus Christ our Lord.   *Amen.*

PROPHECIES.

PROVERBS.

A FALSE balance is abomination to the Lord : but a just weight is his delight.

When pride cometh, then cometh shame : but with the lowly is wisdom.

The integrity of the upright shall guide them : but the perverseness of transgressors shall destroy them.

Riches profit not in the day of wrath : but righteousness delivereth from death.

The righteousness of the upright shall deliver them : but transgressors shall be taken in their own naughtiness.

When a wicked man dieth, his expectation shall perish ; and the hope of unjust men perisheth.

An hypocrite with his mouth destroyeth his neighbor : but through knowledge shall the just be delivered.

By the blessing of the upright the city is exalted: but it is overthrown by the mouth of the wicked.

He that is void of wisdom despiseth his neighbor: but a man of understanding holdeth his peace.

A talebearer revealeth secrets: but he that is of a faithful spirit concealeth the matter.

Where no counsel is, the people fall; but in the multitude of counsellors there is safety.

Now unto the King eternal, immortal, invisible, the only wise God;

Be honor and glory, through Jesus Christ, for ever and ever.

PSALMS.

PLEAD my cause, O Lord, with them that strive with me.
Take hold of shield and buckler, and stand up for mine help.

Say unto my soul, I am thy salvation.
And my soul shall be joyful in the Lord: it shall rejoice in his salvation.

Lord, who is like unto thee, which deliverest the poor from him that is too strong for him, yea, the poor and the needy from him that spoileth him!

I will give thee thanks in the great congregation: I will praise thee among much people.

And my tongue shall speak of thy righteousness, and of thy praise, all the day long.

Thy righteousness is like the great mountains; thy judgments are a great deep. O Lord, thou preservest man and beast.

How excellent is thy loving-kindness, O God! therefore the children of men put their trust under the shadow of thy wings.

They shall be satisfied with the abundance of thy house; and thou shalt make them drink of the river of thy pleasures.

17 *

For with thee is the fountain of life : in thy light shall we see light.

O continue thy loving-kindness unto them that know thee ; and thy righteousness to the upright in heart.

Let not the foot of pride come against me, and let not the hand of the wicked remove me.

Fret not thyself because of evil doers, neither be thou envious against the workers of iniquity.

For they shall soon be cut down like the grass, and wither as the green herb.

Trust in the Lord, and do good ; so shalt thou dwell in the land, and verily thou shalt be fed.

Delight thyself also in the Lord ; and he shall give thee the desires of thine heart.

Commit thy way unto the Lord ; trust also in him ; and he shall bring it to pass.

And he shall bring forth thy righteousness as the light, and thy judgment as the noonday.

Rest in the Lord, and wait patiently for him : fret not thyself because of him who prospereth in his way, because of the man who bringeth wicked devices to pass.

Cease from anger, and forsake wrath : fret not thyself in any wise to do evil.

For evil doers shall be cut off : but those that wait upon the Lord, they shall inherit the earth.

For yet a little while, and the wicked shall not be : yea, thou shalt diligently consider his place, and it shall not be.

But the meek shall inherit the earth ; and shall delight themselves in the abundance of peace.

A little that a righteous man hath is better than the riches of many wicked.

The Lord knoweth the days of the upright ; and their inheritance shall be for ever.

They shall not be ashamed in the evil time ; and in the days of famine they shall be satisfied :

The steps of a good man are ordered by the Lord; and he delighteth in his way.

Though he fall, he shall not be utterly cast down: for the Lord upholdeth him with his hand.

I have been young, and now am old; yet have I not seen the righteous forsaken, nor his seed begging bread.

He is ever merciful, and lendeth; and his seed is blessed.

Depart from evil, and do good; and dwell for evermore.

For the Lord loveth judgment, and forsaketh not his saints; they are preserved for ever: but the seed of the wicked shall be cut off.

The mouth of the righteous speaketh wisdom, and his tongue talketh of judgment.

The law of his God is in his heart; none of his steps shall slide.

Wait on the Lord, and keep his way, and he shall exalt thee to inherit the land.

I have seen the wicked in great power, and spreading himself like a green bay-tree.

Yet he passed away, and lo, he was not: yea, I sought him, but he could not be found.

Mark the perfect man, and behold the upright: for the end of that man is peace.

The transgressors shall be destroyed together.

But the salvation of the righteous is of the Lord: he is their strength in time of trouble.

And the Lord shall help them, and deliver them: he shall deliver them from the wicked, and save them, because they trust in him.

BENEDICTION II.

NINETEENTH SUNDAY AFTER WHITSUNDAY.

COLLECT.

LORD, we beseech thee, grant thy people grace to withstand the temptations of the world without, and of evil passions within ; to make daily advances in wisdom and goodness ; and with pure hearts and minds to follow thee, the only God, through Jesus Christ our Lord.   *Amen.*

PROPHECIES.

PROVERBS.

WISDOM hath builded her house, she hath hewn out her seven pillars.

She crieth upon the highest places of the city,

Whoso is simple, let him turn in hither : as for him that wanteth understanding, she saith to him,

Forsake the foolish, and live ; and go in the way of understanding.

Give instruction to a wise man, and he will be yet wiser : teach a just man, and he will increase in learning.

The fear of the Lord is the beginning of wisdom : and the knowledge of the holy is understanding.

For by me thy days shall be multiplied, and the years of thy life shall be increased.

If thou be wise, thou shalt be wise for thyself : but if thou scornest, thou alone shalt bear it.

A wise son maketh a glad father : but a foolish son is the heaviness of his mother.

Treasures of wickedness profit nothing : but righteousness delivereth from death.

The Lord will not suffer the soul of the righteous to famish : but he casteth away the substance of the wicked.

Blessings are upon the head of the just, but violence covereth the mouth of the wicked.

The memory of the just is blessed : but the name of the wicked shall rot.

The wise in heart will receive commandments : but a prating fool shall fall.

He that walketh uprightly walketh surely : but he that perverteth his ways shall be known.

Hatred stirreth up strifes : but love covereth all sins.

The labor of the righteous tendeth to life : the fruit of the wicked to sin.

He is in the way of life that keepeth instruction : but he that refuseth reproof erreth.

He that hideth hatred with lying lips, and he that uttereth a slander, is a fool.

In the multitude of words there wanteth not sin : but he that refraineth his lips is wise.

The blessing of the Lord, it maketh rich, and he addeth no sorrow with it.

It is as sport to a fool to do mischief : but a man of understanding hath wisdom.

The fear of the wicked, it shall come upon him : but the desire of the righteous shall be granted.

As the whirlwind passeth, so is the wicked no more : but the righteous is an everlasting foundation.

As vinegar to the teeth, and as smoke to the eyes, so is the sluggard to them that send him.

The hope of the righteous shall be gladness : but the expectation of the wicked shall perish.

Praise ye the Lord !
The Lord's name be praised.

PSALMS.

BLESSED is he whose transgression is forgiven, whose sin is covered.

Blessed is the man unto whom the Lord imputeth not iniquity, and in whose spirit there is no guile.

I will bless the Lord at all times: his praise shall continually be in my mouth.

My soul shall make her boast in the Lord: the humble shall hear thereof, and be glad.

O magnify the Lord with me, and let us exalt his name together.

I sought the Lord, and he heard me, and delivered me from all my fears.

They looked unto him, and were lightened; and their faces were not ashamed.

This poor man cried, and the Lord heard him, and saved him out of all his troubles.

The angel of the Lord encampeth round about them that fear him, and delivereth them.

O taste and see that the Lord is good: blessed is the man that trusteth in him.

O fear the Lord, ye his saints: for there is no want to them that fear him.

The young lions do lack, and suffer hunger; but they that seek the Lord shall not want any good thing.

Come, ye children, hearken unto me: I will teach you the fear of the Lord.

What man is he that desireth life, and loveth many days, that he may see good?

Keep thy tongue from evil, and thy lips from speaking guile.

Depart from evil, and do good; seek peace, and pursue it.

The eyes of the Lord are upon the righteous, and his ears are open unto their cry.

The face of the Lord is against them that do evil, to cut off the remembrance of them from the earth.

The righteous cry, and the Lord heareth, and delivereth them out of all their troubles.

The Lord is nigh unto them that are of a broken heart; and saveth such as be of a contrite spirit.

Many are the afflictions of the righteous: but the Lord delivereth him out of them all.

Evil shall slay the wicked; and they that hate the righteous shall be desolate.

The Lord redeemeth the soul of his servants; and none of them that trust in him shall be desolate.

BENEDICTION III.

TWENTIETH SUNDAY AFTER WHITSUNDAY.

COLLECT.

O GOD, forasmuch as without thee we are not able to please thee, mercifully grant that thy Holy Spirit may in all things direct and rule our hearts; that they may be cleansed from everything which defileth, and always inclined to keep thy law, through our Saviour Jesus Christ. *Amen.*

PROPHECIES.

JOB.

THEN the Lord answered Job out of the whirlwind, and said,

Who is this that darkeneth counsel by words without knowledge?

Gird up now thy loins like a man; for I will demand of thee, and answer thou me.

Where wast thou when I laid the foundations of the earth? declare, if thou hast understanding.

Who hath laid the measures thereof, if thou knowest? or who hath stretched the line upon it?

Whereupon are the foundations thereof fastened? or who laid the corner-stone thereof,

When the morning-stars sang together, and all the sons of God shouted for joy?

Or who shut up the sea with doors when it brake forth?

When I made the cloud the garment thereof, and thick darkness a swaddling band for it,

And brake up for it my decreed place, and set bars and doors,

And said, Hitherto shalt thou come, but no further; and here shall thy proud waves be stayed?

Hast thou commanded the morning since thy days; and caused the day-spring to know his place;

That it might take hold of the ends of the earth, that the wicked might be shaken out of it?

Hast thou entered into the springs of the sea? or hast thou walked in the search of the depth?

Have the gates of death been opened unto thee? or hast thou seen the doors of the shadow of death?

Hast thou perceived the breadth of the earth? declare, if thou knowest it all.

Where is the way where light dwelleth? and as for darkness, where is the place thereof,

That thou shouldest take it to the bound thereof, and that thou shouldest know the paths to the house thereof?

Knowest thou it, because thou wast then born? or because the number of thy days is great?

Hast thou entered into the treasures of the snow, or hast thou seen the treasures of the hail,

Which I have reserved against the time of trouble, against the day of battle and war?

By what way is the light parted, which scattereth the east wind upon the earth ?

Who hath divided a water-course for the overflowing of waters ; or a way for the lightning of thunder ;

To cause it to rain on the earth, where no rain is ; on the wilderness, wherein there is no man ;

To satisfy the desolate and waste ground ; and to cause the bud of the tender herb to spring forth ?

Hath the rain a father ? or who hath begotten the drops of dew ?

The waters are hid as with a stone, and the face of the deep is frozen.

Canst thou bind the sweet influences of Pleiades, or loose the bands of Orion ?

Canst thou bring forth Mazzaroth in his season ? or canst thou guide Arcturus with his sons ?

Knowest thou the ordinances of heaven ? canst thou set the dominion thereof in the earth ?

Canst thou lift up thy voice to the clouds, that abundance of waters may cover thee ?

Canst thou send lightnings, that they may go, and say unto thee, Here we are ?

Who hath put wisdom in the inward parts ? or who hath given understanding to the heart ?

Who can number the clouds in wisdom ? or who can stay the bottles of heaven,

When the dust groweth into hardness, and the clods cleave fast together ?

Wilt thou hunt the prey for the lion ? or fill the appetite of the young lions,

When they couch in their dens, and abide in the covert to lie in wait ?

Who provideth for the raven his food ? when his young ones cry unto God, they wander for lack of meat.

Then Job answered the Lord, and said,

18

I know that thou canst do everything, and that no thought can be withholden from thee.

O Lord, open thou our ears !
That we may hear meekly thy word, and receive it with pure affection.

PSALMS.

UNTO thee, O Lord, do I lift up my soul.
O my God, I trust in thee : let me not be ashamed, let not mine enemies triumph over me.

Yea, let none that wait on thee be ashamed : let them be ashamed which transgress without cause.

Show me thy ways, O Lord ; teach me thy paths.

Lead me in thy truth, and teach me : for thou art the God of my salvation ; on thee do I wait all the day.

Remember, O Lord, thy tender mercies and thy loving-kindnesses ; for they have been ever of old.

Remember not the sins of my youth, nor my transgressions : according to thy mercy remember thou me for thy goodness' sake, O Lord.

Good and upright is the Lord : therefore will he teach sinners in the way.

The meek will he guide in judgment : and the meek will he teach his way.

All the paths of the Lord are mercy and truth unto such as keep his covenant and his testimonies.

For thy name's sake, O Lord, pardon mine iniquity ; for it is great.

What man is he that feareth the Lord ? him shall he teach in the way that he shall choose.

His soul shall dwell at ease ; and his seed shall inherit the earth.

The secret of the Lord is with them that fear him ; and he will show them his covenant.

Mine eyes are ever toward the Lord ; for he shall pluck my feet out of the net.

Turn thee unto me, and have mercy upon me ; for I am desolate and afflicted.

The troubles of my heart are enlarged : O bring thou me out of my distresses.

Look upon mine affliction and my pain ; and forgive all my sins.

O keep my soul, and deliver me : let me not be ashamed ; for I put my trust in thee.

Let integrity and uprightness preserve me ; for I wait on thee.

Redeem Israel, O God, out of all his troubles.

BENEDICTION XIII.

TWENTY-FIRST SUNDAY AFTER WHITSUNDAY.

COLLECT.

O ALMIGHTY and most merciful God, of thy bountiful goodness keep us, we beseech thee, from all things that may hurt us ; that we, being ready both in body and soul, may cheerfully accomplish those things which thou commandest ; through Jesus Christ our Lord.   *Amen.*

PROPHECIES.

ISAIAH.

THUS saith the Lord, The heaven is my throne, and the earth is my footstool : where is the house that ye build unto me ? and where is the place of my rest ?

For all those things hath mine hand made, and all those things have been, saith the Lord : but to this man will I look, even to him that is poor and of a contrite spirit, and trembleth at my word.

Hear the word of the Lord, ye that tremble at his word. Let the Lord be glorified.   He shall appear to your joy.

A voice of noise from the city, a voice from the temple, a voice of the Lord that rendereth recompense to his enemies.

Rejoice ye with the city of God, and be glad with her, all ye that love her:

That ye may be satisfied with her consolations ; that ye may be delighted with the abundance of her glory.

For thus saith the Lord, Behold, I will extend peace to her like a river, and glory like a flowing stream.

As one whom his mother comforteth, so will I comfort you ; and ye shall be comforted.

And when ye see this, your heart shall rejoice, and the hand of the Lord shall be known toward his servants, and his indignation toward his enemies.

For, behold, the Lord will come with fire, and with his chariots like a whirlwind, to render his rebuke with flames of fire.

For I know their works and their thoughts: it shall come, that I will gather all nations and tongues ; and they shall come, and see my glory.

And I will set a sign among them, and I will send those that escape of them unto the nations.

And they shall bring all your brethren for an offering unto the Lord, out of all nations, to my holy mountain, saith the Lord, as the children of Israel bring an offering in a clean vessel into the house of the Lord.

For as the new heavens and the new earth, which I will make, shall remain before me, saith the Lord, so shall your seed and your name remain.

And it shall come to pass, that from one new moon to another, and from one sabbath to another, shall all flesh come to worship before me, saith the Lord.

O Lord, open thou our lips ?
And our mouth shall show forth thy praise.

PSALMS.

I WILL extol thee, my God, O King; and I will bless thy name for ever and ever.

Every day will I bless thee, and I will praise thy name for ever and ever.

Great is the Lord, and greatly to be praised; and his greatness is unsearchable.

One generation shall praise thy works to another, and shall declare thy mighty acts.

I will speak of the glorious honor of thy majesty, and of thy wondrous works.

And men shall speak of the might of thy terrible acts: and I will declare thy greatness.

They shall abundantly utter the memory of thy great goodness, and shall sing of thy righteousness.

The Lord is gracious, and full of compassion; slow to anger, and of great mercy.

The Lord is good to all; and his tender mercies are over all his works.

All thy works shall praise thee, O Lord; and thy saints shall bless thee.

They shall speak of the glory of thy kingdom, and talk of thy power;

To make known to the sons of men his mighty acts, and the glorious majesty of his kingdom.

Thy kingdom is an everlasting kingdom, and thy dominion endureth throughout all generations.

The Lord upholdeth all that fall, and raiseth up all those that be bowed down.

The eyes of all wait upon thee; and thou givest them their meat in due season.

18 *

Thou openest thine hand, and satisfiest the desire of every living thing.

The Lord is righteous in all his ways, and holy in all his works.

The Lord is nigh unto all them that call upon him, to all that call upon him in truth.

He will fulfil the desire of them that fear him : he also will hear their cry, and will save them.

The Lord preserveth all them that love him: but all the wicked will he destroy.

Praise ye the Lord from the heavens : praise him in the heights.

Praise ye him, all his angels : praise ye him, all his hosts.

Praise ye him, sun and moon : praise him, all ye stars of light.

Praise him, ye heavens of heavens, and ye waters that be above the heavens.

Let them praise the name of the Lord : for he commanded, and they were created.

He hath also established them for ever and ever : he hath made a decree which shall not pass.

Praise the Lord from the earth, ye dragons, and all deeps :

Fire and hail ; snow and vapors ; stormy wind fulfilling his word :

Mountains, and all hills ; fruitful trees, and all cedars :

Beasts, and all cattle ; creeping things, and flying fowl :

Kings of the earth, and all people ; princes, and all judges of the earth :

Both young men and maidens ; old men and children :

Let them praise the name of the Lord : for his name alone is excellent, his glory is above the earth and heaven.

He also exalteth his people, the praise of all his saints, a people near unto him.   Praise ye the Lord.

BENEDICTION XIV.

TWENTY-SECOND SUNDAY AFTER WHIT-SUNDAY.

COLLECT.

GRANT, we beseech thee, merciful Lord, to thy faithful people, pardon and peace; that they may be cleansed from all their sins, and serve thee with a pure heart and a quiet mind, through Jesus Christ our Lord. *Amen.*

PROPHECIES.

PROVERBS.

IF thou wilt receive my words, and hide my commandments with thee;

So that thou incline thine ear unto wisdom, and apply thine heart to understanding;

Yea, if thou criest after knowledge, and liftest up thy voice for understanding;

If thou seekest her as silver, and searchest for her as for hid treasures;

Then shalt thou understand the fear of the Lord, and find the knowledge of God.

For the Lord giveth wisdom: out of his mouth cometh knowledge and understanding.

He layeth up sound wisdom for the righteous; he is a buckler to them that walk uprightly.

He keepeth the paths of judgment, and preserveth the way of his saints.

Then shalt thou understand righteousness, and judgment, and equity: yea, every good path.

When wisdom entereth into thine heart, and knowledge is pleasant unto thy soul;

Discretion shall preserve thee, understanding shall keep thee:

To deliver thee from the way of the evil man, from the man that speakest froward things ;

Who leave the paths of uprightness, to walk in the ways of darkness ;

Who rejoice to do evil, and delight in the frowardness of the wicked ;

Whose ways are crooked, and they froward in their paths ;

To deliver thee from the strange woman, even from the stranger which flattereth with her words ;

Which forsaketh the guide of her youth, and forgetteth the covenant of her God.

For the upright shall dwell in the land, and the perfect shall remain in it.

But the wicked shall be cut off from the earth, and the transgressors shall be rooted out of it.

My son, forget not my law ; but let thine heart keep my commandments :

For length of days, and long life, and peace, shall they add to thee.

Let not mercy and truth forsake thee ; bind them about thy neck ; write them upon the table of thine heart :

So shalt thou find favor and good understanding in the sight of God and man.

Trust in the Lord with all thine heart ; and lean not unto thine own understanding.

In all thy ways acknowledge him, and he shall direct thy paths.

Be not wise in thine own eyes : fear the Lord, and depart from evil.

Honor the Lord with thy substance, and with the first-fruits of all thine increase.

My son, despise not the chastening of the Lord ; neither be weary of his correction :

For whom the Lord loveth he correcteth, even as a father the son in whom he delighteth.

Happy is the man that findeth wisdom, and the man that getteth understanding :

For the merchandise of it is better than the merchandise of silver, and the gain thereof than fine gold.

She is more precious than rubies: and all the things thou canst desire are not to be compared unto her.

Length of days is in her right hand ; and in her left hand riches and honor.

Her ways are ways of pleasantness, and all her paths are peace.

She is a tree of life to them that lay hold upon her ; and happy is every one that retaineth her.

Now unto the King eternal, immortal, invisible, the only wise God ;

Be honor and glory, through Jesus Christ, for ever and ever.

PSALMS.

O GIVE thanks unto the Lord, for he is good : for his mercy endureth for ever.

Let the redeemed of the Lord say so, whom he hath redeemed from the hand of the enemy ;

And gathered them out of the lands, from the east and from the west, from the north and from the south.

They wandered in the wilderness in a solitary way ; they found no city to dwell in.

Hungry and thirsty, their soul fainted in them.

Then they cried unto the Lord in their trouble, and he delivered them out of their distresses.

And he led them forth by the right way, that they might go to a city of habitation.

O that men would praise the Lord for his goodness, and for his wonderful works to the children of men !

For he satisfieth the longing soul, and filleth the hungry soul with goodness.

Such as sit in darkness and in the shadow of death, being bound in affliction and iron ;

Because they rebelled against the words of God, and contemned the counsel of the Most High :

Therefore he brought down their heart with labor ; they fell down, and there was none to help.

Then they cried unto the Lord in their trouble, and he saved them out of their distresses.

He brought them out of darkness and the shadow of death, and brake their bands in sunder.

O that men would praise the Lord for his goodness, and for his wonderful works to the children of men !

They that go down to the sea in ships, that do business in great waters ;

These see the works of the Lord, and his wonders in the deep.

For he commandeth, and raiseth the stormy wind, which lifteth up the waves thereof.

They mount up to the heaven, they go down again to the depths : their soul is melted because of trouble.

Then they cry unto the Lord in their trouble, and he bringeth them out of their distresses.

He maketh the storm a calm, so that the waves thereof are still.

Then are they glad because they be quiet ; so he bringeth them unto their desired haven.

O that men would praise the Lord for his goodness, and for his wonderful works to the children of men !

Let them exalt him also in the congregation of the people, and praise him in the assembly of the elders.

He turneth rivers into a wilderness, and the water-springs into dry ground ;

A fruitful land into barrenness, for the wickedness of them that dwell therein.

He turneth the wilderness into a standing water, and dry ground into water-springs.

And there he maketh the hungry to dwell, that they may pre-pare a city for habitation ;

And sow the fields, and plant vineyards, which may yield fruits of increase.

He poureth contempt upon princes, and causeth them to wander in the wilderness, where there is no way.

Yet setteth he the poor on high from affliction, and maketh him families like a flock.

The righteous shall see it, and rejoice : and all iniquity shall stop her mouth.

Whoso is wise, and will observe these things, even they shall understand the loving-kindness of the Lord.

BENEDICTION XII.

TWENTY-THIRD SUNDAY AFTER WHIT-SUNDAY.

COLLECT.

LORD, we beseech thee to keep thy household, the Church, in continual godliness ; that through thy protection it may be free from all adversities, and devoutly given to serve thee in good works, to the glory of thy name, through the merits and mediation of Jesus Christ our Lord. *Amen.*

PROPHECIES.

ISAIAH.

WHO is this that is glorious in his apparel, travelling in the greatness of his strength ?

I that speak in righteousness, mighty to save.

Wherefore art thou red in thine apparel, and thy garments like him that treadeth in the wine-vat ?

I have trodden the wine-press alone ; and of the people there was none with me.

I will mention the loving-kindnesses of the Lord, and the praises of the Lord, according to all that the Lord hath bestowed on us, according to his mercies, and according to the multitude of his loving-kindnesses.

For he said, Surely they are my people, children that will not lie : so he was their Saviour.

In all their affliction he was afflicted, and the angel of his presence saved them : in his love and in his pity he redeemed them ; and he bare them, and carried them all the days of old.

Look down from heaven, and behold from the habitation of thy holiness and of thy glory : where is thy zeal and thy strength, and thy mercies toward me ? are they restrained ?

Doubtless thou art our Father, though Abraham be ignorant of us, and Israel acknowledge us not : thou, O Lord, art our Father, our Redeemer ; thy name is from everlasting.

O that thou wouldest rend the heavens, that thou wouldest come down, that the mountains might flow down at thy presence.

When thou didst terrible things which we looked not for, thou camest down, the mountains flowed down at thy presence.

For since the beginning of the world men have not heard, nor perceived by the ear, neither hath the eye seen, O God, besides thee, what he hath prepared for him that waiteth for him.

Thou meetest him that rejoiceth and worketh righteousness, those that remember thee in thy ways.

But we are all as an unclean thing, and all our righteousnesses are as filthy rags ; and we all do fade as a leaf ; and our iniquities, like the wind, have taken us away.

And there is none that calleth upon thy name, that stirreth up himself to take hold of thee : for thou hast hid thy face from us, and hast consumed us, because of our iniquities.

But now, O Lord, thou art our Father ; we are the clay, and thou our potter ; and we all are the work of thy hand.

Be not wroth very sore, O Lord, neither remember iniquity for ever : behold, see, we beseech thee, we are all thy people.

Praise ye the Lord !
The Lord's name be praised.

PSALMS.

BLESS the Lord, O my soul. O Lord my God, thou art very great ; thou art clothed with honor and majesty :

Who coverest thyself with light as with a garment : who stretchest out the heavens like a curtain :

Who layeth the beams of his chambers in the waters : who maketh the clouds his chariot : who walketh upon the wings of the wind :

Who maketh his angels spirits ; his ministers a flaming fire :

Who laid the foundations of the earth, that it should not be removed for ever.

Thou coveredst it with the deep as with a garment : the waters stood above the mountains.

At thy rebuke they fled ; at the voice of thy thunder they hasted away.

They go up by the mountains ; they go down by the valleys unto the place which thou hast founded for them.

Thou hast set a bound that they may not pass over ; that they turn not again to cover the earth.

He sendeth the springs into the valleys, which run among the hills.

They give drink to every beast of the field : the wild asses quench their thirst.

By them shall the fowls of the heaven have their habitation, which sing among the branches.

19

He watereth the hills from his chambers : the earth is satisfied with the fruit of thy works.

He causeth the grass to grow for the cattle, and herb for the service of man : that he may bring forth food out of the earth.

He appointeth the moon for seasons : the sun knoweth his going down.

Thou makest darkness, and it is night : wherein all the beasts of the forest do creep forth.

The young lions roar after their prey, and seek their meat from God.

The sun ariseth, they gather themselves together, and lay them down in their dens.

Man goeth forth unto his work and to his labor until the evening.

O Lord, how manifold are thy works ! in wisdom hast thou made them all : the earth is full of thy riches.

So is this great and wide sea, wherein are things creeping innumerable, both small and great beasts.

There go the ships : there is that leviathan, whom thou hast made to play therein.

These wait all upon thee : that thou mayest give them their meat in due season.

That thou givest them, they gather : thou openest thine hand, they are filled with good.

Thou hidest thy face, they are troubled : thou takest away their breath, they die, and return to their dust.

Thou sendest forth thy spirit, they are created : and thou renewest the face of the earth.

The glory of the Lord shall endure for ever : the Lord shall rejoice in his works.

He looketh on the earth, and it trembleth : he toucheth the hills, and they smoke.

I will sing unto the Lord as long as I live : I will sing praise to my God while I have my being.

My meditation of him shall be sweet : I will be glad in the Lord.

Let the sinners be consumed out of the earth, and let the wicked be no more. Bless thou the Lord, O my soul.
Praise ye the Lord!

BENEDICTION XI.

TWENTY-FOURTH SUNDAY AFTER WHIT-SUNDAY.

COLLECT.

O GOD, our refuge and strength, who art the author of all godliness ; be ready, we beseech thee, to hear the devout prayers of thy Church ; and grant that those things which we ask faithfully, we may obtain effectually, through Jesus Christ our Lord. *Amen.*

PROPHECIES.

ECCLESIASTES.

Cast thy bread upon the waters: for thou shalt find it after many days.

Give a portion to seven, and also to eight ; for thou knowest not what evil shall be upon the earth.

He that observeth the wind shall not sow ; and he that regardeth the clouds shall not reap.

As thou knowest not what is the way of the spirit, even so thou knowest not the works of God who maketh all.

In the morning sow thy seed, and in the evening withhold not thine hand ;

For thou knowest not whether shall prosper, either this or that, or whether they both shall be alike good.

Truly the light is sweet, and a pleasant thing it is for the eyes to behold the sun :

But if a man live many years, and rejoice in them all, yet let him remember the days of darkness; for they shall be many.

Rejoice, O young man, in thy youth, and let thy heart cheer thee in the days of thy youth, and walk in the ways of thine heart, and in the sight of thine eyes: but know thou, that for all these things God will bring thee into judgment.

Therefore remove sorrow from thy heart, and put away evil from thy flesh.

Remember now thy Creator in the days of thy youth, while the evil days come not, nor the years draw nigh, when thou shalt say, I have no pleasure in them:

While the sun, or the light, or the moon, or the stars, be not darkened, nor the clouds return after the rain:

In the day when the keepers of the house shall tremble, and the strong men shall bow themselves, and the grinders cease, because they are few, and those that look out of the windows be darkened;

And the doors shall be shut in the streets, when the sound of the grinding is low; and they shall rise up at the voice of the bird: and all the daughters of music shall be brought low:

Also when they shall be afraid of that which is high, and fears shall be in the way, and the almond-tree shall flourish, and the grasshopper shall be a burden, and desire shall fail; because man goeth to his long home, and the mourners go about the streets:

Or ever the silver cord be loosed, or the golden bowl be broken, or the pitcher be broken at the fountain, or the wheel broken at the cistern:

Then shall the dust return to the earth as it was; and the spirit shall return unto God who gave it.

The Preacher sought to find out acceptable words; and that which was written was upright, even words of truth.

Let us hear the conclusion of the whole matter: Fear God, and keep his commandments: for this is the whole duty of man.

For God shall bring every work into judgment, with every secret thing, whether it be good, or whether it be evil.

O Lord, open thou our ears!

That we may hear thy word, and receive it with pure affection.

PSALMS.

O COME, let us sing unto the Lord: let us make a joyful noise to the Rock of our salvation.

Let us come before his presence with thanksgiving,

And make a joyful noise unto him with psalms.

For the Lord is a great God, and a great King above all gods.

In his hand are the deep places of the earth:

The strength of the hills is his also.

The sea is his, and he made it:

And his hands formed the dry land.

O come, let us worship and bow down: let us kneel before the Lord our maker.

For he is our God; and we are the people of his pasture, and the sheep of his hand.

To-day, if ye will hear his voice, harden not your heart, as in the provocation, and as in the day of temptation in the wilderness.

O sing unto the Lord a new song: sing unto the Lord, all the earth.

Sing unto the Lord, bless his name; show forth his salvation from day to day.

Declare his glory among the heathen, his wonders among all people.

For the Lord is great, and greatly to be praised: he is to be feared above all gods.

For all the gods of the nations are idols: but the Lord made the heavens.

Honor and majesty are before him;

19 *

Strength and beauty are in his sanctuary.

Give unto the Lord, O ye kindreds of the people, give unto the Lord glory and strength.

Give unto the Lord the glory due unto his name.

Bring an offering, and come into his courts.

O worship the Lord in the beauty of holiness :

Fear before him, all the earth.

Say among the heathen that the Lord reigneth : the world also shall be established that it shall not be moved : he shall judge the people righteously.

Let the heavens rejoice, and let the earth be glad ;

Let the sea roar, and the fulness thereof.

Let the field be joyful, and all that is therein ;

Then shall all the trees of the wood rejoice before the Lord ;

For he cometh, for he cometh to judge the earth :

He shall judge the world with righteousness, and the people with his truth.

The Lord reigneth ; let the earth rejoice ; let the multitude of isles be glad thereof.

Clouds and darkness are round about him : righteousness and judgment are the habitation of his throne.

A fire goeth before him, and burneth up his enemies round about.

His lightnings enlightened the world ; the earth saw, and trembled.

The hills melted like wax at the presence of the Lord, at the presence of the Lord of the whole earth.

The heavens declare his righteousness, and all the people see his glory.

Confounded be all they that serve graven images, that boast themselves of idols ;

For thou, Lord, art high above all the earth : thou art exalted far above all gods.

Ye that love the Lord, hate evil : he preserveth the souls of his saints ; he delivereth them out of the hand of the wicked.

Light is sown for the righteous, and gladness for the upright in heart.

Rejoice in the Lord, ye righteous; and give thanks at the remembrance of his holiness.

BENEDICTION X.

TWENTY-FIFTH SUNDAY AFTER WHITSUNDAY.

COLLECT.

O LORD, we beseech thee, absolve thy people from their offences ; that through thy bountiful goodness we may all be delivered from the bands of those sins which by our frailty we have committed, and be brought into the glorious liberty of the children of God. Grant this, O Heavenly Father, for thine infinite mercy's sake in Jesus Christ our Saviour. *Amen.*

PROPHECIES.

JOB.

Is there not an appointed time to man upon earth ? are not his days also like the days of an hireling?

The eye of him that hath seen me shall see me no more : thine eyes are upon me, and I am not.

What is man, that thou shouldest magnify him ? and that thou shouldest set thine heart upon him ?

And that thou shouldest visit him every morning, and try him every moment?

If thou wert pure and upright, surely now he would awake for thee, and make the habitation of thy righteousness prosperous.

Though thy beginning was small, yet thy latter end should greatly increase.

For inquire, I pray thee, of the former age, and prepare thyself to the search of their fathers.

Behold, God will not cast away a perfect man, neither will he help the evil doers.

I know it is so of a truth : but how should man be just with God ?

If he will contend with him, he cannot answer him one of a thousand.

He is wise in heart, and mighty in strength : who hath hardened himself against him, and hath prospered ?

Which removeth the mountains, and they know not : which overturneth them in his anger ;

Which shaketh the earth out of her place, and the pillars thereof tremble ;

Which commandeth the sun, and it riseth not, and sealeth up the stars ;

Which alone spreadeth out the heavens, and treadeth upon the waves of the sea ;

Which maketh Arcturus, Orion, and Pleiades, and the chambers of the south ;

Which doeth great things past finding out ; yea, and wonders without number.

Lo, he goeth by me, and I see him not : he passeth on also, but I perceive him not.

Behold, he taketh away, who can hinder him ? who will say unto him, What doest thou ?

If God will not withdraw his anger, the proud helpers do stoop under him.

How much less shall I answer him, and choose out my words to reason with him ?

Whom, though I were righteous, yet would not I answer, but I would make supplication to my judge.

If I speak of strength, lo, he is strong : and if of judgment, who shall set me a time to plead ?

If I justify myself, mine own mouth shall condemn me : if I say, I am perfect, it shall also prove me perverse.

For he is not a man, as I am, that I should answer him, and we should come together in judgment.

Neither is there any daysman betwixt us, that might lay his hand upon us both.

Let him take his rod away from me, and let not his fear terrify me.

O Lord, open thou our lips !
And our mouth shall show forth thy praise.

PSALMS.

THE earth is the Lord's, and the fulness thereof; the world, and they that dwell therein :

For he hath founded it upon the seas, and established it upon the floods.

Who shall ascend into the hill of the Lord ? or who shall stand in his holy place ?

He that hath clean hands, and a pure heart ; who hath not lifted up his soul unto vanity, nor sworn deceitfully.

He shall receive the blessing from the Lord, and righteousness from the God of his salvation.

This is the generation of them that seek him, that seek thy face.

Lift up your heads, O ye gates ; and be ye lifted up, ye everlasting doors ; and the King of glory shall come in.

Who is this King of glory ?

The Lord strong and mighty, the Lord mighty in battle.

Lift up your heads, O ye gates ; even lift them up, ye everlasting doors ; and the King of glory shall come in.

Who is this King of glory ?

The Lord of hosts, he is the King of glory.

The Lord hear thee in the day of trouble ; the name of the God of Jacob defend thee.

Send thee help from the sanctuary, and strengthen thee out of Zion.

Grant thee according to thine own heart, and fulfil all thy counsel.

We will rejoice in thy salvation, and in the name of our God we will set up our banners : the Lord fulfil all thy petitions.

Now know I that the Lord saveth his anointed : he will hear him from his holy heaven with the saving strength of his right hand.

Some trust in chariots, and some in horses : but we will remember the name of the Lord our God.

They are brought down and fallen; but we are risen, and stand upright.

Save, Lord : let the king hear us when we call.

The heavens declare the glory of God : and the firmament showeth his handiwork.

Day unto day uttereth speech, and night unto night showeth knowledge.

There is no speech nor language where their voice is not heard.

Their line is gone out through all the earth, and their words to the end of the world.   In them hath he set a tabernacle for the sun ;

Which is as a bridegroom coming out of his chamber, and rejoiceth as a strong man to run a race.

His going forth is from the end of the heaven, and his circuit unto the ends of it : and there is nothing hid from the heat thereof.

The law of the Lord is perfect, converting the soul : the testimony of the Lord is sure, making wise the simple :

The statutes of the Lord are right, rejoicing the heart : the commandment of the Lord is pure, enlightening the eyes :

The fear of the Lord is clean, enduring for ever : the judgments of the Lord are true and righteous altogether.

More to be desired are they than gold, yea, than much fine gold ; sweeter also than honey and the honeycomb.

Moreover, by them is thy servant warned : and in keeping of them there is great reward.

Who can understand his errors ? cleanse thou me from secret faults.

Keep back thy servant also from presumptuous sins ; let them not have dominion over me : then shall I be upright, and I shall be innocent from the great transgression.

Let the words of my mouth, and the meditation of my heart, be acceptable in thy sight, O Lord, my strength and my redeemer.

BENEDICTION IX.

TWENTY-SIXTH SUNDAY AFTER WHIT-SUNDAY.

COLLECT.

O LORD, we beseech thee to encourage the hearts of thy faithful people, that they, always relying on thy power, and trusting in thy grace, may bring forth plenteously the fruit of good works, and of thee be plenteously rewarded, both in the world which now is, and that which is to come, through Jesus Christ our Lord. *Amen.*

PROPHECIES.

JOB.

MY righteousness I hold fast, and will not let it go : my heart shall not reproach me so long as I live.

For what is the hope of the hypocrite, though he hath gained, when God taketh away his soul?

Will God hear his cry when trouble cometh upon him ?

I will teach you by the hand of God; that which is with the Almighty will I not conceal.

Surely there is a vein for the silver, and a place for gold where they fine it.

Iron is taken out of the earth, and brass is molten out of the stone.

He setteth an end to darkness, and searcheth out all perfection: the stones of darkness, and the shadow of death.

As for the earth, out of it cometh bread: and under it is turned up as it were fire.

The stones of it are the place of sapphires: and it hath dust of gold.

There is a path which no fowl knoweth, and which the vulture's eye hath not seen:

The lion's whelps have not trodden it, nor the fierce lion passed by it.

He putteth forth his hand upon the rocks; he overturneth the mountains by the roots.

He cutteth out rivers among the rocks; and his eye seeth every precious thing.

He bindeth the floods from overflowing; and the thing that is hid bringeth he forth to light.

But where shall wisdom be found? and where is the place of understanding?

Man knoweth not the price thereof; neither is it found in the land of the living.

The depth saith, It is not in me: and the sea saith, It is not with me.

It cannot be gotten for gold, neither shall silver be weighed for the price thereof.

It cannot be valued with the gold of Ophir, with the precious onyx, or the sapphire.

The gold and the crystal cannot equal it: and the exchange of it shall not be for jewels of fine gold.

No mention shall be made of coral, or of pearls: for the price of wisdom is above rubies.

The topaz of Ethiopia shall not equal it, neither shall it be valued with pure gold.

Whence then cometh wisdom? and where is the place of understanding?

Seeing it is hid from the eyes of all living, and kept close from the fowls of the air.

Destruction and death say, We have heard the fame thereof with our ears.

God understandeth the way thereof, and he knoweth the place thereof.

For he looketh to the ends of the earth, and seeth under the whole heaven;

To make the weight for the winds; and he weigheth the waters by measure.

When he made a decree for the rain, and a way for the lightning of the thunder;

Then did he see it, and declare it; he prepared it, yea, and searched it out.

And unto man he said, Behold, the fear of the Lord, that is wisdom; and to depart from evil is understanding.

Now unto the King eternal, immortal, invisible, the only wise God.

Be honor and glory, through Jesus Christ, for ever and ever.

PSALMS.

It is a good thing to give thanks unto the Lord, and to sing praises unto thy name, O Most High;

To show forth thy loving-kindness in the morning, and thy faithfulness every night.

For thou, Lord, hast made me glad, through thy work; I will triumph in the works of thy hand.

O Lord, how great are thy works! and thy thoughts are very deep.

20

When the wicked spring as the grass, and when all the workers of iniquity do flourish ; it is that they shall be destroyed for ever :

But thou, Lord, art most high for evermore.

For, lo, thine enemies, O Lord, for, lo, thine enemies shall perish : all the workers of iniquity shall be scattered.

Those that be planted in the house of the Lord shall flourish in the courts of our God.

They shall still bring forth fruit in old age ; they shall be fat and flourishing ;

To show that the Lord is upright : he is my rock, and there is no unrighteousness in him.

How amiable are thy tabernacles, O Lord of hosts !

My soul longeth, yea, even fainteth for the courts of the Lord ; my heart and my flesh crieth out for the living God.

Yea, the sparrow hath found an house, and the swallow a nest for herself, where she may lay her young, even thine altars, O Lord of hosts, my King, and my God.

Blessed are they that dwell in thy house : they will be still praising thee.

Blessed is the man whose strength is in thee ; in whose heart are thy ways,

Who passing through the valley of Baca make it a well ; the rain also filleth the pools.

They go from strength to strength, every one of them in Zion appeareth before God.

Behold, O God our shield, and look upon the face of thine anointed.

For a day in thy courts is better than a thousand.   I had rather be a door-keeper in the house of my God, than to dwell in the tents of wickedness.

For the Lord God is a sun and shield : the Lord will give grace and glory ; no good thing will he withhold from them that walk uprightly.

O Lord of hosts, blessed is the man that trusteth in thee.

The Lord is my shepherd ; I shall not want.

He maketh me to lie down in green pastures : he leadeth me beside the still waters.

He restoreth my soul : he leadeth me in the paths of righteousness for his name's sake.

Yea, though I walk through the valley of the shadow of death, I will fear no evil : for thou art with me ; thy rod and thy staff they comfort me.

Thou preparest a table before me in the presence of mine enemies : thou anointest my head with oil ; my cup runneth over.

Surely goodness and mercy shall follow me all the days of my life ; and I will dwell in the house of the Lord for ever.

BENEDICTION VIII.

TWENTY–SEVENTH SUNDAY AFTER WHIT-SUNDAY.

COLLECT.

O ALMIGHTY God, who alone canst order the wills and affections of men, grant unto thy people that they may love the thing which thou commandest, and desire that which thou dost promise, that so among the sundry and manifold changes of this world our hearts may surely there be fixed, where alone true joys are to be found, through Jesus Christ our Lord. *Amen.*

PROPHECIES.

ECCLESIASTES.

A GOOD name is better than precious ointment ; and the day of death than the day of one's birth.

It is better to go to the house of mourning, than to go to the house of feasting: for that is the end of all men; and the living will lay it to his heart.

Sorrow is better than laughter: for by the sadness of the countenance the heart is made better.

The heart of the wise is in the house of mourning; but the heart of fools is in the house of mirth.

It is better to hear the rebuke of the wise, than for a man to hear the song of fools:

Better is the end of a thing than the beginning thereof: and the patient in spirit is better than the proud in spirit.

Be not hasty in thy spirit to be angry: for anger resteth in the bosom of fools.

Say not thou, What is the cause that the former days were better than these? for thou dost not inquire wisely concerning this.

For wisdom is a defence, and money is a defence: but the excellency of knowledge is, that wisdom giveth life to them that have it.

In the day of prosperity be joyful, but in the day of adversity consider: God also hath set the one over against the other.

Wisdom strengtheneth the wise more than ten mighty men which are in the city.

For there is not a just man upon earth, that doeth good, and sinneth not.

All this have I proved by wisdom: I said, I will be wise; but it was far from me.

That which is far off, and exceeding deep, who can find it out?

I applied mine heart to know, and to search, and to seek out wisdom, and the reason of things, and to know the wickedness of folly, even of foolishness and madness.

Who is as the wise man? and who knoweth the interpretation of a thing?

Whoso keepeth the commandment shall feel no evil thing : and a wise man's heart discerneth both time and judgment.

Because to every purpose there is time and judgment, therefore the misery of man is great upon him.

For he knoweth not that which shall be : for who can tell him when it shall be ?

There is no man that hath power over the spirit to retain the spirit : neither hath he power in the day of death : and there is no discharge in that war ; neither shall wickedness deliver those that are given to it.

All this have I seen, and applied my heart unto every work that is done under the sun : there is a time wherein one man ruleth over another to his own hurt.

And so I saw the wicked buried, who had come and gone from the place of the holy, and they were forgotten in the city where they had so done : this is also vanity.

Because sentence against an evil work is not executed speedily, therefore the heart of the sons of men is fully set in them to do evil.

Though a sinner do evil an hundred times, and his days be prolonged, yet surely I know that it shall be well with them that fear God, which fear before him :

But it shall not be well with the wicked, neither shall he prolong his days, which are as a shadow ; because he feareth not before God.

When I applied mine heart to know wisdom, and to see the business that is done upon the earth :

Then I beheld all the work of God, that a man cannot find out the work that is done under the sun : because though a man labor to seek it out, yet he shall not find it ; yea, further ; though a wise man think to know it, yet shall he not be able to find it.

Whatsoever thy hand findeth to do, do it with thy might ; for there is no work, nor device, nor knowledge, nor wisdom, in the grave, whither thou goest.

20 *

I returned, and saw under the sun, that the race is not to the swift, nor the battle to the strong, neither yet bread to the wise, nor yet riches to men of understanding, nor yet favor to men of skill; but time and chance happeneth to them all.

This wisdom have I seen also under the sun, and it seemed great unto me:

There was a little city, and few men within it; and there came a great king against it, and besieged it, and built great bulwarks against it.

Now there was found in it a poor wise man, and he by his wisdom delivered the city; yet no man remembered that same poor man.

Then said I, Wisdom is better than strength: nevertheless the poor man's wisdom is despised, and his words are not heard.

The words of wise men are heard in quiet, more than the cry of him that ruleth among fools.

Wisdom is better than weapons of war.

Praise ye the Lord!

The Lord's name be praised.

PSALMS.

Except the Lord build the house, they labor in vain that build it: except the Lord keep the city, the watchman waketh but in vain.

It is vain for you to rise up early, to sit up late, to eat the bread of sorrows: he giveth his beloved sleep.

Out of the depths have I cried unto thee, O Lord.

Lord, hear my voice: let thine ears be attentive to the voice of my supplications.

If thou, Lord, shouldest mark iniquities, O Lord, who shall stand?

But there is forgiveness with thee, that thou mayest be feared.

I wait for the Lord, my soul doth wait, and in his word do I hope.

My soul waiteth for the Lord more than they that watch for the morning ; I say, more than they that watch for the morning.

Let Israel hope in the Lord : for with the Lord there is mercy, and with him is plenteous redemption.

And he shall redeem Israel from all his iniquities.

Arise, O Lord, into thy rest; thou, and the ark of thy strength.

Let thy priests be clothed with righteousness ; and let thy saints shout for joy.

Behold, how good and how pleasant it is for brethren to dwell together in unity !

As the dew of Hermon, and as the dew that descended upon the mountains of Zion : for there the Lord commanded the blessing, even life for evermore.

Behold, bless ye the Lord, all ye servants of the Lord, which by night stand in the house of the Lord.

Lift up your hands in the sanctuary, and bless the Lord.

The Lord, that made heaven and earth, bless thee out of Zion.

Praise ye the Lord. Praise ye the name of the Lord: praise him, O ye servants of the Lord.

Ye that stand in the house of the Lord, in the courts of the house of our God,

Praise the Lord ; for the Lord is good: sing praises unto his name ; for it is pleasant.

Whatsoever the Lord pleased, that did he in heaven, and in earth, in the seas, and all deep places.

He causeth the vapors to ascend from the ends of the earth: he maketh lightnings for the rain ; he bringeth the wind out of his treasuries.

Thy name, O Lord, endureth for ever; and thy memorial, O Lord, throughout all generations.

O give thanks unto the Lord ; for he is good: for his mercy endureth for ever.

Who remembered us in our low estate : for his mercy endureth for ever :

And hath redeemed us from our enemies : for his mercy endureth for ever.

Who giveth food to all flesh : for his mercy endureth for ever.

O give thanks unto the God of heaven : for his mercy endureth for ever.

BENEDICTION VII.

TWENTY–EIGHTH SUNDAY AFTER WHIT- SUNDAY.

COLLECT.

BLESSED Lord, who hast caused all holy Scriptures to be written for our instruction, grant that we may in such wise hear them, read, mark, learn, and inwardly digest, that by patience and comfort of thy holy word we may embrace and ever hold fast the blessed hope of everlasting life which thou hast given us in our Saviour Jesus Christ.   *Amen.*

PROPHECIES.

PROVERBS.

HE that, being often reproved, hardeneth his neck, shall suddenly be destroyed, and that without remedy.

When the righteous are in authority, the people rejoice : but when the wicked beareth rule, the people mourn.

Whoso loveth wisdom .rejoiceth his father: but he that keepeth company with harlots spendeth his substance.

The king by judgment establisheth the land : but he that receiveth gifts overthroweth it.

A man that flattereth his neighbor spreadeth a net for his feet.

In the transgression of an evil man there is a snare: but the righteous doth sing and rejoice.

The righteous considereth the cause of the poor: but the wicked regardeth not to know it.

Scornful men bring a city into a snare: but wise men turn away wrath.

If a wise man contendeth with a foolish man, whether he rage or laugh, there is no rest.

The bloodthirsty hate the upright: but the just seek his soul.

A fool uttereth all his mind: but a wise man keepeth it in till afterwards.

The poor and the deceitful man meet together: the Lord lighteneth both their eyes.

The king that faithfully judgeth the poor, his throne shall be established for ever.

The rod and reproof give wisdom: but a child left to himself bringeth his mother to shame.

When the wicked are multiplied, transgression increaseth: but the righteous shall see their fall.

Correct thy son, and he shall give thee rest; yea, he shall give delight unto thy soul.

Where there is no vision, the people perish: but he that keepeth the law, happy is he.

Seest thou a man that is hasty in his words? there is more hope of a fool than of him.

An angry man stirreth up strife, and a furious man aboundeth in transgression.

A man's pride shall bring him low: but honor shall uphold the humble in spirit.

Whoso is partner with a thief, hateth his own soul: he heareth cursing, and bewrayeth it not.

The fear of man bringeth a snare: but whoso putteth his trust in the Lord shall be safe.

Many seek the ruler's favor; but every man's judgment cometh from the Lord.

O Lord, open thou our ears !

That we may hear meekly thy word, and receive it with pure affection.

PSALMS.

REMEMBER the word unto thy servant, upon which thou hast caused me to hope.

This is my comfort in my affliction : for thy word hath quickened me.

I remembered thy judgments of old, O Lord ; and have comforted myself.

Thy statutes have been my song in the house of my pilgrimage.

I have remembered thy name, O Lord, in the night, and have kept thy law.

This I had, because I kept thy precepts.

Thou art my portion, O Lord : I have said that I would keep thy words.

I entreated thy favor with my whole heart : be merciful unto me according to thy word.

I thought on my ways, and turned my feet unto thy testimonies.

I made haste, and delayed not to keep thy commandments.

I am a companion of all them that fear thee, and of them that keep thy precepts.

The earth, O Lord, is full of thy mercy.

Thou hast dealt well with thy servant, O Lord, according unto thy word.

Teach me good judgment and knowledge : for I have believed thy commandments.

Thou art good, and doest good : teach me thy statutes.

It is good for me that I have been afflicted ; that I might learn thy statutes.

The law of thy mouth is better unto me than thousands of gold and silver.

Thy hands have made me and fashioned me ; give me understanding, that I may learn thy commandments.

I know, O Lord, that thy judgments are right, and that thou in faithfulness hast afflicted me.

Let, I pray thee, thy merciful kindness be for my comfort, according to thy word unto thy servant.

Let thy tender mercies come unto me, that I may live : for thy law is my delight.

Let my heart be sound in thy statutes ; that I be not ashamed.

For ever, O Lord, thy word is settled in heaven.

Thy faithfulness is unto all generations : thou hast established the earth, and it abideth.

They continue this day according to thine ordinances : for all are thy servants.

I will never forget thy precepts : for with them thou hast quickened me.

I have seen an end of all perfection : but thy commandment is exceeding broad.

O how love I thy law ! it is my meditation all the day.

How sweet are thy words unto my taste ! yea, sweeter than honey to my mouth.

Through thy precepts I get understanding : therefore I hate every false way.

BENEDICTION VI.

TWENTY–NINTH SUNDAY AFTER WHIT-SUNDAY.

COLLECT.

ALMIGHTY God, the Fountain of all wisdom, who knowest our necessities before we ask, and our ignorance in asking, we beseech thee to have compassion on our infirmities, and grant that those things which we faithfully ask may be effectually obtained, and those things which for our unworthiness we dare not, and for our blindness we cannot ask, vouchsafe to give us for the sake of thine infinite mercy in Jesus Christ our Lord. *Amen.*

PROPHECIES.

PROVERBS.

BOAST not thyself of to-morrow ; for thou knowest not what a day may bring forth.

Let another man praise thee, and not thine own mouth ; a stranger, and not thine own lips.

A stone is heavy, and the sand weighty ; but a fool's wrath is heavier than them both.

Wrath is cruel, and anger is outrageous ; but who is able to stand before envy?

Faithful are the wounds of a friend ; but the kisses of an enemy are deceitful.

Thine own friend, and thy father's friend, forsake not.

The wicked flee when no man pursueth : but the righteous are bold as a lion.

For the transgression of a land many are the princes thereof: but by a man of understanding and knowledge the state thereof shall be prolonged.

A poor man that oppresseth the poor is like a sweeping rain, which leaveth no food.

They that forsake the law praise the wicked: but such as keep the law contend with them.

Evil men understand not judgment: but they that seek the Lord understand all things.

Better is the poor that walketh in his uprightness, than he that is perverse in his ways, though he be rich.

He that by usury and unjust gain increaseth his substance, he shall gather it for him that will pity the poor.

He that turneth away his ear from hearing the law, even his prayer shall be abomination.

Whoso causeth the righteous to go astray in an evil way, he shall fall himself into his own pit: but the upright shall have good things in possession.

The rich man is wise in his own conceit; but the poor that hath understanding searcheth him out.

He that covereth his sins shall not prosper; but whoso confesseth and forsaketh them shall have mercy.

Happy is the man that feareth alway: but he that hardeneth his heart shall fall into mischief.

Whoso walketh uprightly shall be saved: but he that is perverse in his ways shall fall at once.

He that tilleth his land shall have plenty of bread; but he that followeth after vain persons shall have poverty enough.

A faithful man shall abound with blessings: but he that maketh haste to be rich shall not be innocent.

To have respect of persons is not good; for, for a piece of bread that man will transgress.

He that hasteth to be rich hath an evil eye, and considereth not that poverty shall come upon him.

He that rebuketh a man, afterwards shall find more favor than he that flattereth with the tongue.

Whoso robbeth his father or his mother, and saith, It is no transgression; the same is the companion of a destroyer.

He that trusteth in his own heart is a fool: but whoso walketh wisely, he shall be delivered.

21

He that giveth unto the poor shall not lack : but he that hideth his eyes shall have many a curse.

When the wicked rise, men hide themselves : but when they perish, the righteous increase.

O Lord, open thou our ears !

That we may hear meekly thy word, and receive it with pure affection.

PSALMS.

THY word is a lamp unto my feet, and a light unto my path.

I have sworn, and I will perform it, that I will keep thy righteous judgments.

Accept, I beseech thee, the free-will offerings of my mouth, O Lord, and teach me thy judgments.

My soul is continually in my hand : yet do I not forget thy law.

Thy testimonies have I taken as an heritage for ever : for they are the rejoicing of my heart.

I have inclined mine heart to perform thy statutes alway, even unto the end.

Thou art my hiding-place and my shield : I hope in thy word.

Depart from me, ye evil-doers : for I will keep the commandments of my God.

Uphold me according unto thy word, that I may live : and let me not be ashamed of my hope.

Hold thou me up, and I shall be safe : and I will have respect unto thy statutes continually.

Thou puttest away all the wicked of the earth like dross : therefore I love thy testimonies.

Be surety for thy servant for good : let not the proud oppress me.

Deal with thy servant according unto thy mercy, and teach me thy statutes.

I am thy servant ; give me understanding, that I may know thy testimonies.

Therefore I esteem all thy precepts concerning all things to be right ; and I hate every false way.

Thy testimonies are wonderful : therefore doth my soul keep them.

The entrance of thy words giveth light ; it giveth understanding unto the simple.

Look thou upon me, and be merciful unto me, as thou usest to do unto those that love thy name.

Order my steps in thy word : and let not any iniquity have dominion over me.

Deliver me from the oppression of man.

Make thy face to shine upon thy servant ; and teach me thy statutes.

Righteous art thou, O Lord, and upright are thy judgments.

Thy righteousness is an everlasting righteousness, and thy law is the truth.

The righteousness of thy testimonies is everlasting : give me understanding, and I shall live.

Hear my voice according unto thy loving-kindness : O Lord, quicken me according to thy judgment.

Thou art near, O Lord ; and all thy commandments are truth.

Concerning thy testimonies, I have known of old that thou hast founded them for ever.

BENEDICTION VIII.

FEASTS OF THE CHURCH.

All Sundays in the Year.

The Circumcision of our Lord	Jan. 1.
Epiphany	Jan. 6.
Conversion of St. Paul	Jan. 25.
Purification of the Virgin	Feb. 2.
Saint Matthias	Feb. 24.
Annunciation of the Virgin	Mar. 25.
Saint Mark	Apr. 25.
St. Philip and St. James	May 1.
St. Barnabas	June 11.
Nativity of St. John Baptist	June 24.
St. Peter	June 29.
St. James	July 25.
St. Bartholomew	Aug. 24.
St. Matthew	Sept. 21.
St. Michael and All Angels	Sept. 29.
St. Luke	Oct. 18.
St. Simon and St. Jude	Oct. 28.
All Saints' Day	Nov. 1.
St. Andrew	Nov. 30.
St. Thomas	Dec. 21.
Christmas	Dec. 25.
St. Stephen	Dec. 26.
St. John	Dec. 27.
The Holy Innocents	Dec. 28.

Monday and Tuesday in Easter Week.

Monday and Tuesday in Whitsun-Week.

MOVABLE FEASTS.

Easter Day is always the first Sunday after the full moon which happens upon or next after the twenty-first day of March; and if the full moon happen upon a Sunday, Easter Day is the Sunday after.

Advent Sunday is always the nearest Sunday to the Feast of St. Andrew, whether before or after.

Septuagesima Sunday is nine weeks before Easter.
Sexagesima   "   " eight "   "   "
Quinquagesima   "   " seven "   "   "
Quadragesima   "   " six   "   "   "
Rogation   "   " five weeks after Easter.
Ascension Day is forty days after Easter.
Whitsunday is seven weeks   "   "

FASTS OF THE CHURCH.

Ash Wednesday, the fortieth day before Easter.
Good Friday, two days before Easter.
The forty days of Lent.
The Ember days the four seasons, being the Wednesday, Friday, and Saturday after the first Sunday in Lent, after the Feast of Pentecost, after September 14th, and after December 13th.
Rogation Days, being Monday, Tuesday, and Wednesday before Holy Thursday or Ascension.
All the Fridays in the year, except Christmas day.

COLLECTS FOR SPECIAL DAYS.

ST. ANDREW'S DAY.

ALMIGHTY God, who didst give such grace unto thy holy Apostle Saint Andrew, that he readily obeyed the calling of thy Son Jesus Christ, and followed him without delay; grant unto us all, that we, being called by thy holy Word, may forthwith give up ourselves obediently to fulfil thy holy commandments, through the same Jesus Christ our Lord. *,Amen.*

ST. THOMAS THE APOSTLE.

ALMIGHTY and ever-living God, who, for the greater confirmation of the faith, didst suffer thy holy Apostle Thomas to be doubtful in thy Son's resurrection; grant us so perfectly, and without all doubt, to believe in thy Son Jesus Christ, that our faith in thy sight may never be reproved. Hear us, O Lord, through the same Jesus Christ, to whom, with thee, be all honor and glory, now and for evermore. *Amen.*

CHRISTMAS DAY.

THE NATIVITY OF OUR LORD.

ALMIGHTY God, who hast given us thine only begotten Son to take our nature upon him, and as at this time to be born of a virgin; grant that we, being regenerate, and made thy children by adoption and grace, may daily be renewed by thy Holy Spirit. And this we beg in the name of Jesus Christ, through whom we ascribe unto thee all honor and glory, now and ever. *Amen.*

ST. STEPHEN'S DAY.

GRANT, O Lord, that, in all our sufferings here upon earth for the testimony of thy truth, we may steadfastly look up to heaven, and by faith behold the glory that shall be revealed; and, being filled with the Holy Ghost, may learn to love and bless our persecutors by the example of thy first martyr, Saint Stephen, who prayed for his murderers, which we ask through the blessed Jesus Christ our Lord, who standeth at the right hand of God to succor all those who suffer for him, the everlasting Mediator and Advocate. *Amen.*

ST. JOHN THE EVANGELIST'S DAY.

MERCIFUL Lord, we beseech thee to cast thy bright beams of light upon thy Church, that it, being instructed by the doctrine of thy blessed Apostle and Evangelist Saint John, may so walk in the light of thy truth, that it may at length attain to everlasting life, through Jesus Christ our Lord. *Amen.*

THE INNOCENTS' DAY.

O ALMIGHTY God, who out of the mouths of babes and sucklings hast ordained strength, and madest infants to glorify thee by their deaths; mortify and kill all vices in us, and so strengthen us by thy grace, that by the innocency of our lives, and constancy of our faith even unto death, we may glorify thy holy name, through Jesus Christ our Lord. *Amen.*

THE CIRCUMCISION OF CHRIST.

ALMIGHTY God, who madest thy blessed Son to be circumcised, and obedient to the Law for man, grant us the true Circumcision of the Spirit: that, our hearts, and all our members, being mortified from all worldly and carnal lusts, we may in all things obey thy blessed will, through the same thy Son Jesus Christ our Lord. *Amen.*

THE EPIPHANY,

OR THE MANIFESTATION OF CHRIST TO THE GENTILES.

O GOD, who by the leading of a star didst manifest thy only begotten Son to the Gentiles, mercifully grant that we, who know thee now by faith, may after this life have the fruition of thy glorious Godhead, through Jesus Christ our Lord. *Amen.*

THE CONVERSION OF ST. PAUL.

O GOD, who, through the preaching of the blessed Apostle Saint Paul, hast caused the light of the Gospel to shine throughout the world ; grant, we beseech thee, that we, having his wonderful conversion in remembrance, may show forth our thankfulness unto thee for the same, by following the holy doctrine which he taught, through Jesus Christ our Lord. *Amen.*

THE PRESENTATION OF CHRIST IN THE TEMPLE,

COMMONLY CALLED, THE PURIFICATION OF SAINT MARY THE VIRGIN.

A LMIGHTY and ever-living God, we humbly beseech thy Majesty, that as thy only-begotten Son was this day presented in the temple in substance of our flesh, so we may be presented unto thee with pure and clean hearts, by the same thy Son Jesus Christ our Lord. *Amen.*

ST. MATTHIAS'S DAY.

O ALMIGHTY God, who into the place of the traitor Judas didst choose thy faithful servant Matthias to be of the number of the twelve Apostles ; grant that thy Church, being always preserved from false apostles, may be ordered and guided by faithful and true pastors, through Jesus Christ our Lord. *Amen.*

THE ANNUNCIATION OF THE BLESSED VIRGIN MARY.

WE beseech thee, O Lord, pour thy grace into our hearts ; that as we have known the incarnation of thy Son Jesus Christ by the message of an angel, so by his cross and passion we may be brought unto the glory of his resurrection, through the same Jesus Christ our Lord. *Amen.*

ST. MARK'S DAY.

O ALMIGHTY God, who hast instructed thy holy Church with the heavenly doctrine of the Evangelist Saint Mark, give us grace that, being not like children carried away with every blast of vain doctrines, we may be established in the truth of thy holy Gospel, through Jesus Christ our Lord. *Amen.*

ST. PHILIP AND ST. JAMES'S DAY.

O ALMIGHTY God, whom truly to know is everlasting life, grant us perfectly to know thy Son Jesus Christ to be the way, the truth, and the life ; that, following the steps of thy holy Apostles Saint Philip and Saint James, we may steadfastly walk in the way that leadeth to eternal life, through the same thy Son Jesus Christ our Lord. *Amen.*

THE ASCENSION DAY.

GRANT, we beseech thee, Almighty God, that like as we do believe thy only begotten Son our Lord Jesus Christ to have ascended into the heavens, so we may also in heart and mind thither ascend, and with him continually dwell, who liveth and reigneth with thee, world without end. *Amen.*

ST. BARNABAS THE APOSTLE.

O LORD God Almighty, who didst endue thy holy Apostle Barnabas with singular gifts of the Holy Ghost, leave us not, we beseech thee, destitute of thy manifold gifts, nor yet of grace to use them alway to thy honor and glory, through Jesus Christ our Lord. *Amen.*

ST. JOHN BAPTIST'S DAY.

ALMIGHTY God, by whose providence thy servant John Baptist was wonderfully born, and sent to prepare the way of thy Son our Saviour, by preaching repentance; make us so to follow his doctrine and holy life, that we may truly repent according to his preaching; and after his example constantly speak the truth, boldly rebuke vice, and patiently suffer for the truth's sake; through Jesus Christ our Lord. *Amen.*

ST. PETER'S DAY.

O ALMIGHTY God, who by thy Son Jesus Christ didst give to thy Apostle Saint Peter many excellent gifts, and commandedst him earnestly to feed thy flock; make, we beseech thee, all pastors diligently to preach thy holy word, and the people obediently to follow the same, that they may receive the crown of everlasting glory, through Jesus Christ our Lord. *Amen.*

ST. JAMES THE APOSTLE.

GRANT, O merciful God, that as thine holy Apostle Saint James, leaving his father and all that he had, without delay was obedient unto the calling of thy Son Jesus Christ, and followed him; so we, forsaking all worldly and carnal affections, may be evermore ready to follow thy holy commandments, through Jesus Christ our Lord. *Amen.*

ST. BARTHOLOMEW THE APOSTLE.

O ALMIGHTY and everlasting God, who didst give to thine Apostle Bartholomew grace truly to believe and to preach thy Word; grant, we beseech thee, unto thy Church, to love that Word which he believed, and both to preach and receive the same, through Jesus Christ our Lord. *Amen.*

ST. MATTHEW THE APOSTLE.

O ALMIGHTY God, who by thy blessed Son didst call Matthew from the receipt of custom to be an Apostle and Evangelist; grant us grace to forsake all covetous desires, and inordinate love of riches, and to follow the same thy Son Jesus Christ, who liveth and reigneth with thee, world without end. *Amen.*

ST. MICHAEL AND ALL ANGELS.

O EVERLASTING God, who hast ordained and constituted the services of angels and men in a wonderful order, mercifully grant, that as thy holy angels always do thee service in heaven, so, by thy appointment, they may succor and defend us on earth, through Jesus Christ our Lord. *Amen.*

ST. LUKE THE EVANGELIST.

A LMIGHTY God, who calledst Luke the physician, whose praise is in the Gospel, to be an Evangelist, and physician of the soul; may it please thee, that, by the wholesome medicines of the doctrine delivered by him, all the diseases of our souls may be healed, through the merits of thy Son Jesus Christ our Lord. *Amen.*

ST. SIMON AND ST. JUDE.

O ALMIGHTY God, who hast built thy Church upon the foundation of the Apostles and Prophets, Jesus Christ himself being the head corner-stone; grant us so to be joined together in unity of spirit by their doctrine, that we may be made an holy temple acceptable unto thee, through Jesus Christ our Lord. *Amen.*

ALL SAINTS' DAY.

O ALMIGHTY God, who hast knit together thine elect in one communion and fellowship, in the mystical body of thy Son Christ our Lord; grant us grace so to follow thy blessed Saints in all virtuous and godly living, that we may come to those unspeakable joys which thou hast prepared for those who unfeignedly love thee, through Jesus Christ our Lord. *Amen.*

ASH–WEDNESDAY.

A LMIGHTY and everlasting God, who hatest nothing that thou hast made, and dost forgive the sins of all those who are penitent; create and make in us new and contrite hearts, that we worthily lamenting our sins, and acknowledging our wretchedness, may obtain of thee, the God of all mercy, perfect remission and forgiveness, through Jesus Christ our Lord. *Amen.*

GOOD FRIDAY.

A LMIGHTY God, we beseech thee graciously to behold this thy family, for which our Lord Jesus Christ was contented to be betrayed, and given up into the hands of wicked men, and to suffer death upon the cross, who now liveth and reigneth with thee, world without end. *Amen.*

SERVICE FOR CHRISTMAS.

COLLECT.

ALMIGHTY God, who hast given us thine only begotten Son to take our nature upon him, and, as at this time, to be born of a virgin, grant that we, being regenerate, and made thy children by adoption and grace, may daily be renewed by thy Holy Spirit. And this we beg in the name of Jesus Christ, through whom we ascribe unto Thee all honor and glory, now and ever. *Amen.*

ANTHEM.

GLORY be to God in the highest, on earth peace, good-will toward men.

Blessed are the people who know the joyful sound; they shall walk, O Lord, in the light of thy countenance;

Through the tender mercies of our God, whereby the day-spring from on high hath visited us;

To give light to those who sit in darkness and in the shadow of death, and to guide our feet in the way of peace.

How beautiful on the mountains are the feet of him who bringeth good tidings; who publisheth peace; who bringeth good tidings of good; who publisheth salvation; who saith unto Zion, Thy God reigneth.

There is sprung up a light for the righteous, and joyful gladness for such as are true of heart.

Rejoice in the Lord, ye righteous, and give thanks at the remembrance of his holiness.

Sing unto the Lord, and praise his name ; be telling of his salvation from day to day.

Let all those who seek him be joyful and glad in him, and let all such as love his salvation say always, The Lord be praised.

PROPER PSALMS.

My heart is inditing joyful words; I speak of the things concerning the King.

Thou art the fairest of the children of men ; full of grace are thy lips ; for God hath blessed thee for ever.

Gird thy sword upon thy thigh, O thou Mighty One, with thy glory and thy majesty.

And in thy majesty ride prosperously, for the cause of truth and meekness and righteousness ; and thy right hand shall teach thee terrible things.

Thy throne, O God, endureth for ever ; the sceptre of thy kingdom is a right sceptre.

Thou hast loved righteousness, and hated iniquity ; wherefore God, even thy God, hath anointed thee with the oil of gladness above thy fellows.

I will make thy name to be remembered to all generations ; so that the people shall praise thee for ever and ever.

Lord, thou art become gracious unto thy land ;

Thou hast forgiven the offence of thy people, and covered all their sins.

Turn us then, O God our Saviour, and let thine anger cease from us.

Wilt thou not turn again and quicken us, that thy people may rejoice in thee ?

Show us thy mercy, O Lord, and grant us thy salvation.

I will hear what God the Lord will speak ; for he will speak peace to his people and his saints ; only let them not return to their folly again.

For his salvation is nigh those who fear him, that glory may dwell in our land.

Mercy and truth are met together; righteousness and peace have kissed each other.

Truth shall flourish out of the earth; and righteousness shall look down from heaven.

Yea, the Lord shall show his loving-kindness; and our land shall yield her increase.

Righteousness shall go before him; and shall keep his path continually.

We will go into his tabernacle, we will worship before his footstool.

Arise, O Lord, into thy resting-place; thou, and the ark of thy strength.

Let thy priests be clothed with righteousness; and let thy saints sing for joy.

BENEDICTION VII.

SERVICE FOR CHRISTMAS EVE.

It is very meet, right, and our bounden duty, that we should at all times, and in all places, give thanks unto thee, O Lord, holy Father Almighty, everlasting God, because thou didst give Jesus Christ, thine only Son, to be born as at this time for us, who by the operation of thy Holy Spirit was made very man of the Virgin Mary his mother, and without spot of sin to make us clean from all sin. Therefore with angels and archangels, and with all the company of heaven, we worship and magnify thy great and glorious name; evermore praising thee, and saying, Holy, holy, holy, Lord God of hosts, heaven and earth are full of the majesty of thy glory. Glory be to thee, O Lord most high, most mighty, most merciful, through our Saviour and Redeemer.

Glory be to God in the highest, and on earth peace, good-will toward men; for unto us is born a Saviour, who is Christ the Lord. We praise thee, we bless thee, we glorify thee, we give thanks unto thee, for this greatest of thy mercies, O Lord God, Heavenly King, God the Father Almighty.

O Eternal God, Father Almighty, who in compassion to lost man didst send thy Son to become his Redeemer, have mercy upon us. Thou, who at sundry times and in divers manners didst speak in times past unto the fathers by the prophets, hast in these last days spoken unto us, by thy well beloved and only begotten, whom thou hast appointed heir of all things, by whom also thou didst make and wilt finally judge the world. In thine infinite wisdom, and perfect love towards us, thou hast wondrously appointed that the Word should be made flesh and dwell among us, that we might behold his glory full of grace and truth. We thank thee that the same blessed Jesus was born a helpless infant, subject to all our infirmities, was born in a manger, was born in poverty and want; that he did lay aside the glory which he had with thee before the world was, and, in the example of a great humility, did condescend to take the form of a servant, that we might from him learn to renounce all our pride, and become lowly and meek after him. Look down, we beseech thee, and vouchsafe to give us thy grace, that we may make him our pattern in all things, and become his obedient disciples. Have compassion on us, and perfect in us the work of our redemption. May he, who had his birth at Bethlehem, his baptism at the Jordan, his agony at Gethsemane, and his crucifixion at Calvary, be preached unto all nations, and be received into all hearts. May violence, oppression, cruelty, and all wrong, disappear at the bidding of this Prince of Peace. May those that are afar off be brought nigh by his precious blood, and the world be converted unto him; that at the name of Jesus every knee may bow, and every tongue confess that he is Lord, to the glory of God the Father. *Amen.*

BENEDICTION VI.

SERVICE FOR A DAY OF THANKSGIVING.

COLLECT.

LORD of all power and might, who art the Author and Giver of all good things, incline us all this day, we beseech thee, to a sincere and fervent thanksgiving for thine innumerable mercies, graft in our hearts the love of thy name, increase in us true religion, nourish us with all goodness, and of thy great mercy keep us in the same, through Jesus Christ our Lord. *Amen.*

[The Psalms of the Sunday after Easter may be read, with any other appropriate passages of Scripture, and Prayers.]

O GIVE thanks unto the Lord; for he is gracious, and his mercy endureth for ever.

O give thanks unto the God of all gods; for his mercy endureth for ever.

O thank the Lord of all lords; for his mercy endureth for ever.

Who by his excellent wisdom made the heavens; for his mercy endureth for ever.

Who laid out the earth above the waters; for his mercy endureth for ever.

Who hath made great lights; for his mercy endureth for ever.

The sun to rule by day; for his mercy endureth for ever.

22 *

The moon and the stars to govern the night; for his mercy endureth for ever.

Who remembereth us when we are in trouble; for his mercy endureth for ever.

And hath delivered us from our enemies; for his mercy endureth for ever.

Who giveth food to all flesh; for his mercy endureth for ever.

O give thanks unto the God of heaven; for his mercy endureth for ever.

The Lord be with you,

And with thy Spirit.

Glory be to God in the highest;

And on earth peace, good-will toward men.

Let us pray.

O Lord, show thy mercy upon us;

And grant us thy salvation.

O God, make clean our hearts within us;

And take not thy Holy Spirit from us.

A THANKSGIVING.

O THOU who art good unto all, who exercisest loving-kindness in all the earth, and who hast come nigh to us by Jesus Christ thy Son, it is thou who givest our daily bread, health in our habitations, and peace in our borders, and who crownest the year with thy goodness. We desire this day gratefully to recount thy mercies, and to ascribe blessing and honor and glory and praise to thee, our rock and fortress, our strength and redeemer.

How precious have been thy thoughts unto us, O God, how great has been the sum of them! We bless thee for preserving our houses from the ravages of fire, for all the health and pleasure which we have enjoyed in them, for the bread which has given strength to our bodies, for the medicine which has arrested the progress of disease, for the sympathy which has comforted us under trouble, for divine preservation in our journeys by land, for favorable winds on the ocean, for refreshing showers upon the fields. We thank thee for every cheerful sensation when alone, for the pleasures of friendly intercourse, for the benefits of good neighborhood, for the privileges of public worship, for the maintenance of civil order, the continuance of peace, the administration of justice, for every encouragement to well-doing, every manifestation of useful truth, and for all the advantages of our condition.

Graciously direct us, O God, to a right improvement of all thy mercies. Preserve us from the wicked indulgence of all fleshly lusts, and from wasting our substance in riotous living. May we enjoy our temporal possessions with temperance, cheerfulness, and contentment. Protect us from the snares of prosperity. May we honor thee with our substance, be rich in good works, and duly esteem and praise thee, the rock of our salvation.

Continue to us the enjoyment of our civil rights; rule in the hearts of our rulers, and direct them in all their designs and measures by thy wisdom and grace; make our land a quiet habitation; grant peace, order, and plenty in our families, our villages and towns, and throughout our country; bless all fountains of useful science; heal and cleanse their waters; dispel the mists of ignorance; arrest the progress of profaneness and vice; make the people of our land humble before thee, peaceable in their civil and social relations, and zealous for the establishment of liberty, order, and truth. May we never by our ingratitude incur that censure, I have nourished and brought up children, but they have rebelled against me. Grant this, O Father, for thine infinite mercy's sake in Jesus Christ our Lord. *Amen.*

BENEDICTION IV.

SERVICE FOR A DAY OF FASTING.

[The Collects for Ash-Wednesday, and for the First Sunday in Lent, and the Psalms and Prophecies for the latter, may be read, together with other appropriate Scriptures and Prayers, at the discretion of the minister.]

PROPHECIES.

ISAIAH.

For thus saith the high and lofty One that inhabiteth eternity, whose name is Holy: I dwell in the high and holy place, with him also that is of a contrite and humble spirit, to revive the spirit of the humble, and to revive the heart of the contrite ones.

For I will not contend for ever, neither will I be always wroth : for the spirit should fail before me, and the souls which I have made.

I create the fruit of the lips : Peace, peace to him that is far off, and to him that is near, saith the Lord ; and I will heal him.

But the wicked are like the troubled sea, when it cannot rest, whose waters cast up mire and dirt.

There is no peace, saith my God, to the wicked.

Cry aloud, spare not, lift up thy voice like a trumpet, and show my people their transgression, and the house of Jacob their sins.

Yet they seek me daily, and delight to know my ways, as a nation that did righteousness, and forsook not the ordinance of their God: they ask of me the ordinances of justice : they take delight in approaching to God.

Wherefore have we fasted, say they, and thou seest not? wherefore have we afflicted our soul, and thou takest no knowledge? Behold, in the day of your fast ye find pleasure, and exact all your labors.

Behold, ye fast for strife and debate, and to smite with the fist of wickedness : ye shall not fast as ye do this day, to make your voice to be heard on high.

Is it such a fast that I have chosen? a day for a man to afflict his soul? is it to bow down his head as a bulrush, and to spread sackcloth and ashes under him? wilt thou call this a fast, and an acceptable day to the Lord?

Is not this the fast that I have chosen? to loose the bands of wickedness, to undo the heavy burdens, and to let the oppressed go free, and that ye break every yoke?

Is it not to deal thy bread to the hungry, and that thou bring the poor that are cast out to thy house? when thou seest the naked, that thou cover him ; and that thou hide not thyself from thine own flesh?

Then shall thy light break forth as the morning, and thine health shall spring forth speedily : and thy righteousness shall go before thee ; the glory of the Lord shall be thy rereward.

Then shalt thou call, and the Lord shall answer ; thou shalt cry, and he shall say, Here I am. If thou take away from the midst of thee the yoke, the putting forth of the finger, and speaking vanity ;

And if thou draw out thy soul to the hungry, and satisfy the afflicted soul ; then shall thy light rise in obscurity, and thy darkness be as the noonday :

And the Lord shall guide thee continually, and satisfy thy soul in drought : and thou shalt be like a watered garden, and like a spring of water, whose waters fail not.

And they that shall be of thee shall build the old waste places : thou shalt raise up the foundations of many generations; and thou shalt be called, The repairer of the breach, The restorer of paths to dwell in.

If thou turn away thy foot from doing thy pleasure on my holy day; and call the Sabbath a delight, the holy of the Lord, honorable; and shalt honor him, not doing thine own ways, nor finding thine own pleasure, nor speaking thine own words:

Then shalt thou delight thyself in the Lord; and I will cause thee to ride upon the high places of the earth: for the mouth of the Lord hath spoken it.

PRAYER.

O THOU, our Heavenly Father and Almighty King, who rulest justly over all, and whose nature it is to have mercy, graciously hearken to our cry, and pardon us all our iniquities. Incline our hearts to confess and mourn the sins we have committed, and to forsake all that we confess; and those that we do thus acknowledge and put away from us, wilt thou, we beseech thee, forgive. Turn thou us, O holy Lord, and we shall be turned. Cleanse thou us, and we shall be clean. Be favorable to thy people, who look to thee in fasting and praying, and help them so to watch and fast and pray, as not to enter into temptation. Thou art a merciful God, full of compassion, long-suffering, and of great pity. Spare thy people, and visit them not in judgment according to their offences. Pardon us all our injustices and infirmities, our irreverence and uncharitableness, our pride and selfishness, and every kind of transgression. Help us, O Lord, who hast created us fearfully and wonderfully, help us to keep under our bodies and bring them into subjection, that all their vile lusts and inordinate appetites may be mortified and subdued to the spirit.

O thou who art the Lord of lords and King of kings, we humbly beseech thee for our country, that it may be still blessed and prospered by the good God of our fathers; that thou wouldst be pleased to preserve and extend its liberties, to purify and maintain its laws, to cause order, industry, contentment, and peace to prevail among all its inhabitants. Be pleased to direct all the consultations of our law-makers, in the nation and in the commonwealth. Rule thou in righteousness among the rulers, and judge among the judges. Deliver us from the mischiefs of sedition, party spirit, maliciousness, and rebellion. And let all things be so ordered, under thy wise and perfect government, that truth and equity, concord and happiness, virtue and religion, may be established upon sure foundations, and stand fast in our heritage for ages to come.

Almighty and Everlasting God, we thine unworthy creatures are strangers and pilgrims on the earth, as all our fathers were. Regard very tenderly, we entreat thee, our low and feeble estate. Send us strength while we live; support us in sickness, and prepare us to die. We ask thee, if it may be thy holy will, to make the earth continue to yield her fruits in their season; to send the early and latter rain, to bless the springing thereof, and to be to the husbandman the joy of harvest. Bless every kind of honest and rightful labor, and stretch out thy wide protection over the ocean and the land. Save us from pestilence and from famine. And dispose all thy children to use thy bounties with moderation, temperance, and thankfulness.

Father of all the families of the earth, send now the blessing of thy Holy Spirit into all our homes. Fill them with the fruits of Christian love. May Christ Jesus thy Son be received and revered and trusted everywhere, as that gracious and blessed Saviour, whom to know aright is life eternal, whose blood cleanseth from all sin, and who hath brought life and immortality to light. And through him unto thee, O Father, be rendered all honor and power and praise, now and for evermore!

Most merciful and righteous Father, who hast taught us

that, if we, through the spirit, do mortify the deeds of the body, we shall live, and who hast commanded us not to be weary nor faint in our minds striving against sin, bring us this day to a true humiliation, and deliver us from evil.   Stand at our right hand, we beseech thee, and work with our hearts, that we may overcome in the time of our temptation ; and being graciously absolved from all our iniquity, made clean from its corruption, loosed from its burden, may we pass our time in quietness and holy trust here on earth, and finally obtain everlasting life, through our Lord and Saviour, the only Mediator and Advocate.   Amen.

BENEDICTION I.

SERVICE FOR A NATIONAL ANNIVERSARY.

[When such anniversary falls on a Sunday, and not on the fifth Sunday after Whitsunday, the Psalms for that fifth Sunday may be read, by exchange with those appointed for the day when it so falls.]

A COLLECT.

O THOU whose throne is in the heavens, God of all nations, who puttest down one and settest up another, who art the Ruler of all the armies of earth and skies, and whose kingdom is from everlasting to everlasting, as thou hast dealt with this people beyond all their deserving, and multiplied thy mercies to us notwithstanding our offences, so we humbly entreat thee still to show thy loving-kindness, by turning us from every false and evil and unjust way; to lighten our darkness, to deliver us from perplexity and peril, to unite all our hearts in a wise and faithful respect both for our liberties and our laws, to keep ever open among us the fountains of knowledge, charity, and grace, to give us peace and prosperity, and to exalt us by righteousness: and this we ask through him who, of thine infinite goodness, is made unto us righteousness, sanctification, and redemption, Jesus Christ our Lord. *Amen.*

23

SERVICE FOR THE COMMUNION OF THE LORD'S SUPPER.*

YE who do truly repent you of your sins, who are in love and charity with your neighbors, who desire to express your gratitude and reverence to your Saviour, Jesus Christ, by commemorating his death in the way which he hath appointed, and who intend, by the aid of God's grace, to live a Christian life, draw near with faith, and take this holy ordinance to your comfort.

Hear the words of invitation and comfort which our Saviour speaks to all who truly turn to him:

Come unto me all ye that labor and are heavy-laden, and I will give you rest.

Blessed are they which do hunger and thirst after righteousness: for they shall be filled.

Peace I leave with you, my peace I give unto you; not as the world giveth give I unto you.

Hear also what his holy Apostles say:

Christ, our Passover, is sacrificed for us: therefore let us keep the Feast, not with old leaven, neither with the leaven of malice and wickedness, but with the unleavened bread of sincerity and truth.

---

* Principally after the old Greek Liturgies, with especial use of that of Antioch, called the Liturgy of St. James, — compiled and translated for a Service-Book by Rev. F. H. Hedge, D.D.

Herein is love, not that we loved God, but that he loved us, and sent his Son to be the propitiation for our sins.

Forasmuch then as ye were not redeemed with corruptible things, as silver and gold, but with the precious blood of Christ, as of a lamb without blemish and without spot, see that ye love one another with a pure heart fervently.

For even hereunto were ye called ; because Christ also suffered for us, leaving us an example, that ye should follow his steps : who his own self bare our sins in his own body on the tree, that we, being dead to sins, should live unto righteousness ; by whose stripes ye were healed.   For ye were as sheep going astray ; but are now returned unto the Shepherd and Bishop of your souls.

Min.   Lift up your hearts.
Ans.   *We lift them up unto the Lord.*
Min.   Let us praise the Lord.
Ans.   *It is meet and just.*
Min.   Yea, it is meet and just and seemly and profitable, day and night, with lips never silent, and heart never dumb, to praise and to bless and to give thanks unto thee, O Lord, who madest heaven and earth, the sea, and all that in them is ; who madest man in thine own image, and when he had transgressed didst not overlook him nor forsake him, but didst recall him by thy Law and school him by thy Prophets, and didst fashion and renew him by the awful and heavenly mysteries of religion ; who madest all things by thy Wisdom, the true Light, thine only begotten Son, our Saviour Jesus Christ, through whom we render unto thee the reasonable service which is rendered, O Lord, by all thy people from north to south, from the rising of the sun to the going down of the same ; through whom every rational creature worshippeth and sendeth up unto thee the eternal song of praise.   Angels, Archangels, Thrones, Dominions, Principalities, Authorities, and Powers, Cherubim and Seraphim, call to one another

with ceaseless voice, and repeat the triumphal hymn, singing and shouting and saying:

Ans. *Holy, holy, holy Lord God of hosts, heaven and earth
are full of thy glory.*

Min. Wherefore, together with the heavenly host, we also
cry aloud and say, Holy indeed art thou, all-holy, and without
measure is the majesty of thy holiness.   Holy also is thine
only begotten Son, our Lord Jesus Christ, and holy the Spirit
that searcheth all things, yea, the deep things of God.

Thou didst send thy Son into the world, that he might renew and reanimate thine image.   Who, born of woman, and
having his conversation with men, did order all things per-
taining to the salvation of our race.   And being about to
undergo the voluntary and life-giving death upon the cross, —
the sinless for us sinners, — on the night in which he was
betrayed, — let us rather say, in which he delivered up himself for the life and salvation of the world, — taking bread in
his holy and innocent and immortal hands, he blessed it and
brake, and gave to his disciples, saying: Take, eat; this is
my body, which is broken and given for you for the remission
of sins.

Ans. *Amen.*

Min. Also taking the cup after he had supped, and blessing it and giving thanks, filled with the Holy Ghost, he gave
it to his disciples, saying: Drink ye all of it; this is the blood
of the New Covenant, which is shed for you and for many,
and given for the remission of sins.

Ans. *Amen.*

Min. This do in remembrance of me.   For as oft as ye
eat of this bread and drink of this cup, ye show forth the
death of the Son of Man, and declare his resurrection, until
he come.

Ans. *Thy death, O Lord, we show forth, and declare thy
resurrection.*

Min. We, therefore, mindful of his life-giving doctrines,

his saving cross and death, his burial and resurrection, his ascension and seat at the right hand of God, — we set apart and devote to the memory of Christ this bread and this cup. And we beseech thee, O Lord, to sanctify these elements, and to sanctify us with thy holy presence. And may this bread be unto us as the sacred body of thy Christ.

Ans. Amen.

Min. And may this cup be unto us as the honored blood of thy Christ.

Ans. Amen.

Min. That so this rite may be profitable to all who partake of it, for the remission of sins, for eternal life, for the sanctification of body and soul, for fruitfulness in good works, for the stablishing of thy holy Church, which thou hast founded on the rock of faith, that the gates of hell may not prevail against it. May we who thus eat of one bread and drink of one cup be made one with each other in the fellowship of the same Holy Spirit, and one with thee in Christ.

And in this our communion we remember, and beseech thee to remember and to bless, the multitudes of every name who are joined with us in one household of faith, — our brethren and sisters in Christ throughout the world.

We remember those who have fallen asleep in Christ, and in the joyful hope of resurrection unto life eternal. O Lord, refresh their spirits with the light of thy countenance.

We remember the fathers from the beginning of the world; the patriarchs, prophets, apostles, martyrs, and all who have wrought righteousness, from righteous Abel even to the present day. Refresh thou their spirits, and give them abundant entrance into the joy of our Lord. And grant unto us, O God, that we may have our part and lot with all thy saints.

We remember all such as journey or are about to journey, and them that sojourn in strange lands. May they have thee for their fellow-voyager and fellow-traveller. May it please thee to abide with them wheresoever they abide, and, whether

23 *

they travel by land or by water, to bring them in safety to their destined goal. Abide with those whom they leave behind, and grant that, in health remaining, they may welcome their own in health returning, and rejoice with them in safety and in peace.

We remember all who are sick and in distress, all who suffer in body or in mind, all who are in prison and in bonds. As bound with them, and as sufferers with them, we bear them in our hearts, and pray for their relief.

We remember our enemies, if there be any who have injured us, or any who look upon us with evil eye, and cherish hatred against us. We beseech thee to turn their hearts, and that we may live peaceably with all men. May we freely forgive all who have wronged us; and if there be any whom we have wronged, may we make amends and seek forgiveness.

We remember the whole family of man, beseeching thee that the spirits of all flesh may taste of thy grace, and that the ends of the earth may see the salvation of God.

And unto us, O Lord, vouchsafe such guidance, that, as Christians, and blameless, we may spend the remainder of our life. Gather us, O Lord, when thou wilt, and as thou wilt, but be it without shame and without reproach, through Jesus Christ our Lord, who alone was found sinless on earth.

Ans. Put away from us, O Lord, our sins, whether wilful or against our wills, in deed and in word, in knowledge and in ignorance, in mind and disposition, and forgive them all according to thy mercy:

Min. In Jesus Christ thy Son, in whom and through whom we bless thee now and ever.

Ans. Amen.

Min. O God and Father of our Lord Jesus Christ, may it please thee to accept us in these our supplications. May our offerings find favor in thy sight, and be as the odor of spiritual incense. Accept them, O Lord, as thou didst accept the offerings of holy men of old, and bless them, as thou didst bless the centurion's alms and the widow's mite. Sanctify us with the grace of thy Christ, and with the frequency of thy Holy Spirit. Sanctify soul and body and spirit, and make us worthy to call upon thee, the Father in heaven, and to say :

Ans. Our Father who art in heaven, hallowed be thy name. Thy kingdom come, thy will be done on earth as in heaven. Give us this day our daily bread. Lead us not into temptation, but deliver us from evil.

Min. Yea, Lord, lead us not into temptation, but deliver us from evil. For thy mercy knoweth that we, through much weakness, are not able of ourselves to overcome. But do thou, together with the trial, provide also a way of escape. For thou givest thy servants power to tread upon serpents and scorpions, and on all the power of the enemy. For thine is the kingdom, and the power, and the glory, for ever and ever

Ans. Amen.

Min. Peace be with you.

Ans. And with thy spirit.

SCRIPTURES.

IT is written by St. Matthew : —

And as they were eating, Jesus took bread, and blessed it, and brake it, and gave it to the disciples, and said, Take, eat; this is my body.

And he took the cup, and gave thanks, and gave it to them, saying, Drink ye all of it; for this is my blood of the new testament, which is shed for many for the remission of sins. But I say unto you, I will not drink henceforth of this fruit of the vine, until that day when I drink it new with you in my Father's kingdom.

It is written by St. Mark : —

And as they did eat, Jesus took bread, and blessed, and brake it and gave to them, and said, Take, eat; this is my body.

And he took the cup, and when he had given thanks, he gave it them; and they all drank of it. And he said unto them, This is my blood of the new testament, which is shed for many. Verily, I say unto you, I will drink no more of the fruit of the vine, until that day that I drink it new in the kingdom of God.

And when they had sung an hymn, they went out into the Mount of Olives.

It is written by St. Luke: —

And when the hour was come, he sat down, and the twelve Apostles with him. And he said unto them, With desire I have desired to eat this passover with you before I suffer. For I say unto you, I will not any more eat thereof, until it be fulfilled in the kingdom of God. And he took the cup, and gave thanks, and said, Take this, and divide it among yourselves. For I say unto you, I will not drink of the fruit of the vine, until the kingdom of God shall come. And he took bread, and gave thanks, and brake it, and gave unto them, saying, This is my body which is given for you: this do in remembrance of me. Likewise also the cup after supper, saying, This cup is the new testament in my blood, which is shed for you.

It is written by Paul, in 1 Cor. xi. : —

For I have received of the Lord that which also I delivered unto you, That the Lord Jesus, the same night in which he was betrayed, took bread: and when he had given thanks, he brake it, and said, Take, eat; this is my body, which is broken for you; this do in remembrance of me. After the same manner also he took the cup, when he had supped, saying, This cup is the new testament in my blood; this do ye, as oft as ye drink it, in remembrance of me. For as often as ye eat this bread, and drink this cup, ye do show the Lord's death till he come.

It is also written in the Gospel of St. John, that Jesus said : —

My Father giveth you the true bread from heaven. For the bread of God is he which cometh down from heaven, and giveth life unto the world. I am the Bread of life : he that cometh to me shall never hunger ; and he that believeth on me shall never thirst. If any man eat of this bread, he shall live for ever; and the bread that I will give is my flesh, which I will give for the life of the world. Except ye eat the flesh of the Son of man, and drink his blood, ye have no life in you. He that eateth my flesh, and drinketh my blood, dwelleth in me, and I in him. As the living Father hath sent me, and I live by the Father, so he that eateth me, even he shall live by me.

For God so loved the world, that he gave his only begotten Son, that whosoever believeth in him should not perish, but have everlasting life.

I am the Way, and the Truth, and the Life : no man cometh unto the Father but by me.

I am the Door : by me if any man enter in, he shall be saved, and go in and out and find pasture.

I am the Good Shepherd : the Good Shepherd giveth his life for the sheep.

I am the True Vine ; ye are the branches. As the branch cannot bear fruit of itself, except it abide in the vine, no more can ye, except ye abide in me. For without me ye can do nothing.

[After the Bread, Prayer, Cup, and Hymn.]

BENEDICTION XIV.*

---

* By the established usage in the University Church, a baptized person may be admitted a member, by the subscription of his or her name to the Covenant printed on page 277, with the announcement to the Church of the fact of such subscription.

Where there is a distinct ceremony of confirmation, or coming to the Lord's Supper, the following form may be used, with prayers or other additions : —

Do you here, in the presence of God and of this congregation, believing in the holy religion of Jesus Christ as taught in the Scriptures of the New Testament, and taking it as the divine guide of your life, and the way of salvation, declare it to be your desire and your present purpose to be henceforth a true disciple of that blessed Saviour, and to remember him in the way which he has appointed ?

Ans. *I do.*

Then the minister may lay his hand on the head of the person answering, who kneels or stands before him, and say : —

Now, therefore, live ; yet not thou, but Christ live in thee ; and the life that thou livest in the flesh, let it be by faith in the Son of God !

Our help is in the name of the Lord, who has made heaven and earth. The Lord Almighty defend and bless you with his heavenly grace, and bring you into his heavenly kingdom ! *Amen.*

SERVICE FOR BAPTISM.

IN the name of Christ, the Founder and Head of the Church, we, who are here assembled, are to observe the holy ordinance of baptism. Hear, then, these words of our Saviour : —

All power is given unto me in heaven and in earth. Go ye, therefore, and teach all nations, baptizing them in the name of the Father, and of the Son, and of the Holy Spirit ; teaching them to observe all things whatsoever I have commanded you : and lo, I am with you alway, even unto the end of the world.

Hear also what is written by his holy Apostles : —

Repent and be baptized, every one of you, for the remission of sins, and ye shall receive the gift of the Holy Spirit. For the promise is unto you, and to your children, and to all that are afar off, as many as the Lord our God shall call.

For ye are all the children of God through faith in Christ Jesus. For as many of you as have been baptized into Christ, have put on Christ.

Know ye not that so many of us as were baptized into Jesus Christ, were baptized into his death? Therefore we are buried with him by baptism into death : that like as Christ was raised up from the dead by the glory of the Father, even so we also should walk in newness of life.

Let us draw near with a true heart, in full assurance of

faith, having our hearts sprinkled from an evil conscience, and our bodies washed with pure water.

The baptism that saveth us is not the putting away the filth of the flesh, but the answer of a good conscience toward God.

FOR INFANTS.

AND Jesus took a child and set him in the midst; and when he had taken him in his arms, he said unto them, Whosoever shall receive one of such children in my name, receiveth me; and whosoever shall receive me, receiveth not me, but Him that sent me.

And they brought young children to him, that he should touch them; and his disciples rebuked those that brought them; but when Jesus saw it, he was much displeased, and said unto them, Suffer the little children to come unto me, and forbid them not, for of such is the kingdom of God. Verily I say unto you, whosoever shall not receive the kingdom of God as a little child, he shall not enter therein.

Whosoever, therefore, shall humble himself as a little child, the same is greatest in the kingdom of heaven.

Take heed that ye despise not one of these little ones; for I say unto you, that in heaven their angels do always behold the face of my Father which is in heaven.

Dearly beloved, ye have brought this child here to be baptized; I demand therefore,

Will ye faithfully and earnestly exhort this child to renounce the hurtful vanities of this world, with all covetous desires of the same, and carnal desires of the flesh, so that *he* may not follow nor be led by them?

I will.

Will ye instruct *him* in the Gospel of our Lord Jesus Christ?

I will.

Will ye exhort *him* to keep God's holy will and commandments, and to walk in the same all the days of *his* life?

I will.

[With the administration of water.]

I BAPTIZE thee in the name of the Father, and of the Son, and of the Holy Spirit.

BENEDICTION X.

FOR ADULTS.

OUR Lord Jesus commanded, that all persons baptized should be instructed in his holy Gospel. You, in the profession of the Christian faith, present yourself to be baptized according to his institution. Do you now promise, that you will receive the instructions of the Christian religion, and strive to govern your faith and practice by its doctrines and laws?

[With the administration of water.]

I BAPTIZE thee in the name of the Father, and of the Son, and of the Holy Spirit.

BENEDICTION X.

COVENANT OF THE CHURCH IN HARVARD UNIVERSITY.*

WE, whose names are underwritten, present ourselves for admission to this Church, in testimony of our faith in Jesus Christ, our acceptance of his religion, and subjection to his laws. We regard this transaction as an expression of our earnest desire to obtain the salvation proposed in the Gospel, and our serious purpose to endeavor to comply with the terms on which it is offered. We design to commemorate the Author and Finisher of our faith, in the manner established in his Church. In a humble and grateful reliance on God for the pardon of sin, and assistance in duty, we solemnly take upon ourselves the engagements of the Christian profession. We will, as we shall have opportunity, acknowledge our relation to this Christian community, by attendance on the services of religion, by the offices of Christian affection, and by submission to the laws of Christian order, beseeching the God and Father of our Lord Jesus Christ, that, being faithful to each other and to our common Master, we may enjoy the consolations of our holy religion here, and be accepted to its rewards hereafter, through the riches of divine favor in Jesus Christ.

* Adopted by vote, November 6, 1814.

THE APOSTLES' CREED.

I BELIEVE in God the Father Almighty, Maker of heaven and earth:

And in Jesus Christ his only Son our Lord; Who was conceived by the Holy Ghost, Born of the Virgin Mary; Suffered under Pontius Pilate, Was crucified, dead, and buried; He descended into hell; The third day he rose from the dead; He ascended into heaven, And sitteth on the right hand of God the Father Almighty; From thence he shall come to judge the quick and the dead.

I believe in the Holy Ghost; The holy Catholic Church; The Communion of Saints; The Forgiveness of sins; The Resurrection of the body; And the Life everlasting. *Amen.*

TE DEUM.

WE praise thee, O God; we acknowledge thee to be the Lord.

All the earth doth worship thee, the Father everlasting.

To thee all angels cry aloud, the heavens and all the powers therein.

To thee cherubim and seraphim continually do cry,

Holy, holy, holy, Lord God of Sabaoth.

Heaven and earth are full of the majesty of thy glory.

The glorious company of the apostles praise thee.

The goodly fellowship of the prophets praise thee.

The noble army of martyrs praise thee.

The holy Church throughout all the world doth acknowledge thee,

The Father of an infinite majesty;

Thine adorable, true, and only Son;

Also the Holy Ghost, the Comforter.

Thou art the King of glory, O Lord;

And Jesus Christ is thy well-beloved Son.

When thou gavest him to deliver man, it pleased thee that he should be born of a virgin.

When he had overcome the sharpness of death, he did open the kingdom of heaven to all believers.

He sitteth at the right hand of God, in the glory of the Father.

We believe that he shall come to be our judge.

We therefore pray thee, help thy servants, whom thou hast redeemed through his most precious blood.

Make them to be numbered with thy saints, in glory ever-lasting.

O Lord, save thy people, and bless thine heritage.

Govern them, and lift them up for ever.

Day by day we magnify thee ;

And we worship thy name, ever, world without end.

Vouchsafe, O Lord, to keep us this day without sin.

O Lord, have mercy upon us ; have mercy upon us.

O Lord, let thy mercy lighten upon us, as our trust is in thee.

O Lord, in thee have we trusted ; let us never be confounded.

LITANY.

O GOD, our Heavenly Father, who by thy Son hast redeemed the world, and by thy Holy Spirit dost govern, direct, and sanctify the hearts of thy faithful servants, have mercy upon us miserable sinners.

O God, through thy blessed Son, the Redeemer of the world, have mercy upon us, thy sinful children, and by thy Holy Spirit sanctify our hearts.

Remember not, Lord, our offences, neither take thou vengeance of our sins; spare us, good Lord, spare thy people whom thou hast redeemed by the most precious blood of thy Son, and be not angry with us for ever.

Spare us, good Lord.

From all evil and mischief; from sin; from the assaults of temptation, from thy wrath, and from everlasting destruction,

Good Lord, deliver us.

From all blindness of heart; from pride, vainglory, and hypocrisy; from envy, hatred, and malice, and all uncharitableness; from all inordinate and sinful affections, and from all the deceitful allurements of this transitory world,

Good Lord, deliver us.

From lightning, and tempest; from plague, pestilence, and famine; from battle, and murder, and from death unprepared for,

Good Lord, deliver us.

From all sedition, privy conspiracy, and rebellion; from all false doctrine, heresy, and schism; from hardness of heart, and contempt of thy word and commandment,

Good Lord, deliver us.

In all time of our tribulation, in all time of our prosperity, in the hour of death, and in the day of judgment,

Good Lord, deliver us.

We sinners do beseech thee to hear us, O Lord God, and that it may please thee to rule and govern thy holy Church Universal in the right way; and to illuminate all ministers of the Gospel with true knowledge, and understanding of thy word; and that both by their preaching and living they may set it forth, and show it accordingly;

We beseech thee to hear us, good Lord.

That it may please thee to endue the President of these United States, the Governor of this Commonwealth, the Judges and Magistrates, and all others in authority, with wisdom and understanding; giving them grace to execute justice and to maintain truth;

We beseech thee to hear us, good Lord.

That it may please thee to bless all colleges and seminaries of learning; all instructors of youth, and all means of true knowledge, virtue, and piety;

We beseech thee to hear us, good Lord.

That it may please thee to bless and keep all thy people; to give to all nations unity, peace, and concord; and to give us a heart to love and fear thee, and diligently to live after thy commandments;

We beseech thee to hear us, good Lord.

That it may please thee to give to all thy people increase of grace, to hear meekly thy word, and to receive it with pure affection, and to bring forth the fruits of the Spirit;

We beseech thee to hear us, good Lord.

That it may please thee to bring into the way of truth all such as have erred, and are deceived; to strengthen such as do stand; to comfort and help the weak-hearted; to raise up those who fall; and finally to give us victory over all temptations;

We beseech thee to hear us, good Lord.

That it may please thee to succor, help, and comfort all who are in danger, necessity, and tribulation; to preserve all who travel by land or by water, all sick persons and young children; to show thy pity upon all prisoners and captives; to defend, and provide for, the fatherless children and widows, and all who are desolate and oppressed;

We beseech thee to hear us, good Lord.

That it may please thee to have mercy upon all men;

We beseech thee to hear us, good Lord.

That it may please thee to forgive our enemies, persecutors, and slanderers, and to turn their hearts;

We beseech thee to hear us, good Lord.

That it may please thee to give and preserve to our use the kindly fruits of the earth, so that in due time we may enjoy them;

We beseech thee to hear us, good Lord.

That it may please thee to give us true repentance, to forgive us all our sins, negligences, and ignorances, and to endue us with the grace of thy Holy Spirit, to amend our lives according to thy holy word;

We beseech thee to hear us, good Lord.

O Lord, grant us thy peace.

Lord, have mercy upon us.

O Lord, deal not with us after our sins;

Neither reward us after our iniquities.

WE humbly beseech thee, O Father, mercifully to look upon our infirmities; and for the glory of thy name, turn from us all those evils which we most justly have deserved ; and grant that in all our troubles we may put our whole trust and confidence in thy mercy, and evermore serve thee in holiness and pureness of living, to thy honor and glory, through our only Mediator and Advocate, Jesus Christ our Lord. *Amen.*

SCRIPTURAL LITANIES.*

I.

[FROM THE EPISTLE TO THE ROMANS.]

O THOU, of whom, and through whom, and to whom are all things, help us with one mind and one mouth to glorify thee, even the Father of our Lord Jesus Christ.

O Thou, who art the God of patience and consolation, grant us to be like-minded one toward another according to Christ Jesus.

O Thou, who art the God of hope, fill us with all joy and peace in believing, that we may abound in hope, through the power of the Holy Ghost.

May we be full of goodness, filled with all knowledge, able also to admonish one another.

May those that are strong bear the infirmities of the weak.

May we follow after the things which make for peace, and things wherewith one may edify another.

Save us, we beseech thee, O Heavenly Father, from being conformed to this world, from thinking of ourselves more highly than we ought to think, from being wise in our own conceits, from being overcome of evil, and enable us to overcome evil with good.

Hear us, good Lord.

If we have, at any time, held the truth in unrighteousness, if when we have known God we have not glorified him as

---

* Taken from the Service-Book of "The Church of the Disciples."

God nor been thankful, if we have changed thy truth into a lie, and worshipped the creature more than the Creator;

Forgive us, we beseech thee, O our Father.

If we have not liked to retain thee in our thoughts, if we have despised thy goodness, forbearance, and long-suffering; if our heart has been impenitent and hard; if we have dishonored thee by breaking thy law;

Forgive us, we beseech thee, O our Father.

If the good which we would, we do not, and the evil which we would not, that we do; if to will is present with us, but how to perform that which we will, we find not; if, when we would do good, evil is present with us; if we find a law in our members warring against the law of our mind, and bringing us into captivity to the law of sin in our members;

Help us, we beseech thee, O our Father.

Being justified by faith, may we have peace with thee, through our Lord Jesus Christ, and rejoice in the hope of the glory of God.

Shed thy love in our hearts by the Holy Ghost.

May the law of the spirit of life in Christ Jesus make us free from the law of sin and death, and make us walk, not after the flesh, but after the spirit; may we not receive the spirit of bondage again to fear, but the spirit of adoption, whereby we call thee Father;

Being led by thy Spirit, may we become thy children.

May nothing separate us from the love of Christ; neither tribulation, nor distress, nor persecution, nor famine, nor nakedness, nor peril, nor the sword;

In all these, may we be more than conquerors through him who has loved us.

May neither death nor life, nor angels nor powers, nor things present nor things to come, nor height nor depth, nor any creature, separate us from the love of God which is in Christ Jesus.

May nothing separate us from thy love.

May we confess with our mouth the Lord Jesus, and believe in our heart that God has raised him from the dead ;

May we believe with our heart unto righteousness, and confess with our mouth unto salvation.

We beseech thee, Heavenly Father, that we may be enabled to present our bodies a living sacrifice, holy and acceptable to thee, being transformed by the renewing of our mind.

Whether we live, may we live unto the Lord; and whether we die, may we die unto the Lord.

May our love be without dissimulation ; may we abhor that which is evil, cleave to that which is good ; be kindly affectioned one toward another ; not slothful in business ; fervent in spirit ; rejoicing in hope ; patient in tribulation ; continuing instant in prayer ; distributing to the necessities of our brethren ; given to hospitality.

May we rejoice with those that rejoice, and weep with those that weep ;

May we render unto all their dues.

May we love our neighbor as ourselves.

May we cast off the works of darkness, and put on the armor of light.

Awaken us, O Lord, from our sleep.

Now unto Him that has power to establish us according to the Gospel, and the preaching of Jesus Christ ;

To God only wise, be glory through Jesus Christ, for ever. Amen.

II.

[FROM THE EPISTLES TO THE CORINTHIANS AND GALATIANS.]

O THOU, who didst command the light to shine out of darkness, and hast shined in our hearts, to give the light of the knowledge of the glory of God in the face of Jesus Christ, establish us in Christ and anoint us.

Seal us thine, O Lord, and give us the earnest of thy Spirit in our hearts.

O God, the Father of our Lord Jesus Christ, the Father of mercies, and the God of all comfort, who comforteth us in all our tribulation, give us grace and peace.

Confirm us unto the end, that we may be blameless in the day of the Lord Jesus.

O Thou, who wilt bring to light the things of darkness, and make manifest the counsels of the heart, and whose Spirit searcheth all things, help us to renounce the hidden things of dishonesty, and to speak as of sincerity, as of God, and as in the sight of God.

Take away, Lord, the veil from our hearts, and let the light of the glorious Gospel of Christ, the image of God, shine upon us.

May we not walk in craftiness, nor handle the word of God deceitfully ; may we judge ourselves, and not be judged ; may we keep under our body and bring it into subjection ; may we watch, quit us like men, and be strong ; and having the spirit of faith, may we believe and therefore speak.

Grant, O Lord, that we faint not ; but though our outward man perish, may our inward man be renewed day by day.

May our light afflictions, which are but for a moment, work out for us a far more exceeding and eternal weight of glory ; while we look, not at the things seen and temporal, but at the things not seen, but eternal.

Reveal to us, O Lord, by thy Spirit, what eye hath not seen, nor ear heard, nor the heart of man conceived.

May we be enriched by thee with all utterance, and with all knowledge ; may we be perfectly joined together in the same mind and in the same judgment ; may we be perfect, may we be of good comfort, may we live in peace ;

May the God of love and peace be with us.

Help us to stand fast in the liberty wherewith Christ has made us free, and not be entangled again with any yoke of bondage; knowing that the kingdom of God is not meat nor drink, but righteousness, peace, and joy in the Holy Spirit.

May we be zealously affected always for that which is good.

Help us to show the fruits of the spirit: love, joy, peace, long-suffering, gentleness, goodness, faith, meekness, and temperance.

If we live in the spirit, may we also walk in the spirit.

As we have opportunity, help us to do good to all men, and especially to those who are of the household of faith; to bear one another's burdens, and so fulfil the law of Christ; to crucify the flesh, with its affections and lusts; to sow to the spirit, and of the spirit to reap life everlasting; and not to be weary in well-doing, believing that we shall in due season reap, if we faint not.

III.

[FROM THE EPISTLE TO THE EPHESIANS.]

O THOU, who art the one God and Father of all; who art above all, and through all, and in us all; who hast adopted us as children in Jesus Christ, thy Son, in whom we have redemption, even the forgiveness of our sins; quicken us, we beseech thee, who have been dead in trespasses and sins.

O Thou, who art rich in mercy, for the sake of thy great love wherewith thou hast loved us, make us alive in Christ.

O God, our Father, the Father of glory, we pray thee to give us the spirit of wisdom and revelation in the knowledge of thyself, that we may know the hope of thy calling, and the riches of thine inheritance, and the greatness of thy power, which thou hast wrought in Christ, when thou didst raise him from the dead, and make him sit at thine own right hand in heavenly places.

25

We pray thee to raise us up also, and make us sit in heavenly places with him.

O Thou, the Father of our Lord Jesus Christ, grant us to be strengthened with might by thy Spirit inwardly; that Christ may dwell in our hearts by faith; that, being rooted and grounded in love, we may be able to understand the breadth and length, and depth and height, of the love of Christ, and be filled with all the fulness of God.

Help us, Heavenly Father, to come, in the unity of the faith, and the knowledge of the Son of God, to the stature of a perfect man, to the measure of the fulness of Christ.

Help us to walk, with all lowliness and meekness, with long-suffering, forbearing one another in love; endeavoring to keep the unity of the spirit in the bond of peace; to put away all bitterness, and wrath, and anger, and evil-speaking, with all malice.

May we be kind to one another, tender-hearted, forgiving one another, even as God, in Christ, hath forgiven us.

May we be followers of thee, as dear children, and walk in love, as Christ has loved us; redeeming the time; having the fruit of the spirit in all goodness and righteousness and truth; speaking to ourselves in psalms and hymns and spiritual songs, singing and making melody in our hearts unto the Lord.

May we give thanks, always, for all things, unto God our Father, in the name of the Lord Jesus.

Help us to be strong in thee and in the power of thy might; to put on thy whole armor, that we may be able to stand in the evil day; girt about with truth, having on the breastplate of righteousness, our feet shod with the Gospel of peace, taking the shield of faith, the helmet of salvation, and the sword of the spirit.

Help us to pray always, with all prayer and supplication, in the spirit, and watch thereunto with all supplication and perseverance.

May peace be to all the brethren, and love, with faith, from God our Father and the Lord Jesus Christ.

Grace be with all them that love our Lord Jesus Christ in sincerity. Amen.

IV.

[FROM SEVERAL OF THE EPISTLES OF PAUL.]

O GOD, our Heavenly Father, who hast loved us, and hast given us everlasting consolation and good hope through grace, we beseech thee to comfort our hearts and to establish us in every good word and work.

Hear us, O God, and direct our hearts into thy love and into the patient waiting of Christ.

O God, our Saviour, who wilt have all men to be saved, and to come to the knowledge of the truth; and hast manifested thyself to us, by the appearing of Jesus Christ, who hath abolished death and brought life and immortality to light through the Gospel, we beseech thee to hear us.

Give to us, O God, the spirit, not of fear, but of power, and of love, and of a sound mind.

O Thou, who art the blessed and only potentate; the King of kings and Lord of lords; who only hast immortality; dwelling in the light which no man can approach unto; whom no man hath seen nor can see; to thee be honor and power everlasting.

We give thee thanks, O our Father, who hast made us meet to be partakers of the inheritance of the saints in light.

Thou hast delivered us from the power of darkness, and hast translated us into the kingdom of thy dear Son, in whom we have redemption, even the forgiveness of our sins.

May we therefore fight the good fight of faith, and lay hold on eternal life, following after righteousness, godliness, faith, love, patience, and meekness.

We pray thee to forgive us, O God, if we have set our affections upon things below, instead of things above; if, professing to know thee, we have denied thee by our works; if through the love of money we have fallen into temptation and a snare; if we have indulged those passions which war against the soul; or if we have done anything through strife or vainglory.

Forgive us, we beseech thee, these and all our sins.

May we work out our salvation with fear and trembling, not counting ourselves to have attained; may we forget the things which are behind, and reach forth unto those which are before; approving the things which are excellent, being sincere and without offence, filled with the fruits of righteousness, and doing all things without murmuring or disputing.

Grant that our conversation be as becometh the Gospel of Christ, and may the peace of God rule in our hearts.

May we watch and be sober; may we put on charity, which is the perfect bond; may we comfort one another, and edify one another; not returning evil for evil, but following ever that which is good; may we rejoice evermore, pray without ceasing, and in everything give thanks; may we prove all things, hold fast that which is good, and abstain from all appearance of evil.

O God of peace, we pray thee to sanctify us wholly.

O God, if thou hast not appointed us unto wrath, but to obtain salvation by our Lord Jesus Christ, preserve our spirit, soul, and body blameless unto his coming; and the grace of our Lord Jesus Christ be with us all, for ever and ever. *Amen.*

V.

[From the Epistles of James and John.]

O God, the Father of lights, with whom is no variableness nor shadow of turning; from whom cometh down every good and perfect gift; we ask of thee wisdom, who givest to all men liberally.

We would ask, O God, in faith, nothing wavering; believing that, if we draw nigh to thee, thou wilt draw nigh to us.

O Almighty God, who canst not be tempted with evil, neither canst tempt any man; we confess that we are drawn away by our own lusts and enticed; but we beseech thee, O our Father, who art very pitiful and of tender mercy, who dost resist the proud, but givest grace to the humble, to hear the prayer of faith and raise us up.

If we have committed sins, may they be forgiven us; if we have known to do good and done it not; if we have been hearers of the word, and not doers also, deceiving our own selves; forgive us, O God, and save us.

May we not have the faith of Jesus Christ with respect of persons; may we not despise the poor; may we not have faith without works, but show our faith by our works; and, laying aside all that is impure, receive with meekness the ingrafted word, which is able to save our souls.

Help us to look into the perfect law of liberty, and continue therein, and so to receive the crown of life which the Lord has promised to them that love him.

Give us, Lord, the wisdom from above, which is first pure, then peaceable, gentle, and easy to be entreated, full of mercy and good fruits, without partiality and without hypocrisy.

O Thou, who art light, and in whom is no darkness at all, may we walk in the light, and have fellowship with thee.

O Thou, who art love; may we dwell in love, and so dwell in thee; may our love be made perfect, and be free from all

25 *

fear; may we be born of God, and overcome the world; may we keep thy commandments, and love thy children.

O God, grant that we love thee, not in word and tongue, but in deed and truth, and hereby know that we are of the truth, and assure our hearts before thee.

May we not love the world, nor the things which are in the world; may we remember that the world passes away, with all that is in it; and that, if we love the world, the love of the Father is not in us.

Grant these our prayers, Heavenly Father, we beseech thee, for thine infinite mercy's sake, in Jesus Christ. Amen.

VI.

[FROM THE EPISTLES OF PETER.]

BLESSED be the God and Father of our Lord Jesus Christ, who according to his abundant mercy hath begotten us again unto a lively hope by the resurrection of Jesus Christ;

To an inheritance incorruptible, undefiled, and that fadeth not away, reserved in heaven for us.

O God, our Father, who hast redeemed us by the precious blood of Christ, and taught us to be holy as thou art holy; and who, without respect of persons, judgest every man's work;

Help us, we pray thee, to pass the time of our sojourning here in fear.

O God, the Father of Jesus Christ, whom, though not having seen, we love; in whom, though now we see him not, believing, we rejoice; who was foreordained before the foundation of the world, but was manifest in these last times; make us, like him, holy in all manner of conversation.

Purify our souls in obeying the truth, through the spirit, unto unfeigned love of the brethren ; and may we love one another with pure hearts fervently.

O Thou, whose eyes are over the righteous, and whose ears are open to their prayers, but whose face is against them that do evil, make us all of one mind, having compassion one of another, loving as brethren, not rendering evil for evil, nor railing for railing, but contrariwise, blessing.

Adorn us with the hidden man of the heart, with that which is not corruptible, with the ornament of a meek and quiet spirit.

Add to our faith, virtue ; and to virtue, knowledge ; and to knowledge, temperance ; and to temperance, patience ; and to patience, godliness ; and to godliness, brotherly kindness ; and to brotherly kindness, charity.

May we all become a holy priesthood, to offer up spiritual sacrifices, acceptable to God, and to show forth the praises of him who hath called us out of darkness into his marvellous light.

May we follow him who has suffered for us, leaving us an example, that we should follow in his steps, and, being dead to sin, should live to righteousness ; when reviled, may we not revile again, but by well-doing put to silence the ignorance of foolish men ; may we refrain our tongue from evil, and our lips that they speak no guile ; may we sanctify the Lord God in our hearts, so that all may be ashamed who falsely accuse our good conversation in Christ.

Grant, O Lord, that, if it be thy will, we may suffer for well-doing, rather than for evil-doing.

May the time past of our lives suffice us to have disobeyed thee ; for the time to come may we be sober and watch unto prayer ; may we have fervent charity among ourselves ; that God may in all things be glorified through Jesus Christ, to whom be praise and dominion for ever and ever.

May the God of all grace, who hath called us to his eternal glory by Christ Jesus, after that we have suffered for a while, make us perfect, establish, strengthen, and settle us, and to him be glory and dominion for ever.   Amen.

SPECIAL PRAYERS.

COLLECT FOR PEACE.

O GOD, who art the author of peace and lover of concord, in knowledge of whom standeth our eternal life, whose service is perfect freedom; defend us thy humble servants in all assaults of our enemies; that we, surely trusting in thy defence, may not fear the power of any adversaries, through the might of Jesus Christ our Lord. *Amen.*

MORNING COLLECT FOR GRACE.

O LORD our Heavenly Father, almighty and everlasting God, who hast safely brought us to the beginning of this day; defend us in the same with thy mighty power; and grant that this day we fall into no sin, neither run into any kind of danger; but that all our doings may be ordered by thy governance, to do always that which is righteous in thy sight, through Jesus Christ our Lord. *Amen.*

A PRAYER FOR RULERS.

O LORD, our Heavenly Father, high and mighty, King of kings, Lord of lords, who dost from thy throne behold all the dwellers upon the earth; most heartily we beseech thee with thy favor to behold the President, Vice-President, and Congress of the United States, and so replenish them with the grace of thy Holy Spirit, that they may always incline to thy will, and walk in thy way. Endue them plenteously with heavenly gifts, that in all their deliberations they may be enabled to promote the national prosperity, and to secure the peace, liberty, and safety of the United States throughout all generations. This we humbly ask in the name of Jesus Christ our Lord. *Amen.*

A PRAYER FOR THE CLERGY AND PEOPLE.

ALMIGHTY and everlasting God, who art the author of every good and perfect gift, send down upon all ministers of the Gospel, and upon all congregations committed to their charge, the needful spirit of thy grace; and, that they may truly please thee, pour upon them the continual dew of thy blessing. Grant this, O Heavenly Father, for thine infinite mercy's sake in Jesus Christ our Lord. *Amen.*

A PRAYER FOR ALL CONDITIONS OF MEN.

O GOD, the Creator and Preserver of all mankind, we humbly beseech thee for all sorts and conditions of men, that thou wouldest be pleased to make thy ways known unto them, thy saving health unto all nations. More especially we pray for the good estate of thy holy Church; that it may be so guided and governed by thy good Spirit, that all who profess and call themselves Christians may be led into the way of truth, and hold the faith in unity of spirit, in the bond of peace, and in righteousness of life. Finally, we commend to thy fatherly goodness all those who are any ways afflicted or distressed in mind, body, or estate; that it may please thee to comfort and relieve them according to their several necessities; giving them patience under their sufferings, and a happy issue out of all their afflictions; and this we humbly ask as disciples of Jesus Christ our Lord. *Amen.*

A GENERAL THANKSGIVING.

ALMIGHTY God, Father of all mercies, we thine unworthy servants do give thee most humble and hearty thanks for all thy goodness and loving-kindness to us and to all men. We bless thee for our creation, preservation, and all the blessings of this life; but above all, for thine inestimable love in the redemption of the world by our Lord Jesus Christ; for the means of grace, and for the hope of glory. And we beseech thee, give us that due sense of all thy mercies, that our hearts may be unfeignedly thankful, and that we may show forth thy praise, not only with our lips, but in our lives, by giving up ourselves to thy service, and by walking before thee in holiness and righteousness all our days, through Jesus Christ our Lord; in whose name we ascribe unto thee all honor and glory, world without end. *Amen.*

A CONCLUDING PRAYER.*

ALMIGHTY God, who hast given us grace at this time with one accord to make our common supplications unto thee, and dost promise that, when two or three are gathered together in thy name, thou wilt grant their requests; fulfil now, O Lord, the desires and petitions of thy servants, as may be most expedient for them, granting us in this world knowledge of thy truth, and in the world to come life everlasting. *Amen.*

PRAYER FOR FORGIVENESS.

ALMIGHTY God, the Father of our Lord Jesus Christ, who desirest not the death of a sinner, but rather that he should turn from his wickedness and live; pardon and absolve all those who truly repent, and unfeignedly believe the holy Gospel. We beseech thee to grant us true repentance, and thy Holy Spirit; that those things may please thee which we do at this present, and that the rest of our life hereafter may be pure and holy; so that at the last we may come to thine eternal joy, through Jesus Christ our Lord. *Amen.*

---

* Known as the Prayer of St. Chrysostom.

ANOTHER.

O ALMIGHTY God, and most merciful Father, unto whom all hearts are open, and from whom no secrets are hid, with simplicity and godly sincerity would we seek thee, confessing our unthankfulness, and our manifold offences. We deplore the sins which we have at any time committed, in thought or affection, in word or deed, against each other and against thee. And we humbly beseech thee, through thy mercy declared unto us by thy Son Jesus Christ, to look graciously upon us, and forgive us, and assist us to lay aside every weight, and the sins which so easily beset us; to mortify our evil and corrupt affections, and to subdue our thoughts and desires to the obedience of the Gospel. May we be convinced, O God, that till we know thee, we know nothing aright; that without thee, we have nothing of any worth; and in wandering from thee, we leave all that is truly good. Let us cast ourselves into the arms of thy mercy, and offer thee our whole being, our bodies and our souls, that they may be thy temple for ever. And wilt thou take us, O Lord, entirely into thy hands, with all that we have, and let nothing henceforward, either in life or death, ever separate us from thee any more. *Amen.*

INTERCESSION FOR FRIENDS.

A LMIGHTY God, fountain of all goodness and all excellency, extend thine abundant favor and loving-kindness to our friends. Reward them for all the good which from thy merciful providence they have conveyed unto us. Let the light of thy countenance shine upon them, and never let them come into any affliction or sadness, but such as may be an instrument of thy glory, and their eternal comfort. Forgive them all their sins. Preserve them from spiritual dangers. Give supply to all their needs, guarding their persons, sanctifying their hearts, and leading them in the way of righteousness, by the waters of comfort, to the land of eternal rest and glory. Through Jesus Christ our Lord. *Amen.*

IN BEREAVEMENT.

SANCTIFY to thy servants, O God, the loss of one of our number by death. Look with pity upon our sorrows ; and grant that the affliction which it has pleased thee to bring upon us may awaken our consciences, and soften our hearts, and impress upon us such convictions of thy holiness and power, that we may place in thee our only felicity, and strive to please thee in all our ways. And give us grace constantly to look forward to that life which is beyond death, and over which death has no power, revealed to us by thy dear Son Jesus Christ. *Amen.*

FOR THE CHRISTIAN MINISTRY.

ALMIGHTY God, and Heavenly Father, who, of thine infinite love and goodness towards us, hast given to us thy only and most dearly beloved Son Jesus Christ, to be our Redeemer, and the author of everlasting life ; who, after he had made perfect our redemption by his death, and was ascended into heaven, sent abroad into the world his Apostles, Prophets, Evangelists, Teachers, and Pastors ; by whose labor and ministry he gathered together a great flock in all the parts of the world, to set forth the eternal praise of thy holy name : for these so great benefits of thy eternal goodness, and for that thou hast vouchsafed to call many of thy servants to the same office and ministry appointed for the salvation of mankind, we render unto thee most hearty thanks, we praise and worship thee ; and we humbly beseech thee, by the same thy blessed Son, to grant unto all, which either here or elsewhere call upon thy holy name, that we may continue to show ourselves thankful unto thee for these and all other thy benefits ; and that we may daily increase and go forward in the knowledge and faith of thee and thy Son, by the Holy Spirit. So that as well by those thy ministers, as by them over whom they are appointed, thy holy name may be for ever glorified, and thy blessed kingdom enlarged ; through the same thy Son Jesus Christ our Lord, who liveth and reigneth with thee in the unity of the same Holy Spirit, world without end. *Amen.*

FOR THE CLOSE OF THE YEAR.

O THOU in whose sight a thousand years are but as a day, all things on earth are passing away, but thou remainest one and the same, and to thy years there is no end. Thy providence has brought us to the close of another mortal year, and we would raise our thoughts above the flight of time, to the eternity in which thou dwellest, and to those things which know no change, but from glory to glory.

Merciful God! open our hearts to hear the awful voice of the departing year. Bring home to us a sense of our mortality. And teach us so to number our days that we may apply our hearts, with all diligence, to the search after wisdom. Make the point of time at which we now stand a gate of heaven. Bless to our sanctification the solemn lessons of the past. Inspire our hearts, O God, with the life of faith, that we may obtain a lasting dominion over the evil that is in the world and in ourselves. Daily, hourly, may we watch and pray lest we fall into temptation.

O that it may be given us, in thy grace, to walk henceforth as becometh our great vocation, as the children of God and the friends of Jesus. Through whom unto thee, O Father everlasting, be all praise and glory, now and for ever. *Amen.*

FOR A NEW YEAR.

BLESSED be God, who has brought us safe to the beginning of another year. Make us sensible, O thou eternal and holy One, how short and uncertain is our mortal life. Pardon our misspent time, and make us henceforth careful to redeem it. Grant that we may begin this new year with new resolutions of serving thee more faithfully. Make us wise unto salvation ; that we may consider in this our day the things that belong to our peace; and that we may pass the time of our sojourning here in thy fear and love ; and be ready to depart hence, whenever thou shalt say unto us, Return, ye children of men. And this we ask in the holy name of Jesus Christ our Lord. *Amen.*

26

FOR SUNDAY EVENING.

GLORY be to thy name for the especial blessings which this sacred day has brought to us. Pardon us, if in any manner we have abused its privileges. Cause the truths which we have heard to sink deep into our hearts, and bring forth in us the fruits of a holy and religous life, a peaceful and blessed death, and a glorious resurrection. These, and all our prayers, would we humbly offer unto thee, O Father of Infinite Mercy, through the most gracious and glorious mediation and intercession of our Redeemer, who liveth and reigneth for ever at thy right hand. *Amen.*

ANOTHER.

BLESSED be God, the God and Father of our Lord Jesus Christ, who hath vouchsafed to us the rest and the instruction of this Christian Sabbath. Blessed be God for the means of happiness and improvement which have been offered this day to us and our fellow-Christians. Make us mindful, we pray thee, of our duty ; that as we often hear how we ought to walk and to please God, we may continue to do so unto our lives' end. And wilt thou ever keep, defend, and bless us, and all thy children throughout the world, bringing us safely, by thy mighty power and grace, into the Sabbath which hath no end, and into the temple from which thy people go no more out, that we may there worship and glorify thee for ever, through him who is the Resurrection and the Life, the Son of thy perfect love, our Saviour and Lord. *Amen.*

AN EVENING PRAYER.

O MERCIFUL God! Eternal Light, shining in darkness! Thou who dispellest the night of sin, and all blindness of heart! since thou hast appointed the night for rest, and the day for labor, we beseech thee, grant that our bodies may rest in peace and quietness, that afterward they may be able to endure the labor they must bear. Temper our sleep, that it be not disorderly, that we may remain spotless both in body and soul; yea, that our sleep itself may be to thy glory. Enlighten the eyes of our understanding, that we may not sleep in death; but always look for deliverance from this misery. Defend us against all assaults of the devil, and take us into thine holy protection. And, although we have not passed this day without greatly sinning against thee, we beseech thee to hide our sins with thy mercy, as thou hidest all things on earth with the darkness of the night, that we may not be cast out from thy presence. Relieve and comfort all those who are afflicted or distressed in mind, body, or estate. Through Jesus Christ our Lord.

Consider and hear us, O Lord; lighten our eyes, lest we sleep the sleep of death.

We will both lay us down in peace and sleep; for thou, Lord, only makest us to dwell in safety. Amen.

SENTENCES OF BENEDICTION.

I.

O LORD, have mercy upon us! have mercy upon us!
O Lord, save thy people and bless thine heritage!
The Lord will bless his people with peace! *Amen.*

II.

BLESSED is the people that know the joyful sound! They shall walk, O Lord, in the light of thy countenance!
O Lord, let thy mercy lighten upon us, as our trust is in thee!
The Lord lift up the light of his countenance upon you, and give you peace! *Amen.*

III.

NOW unto Him that is able to do exceeding abundantly above all that we ask or think, according to the power that worketh in us;
Unto Him be glory in the Church, by Christ Jesus, throughout all ages, world without end.
Blessing, and glory, and honor be unto our God for ever and ever. *Amen.*

IV.

GREAT and marvellous are thy works, Lord God Almighty, just and true are all thy ways, thou King of saints.

Who shall not fear thee, O Lord, and glorify thy name? for thou only art holy: for all nations shall come and worship before thee.

Salvation to our God, who sitteth upon the throne, and unto the Lamb. *Amen.*

V.

Now the God of patience and consolation grant you to be like-minded one towards another, according to Christ Jesus.

By this shall all men know that we are his disciples, if we have love one to another.

And the Lord make you to increase and abound in love one towards another, and towards all men. To the end he may stablish your hearts unblamable in holiness before God, even our Father, at the coming of our Lord Jesus Christ with all his saints. *Amen.*

VI.

GRACE be unto you, and peace, from Him which is, and which was, and which is to come ; and from the seven spirits which are before his throne ;

And from Jesus Christ, who is the faithful witness, and the first-begotten of the dead, and the Prince of the kings of the earth, and who hath made us kings and priests unto God and his Father ;

To him be glory and dominion for ever and ever. *Amen.*

VII.

GLORY be to God, who hath saved us, and called us with a holy calling, not according to our works, but according to his own purpose and grace, which was given us in Christ Jesus before the world began ;

But is now made manifest by the appearing of our Saviour Jesus Christ, who hath abolished death, and hath brought life and immortality to light through the Gospel.

Grace be with you ! *Amen.*

VIII.

BLESSED be the God and Father of our Lord Jesus Christ, who according to his abundant mercy hath begotten us again unto a lively hope by the resurrection of Jesus Christ from the dead.

When Christ, who is our life, shall appear, then may we also appear with him in glory !

Which he shall show who is the blessed and only Potentate ; the King of kings, and Lord of lords ; who only hath immortality, dwelling in the light which no man can approach unto: whom no man hath seen nor can see; to whom be honor and power everlasting. *Amen.*

IX.

GRACE be with all them that love our Lord Jesus Christ in sincerity.

In whom we have redemption, through his blood, even the forgiveness of sins.

Now our Lord Jesus Christ himself, and God, even our Father, which hath loved us, and hath given us everlasting consolation and good hope through grace, comfort your hearts and stablish you in every good word and work. *Amen.*

X.

Now the God of hope fill you with all joy and peace in believing, that ye may abound in hope, through the power of the Holy Spirit.

Behold the tabernacle of God is with men, and he will dwell with them, and they shall be his people, and God himself shall be with them and be their God.

`And in him shall all the families of the earth be blessed. *Amen.*

XI.

Open, O Lord, the gates of righteousness, that the righteous may enter in !

Blessed are they that do his commandments, that they may have right to the tree of life, and may enter in through the gates into the city.

Glory be to him that is the Resurrection and the Life, to him that is holy, to him that is true, to him that openeth and no man shutteth, and shutteth and no man openeth, that liveth, and was dead, and is alive for evermore !   *Amen.*

XII.

The Lord bless you, and keep you : the Lord make his face to shine upon you and be gracious unto you.

The Lord is merciful and gracious, slow to anger and plenteous in mercy.

The grace of our Lord Jesus Christ be with you all.   *Amen.*

XIII.

Now the Lord of peace himself give you peace by all means.

The Lord deliver us from every evil work, and preserve us unto his heavenly kingdom, to whom be glory for ever and ever.

The Lord be with you all !   *Amen.*

XIV.

Now the God of peace, that brought again from the dead our Lord Jesus, that Great Shepherd of the sheep, through the blood of the everlasting covenant, make you perfect in every good work to do his will.

And there shall be one Fold and one Shepherd.

Glory be to God in the highest! on earth peace, good-will to men! *Amen.*

XV.

The God of all grace, who hath called us unto his eternal glory by Christ Jesus, after that ye have suffered awhile, make you perfect, stablish, strengthen, settle you.

To him be glory and dominion for ever and ever.

Now unto him that is able to keep you from falling, and to present you faultless before the presence of his glory with exceeding joy, to the only wise God our Saviour, be glory and majesty, dominion and power, both now and ever. *Amen.*

THE END.

Im The Story

personalised classic books

"Beautiful gift.. lovely finish.
My Niece loves it, so precious!"

Helen R Brumfieldon

⭐⭐⭐⭐⭐

UNIQUE
GIFT

FOR KIDS, PARTNERS
AND FRIENDS

Timeless books such as:

Kids

Alice in Wonderland · The Jungle Book · The Wonderful Wizard of Oz
Peter and Wendy · Robin Hood · The Prince and The Pauper
The Railway Children · Treasure Island · A Christmas Carol

Adults

Romeo and Juliet · Dracula

Highly
Customizable

Change
Books Title

Replace
Characters Names
with yours

Upload
Photo for
inside page

Add
Inscriptions

Visit
Im The Story .com
and order yours today!